Statistics for Social Science and Public Policy

Advisors:
S.E. Fienberg   D. Lievesley   J.E. Rolph

Springer

New York
Berlin
Heidelberg
Barcelona
Hong Kong
London
Milan
Paris
Singapore
Tokyo

Statistics for Social Science and Public Policy

Sally C. Morton
John E. Rolph
Editors

Public Policy and Statistics

Case Studies from RAND

Foreword by Bradley Efron

With 36 Figures

 Springer

Sally C. Morton
RAND
1700 Main Street
Santa Monica, CA 90401-2138
USA
Sally_Morton@rand.org

John E. Rolph
Marshall School of Business
University of Southern California
Los Angeles, CA 90089-0809
USA
jrolph@usc.edu

Advisors

Stephen E. Fienberg
Department of Statistics
Carnegie Mellon University
Pittsburgh, PA 15213
USA

John E. Rolph
Marshall School of Business
University of Southern California
Los Angeles, CA 90089-0809
USA
jrolph@usc.edu

Denise Lievesley
Institute for Statistics
Room H. 113
UNESCO
7 Place de Fontenoy
75352 Paris 07 SP
France

Library of Congress Cataloging-in-Publication Data
Public Policy and Statistics: case studies from RAND / editors Sally C. Morton, John E. Rolph.
    p. cm. — (Statistics for social science and public policy)
    Includes bibliographical references and index.
    ISBN 0-387-98777-0 (alk. paper)
    1. Policy sciences—Methodology. 2. Social sciences—Statistical methods—Case studies.
    I. Morton, Sally C. II. Rolph, John E. III. Series.
    H97.S764 2000
    320'.6—dc21   00-020827

Printed on acid-free paper.

Production managed by A. Orrantia; manufacturing supervised by Jeffrey Taub.
Photocomposed copy prepared in Microsoft Word 5.1 by RAND.
Printed and bound by Edwards Brothers, Inc., Ann Arbor, MI.
Printed in the United States of America.

9 8 7 6 5 4 3 2 1

ISBN 0-387-98777-0 Springer-Verlag New York Berlin Heidelberg   SPIN 10557790

To our RAND colleagues: past, present, and future

Foreword

This is the information age. America is awash in information, pouring out of our newspapers, magazines, networks, call-in radios, and the Internet by the hour and the minute, 24 hours a day. The only trouble is that most of it is misinformation, or its uglier cousin, disinformation. There are many reasons to mis- or disinform the public, and small rewards for accuracy. Advocacy groups, the media, politicians, and chat-room residents follow their own agendas. The truth is out there, as *The X-Files* assures us, but finding it can exhaust a modern Diogenes.

Search no further. The RAND Corporation, America's original think tank, earns its money fishing truths out of murky political and social waters. Its clients, often Federal and state governments, pay for clear views and accurate analysis, not propaganda. The quantitative conscience of RAND, often the final arbiter of what constitutes the true story, is its small but powerful Statistics Group, and this is their book.

The collection of ten case histories that follows concerns important issues, some of which are the stuff of controversy and confusion. Here is where RAND's clients have gotten the most for the money, and where you, the misinformation-jaded reader, may be most informed. Racial bias in death sentences is an American scandal and deserves Amnesty International's recent condemnation. Or does it? Could it be that race is actually not a significant factor in assigning death sentences? See what Morton and Rolph found out in Chapter 5. Hundreds of thousands of homeless, maybe millions, are flooding the streets of our cities and even suburban areas. Or are they? Maybe media and advocacy groups have grossly magnified a serious situation. Get an accurate count from Abrahamse in Chapter 3. What about global warming? Isn't it possible that most of the problem reflects natural variations, not human carelessness? Possible, yes, but see what Adams, Hammitt, and Hodges have to say in Chapter 4.

Missing from this volume are heated prose, moral indignation, and the testimony of celebrity experts. The language is quiet, mainly nontechnical, and clear enough to explain even difficult issues of statistical modeling to a general audience. This is also a casebook, designed to help serious students of public policy. The editors have faithfully adhered to the casebook format, beginning each chapter with a careful background description of the problem under discussion, the relevant research questions, and the statistical techniques to be used. The techniques themselves range over modern as well as classical methodology, including imputation, the bootstrap, and empirical Bayes methods. These ideas have been perfected and even invented at RAND, and they are deftly employed here.

The RAND Corporation was founded in 1946, with one main client, the U. S. Air Force, and one job, to forecast the military problems of the cold-war era. One forecast would have seemed most implausible in those days of a top-secret facility and nuclear scenarios: a RAND-sponsored volume in which its Statistics Group examined school drug usage, eye care, and hospital mortality rates. RAND didn't have a Statistics Group until 1976, although many of the world's best statisticians frequented its nationally respected mathematics department. It was a department reflecting the founding presence of John von Neuman from its game theoretic research to the literally futuristic JOSS computing system.

That era ended suddenly with the Pentagon papers affair, flowing from a RAND photocopier, and a dramatic drop in military interest. (Chapter 7 reflects the large part of RAND still devoted to military forecasting.) The term "reinventing oneself" might have been invented at RAND, which successfully transformed itself into the premier social science/public-policy research engine. An important part of that story has been the Statistics Group, founded in 1976. One of the founding members, Carl Morris, along with Jennifer Hill, reports on the Health Insurance Study in Chapter 2. This study, which cast brilliant light on a subject lost in confusion, remains RAND's single greatest contribution to clear thinking on public policy. Chapter 2 is indeed a casebook illustration of tough-minded statistical planning in action.

The coffee cups in the editors' office celebrate the 25th anniversary of the RAND Statistics Group, due in 2001. Looking ahead still seems to be in vogue at RAND. The cups' motto reads "Confronting Uncertainty in Public Policy," a fitting encomium for this far-reaching volume.

BRADLEY EFRON

Stanford University

Preface

"The country is hungry for information; everything of a statistical character, or even a statistical appearance, is taken up with an eagerness that is almost pathetic; the community have not yet learned to be half skeptical and critical enough in respect to such statements."

General Francis A. Walker, Superintendent of the 1870 Census
Freedman, Pisani, Purves, and Adhikari (1991)

This book consists of case studies of public policy issues arising out of collaborations between current or former RAND statisticians and our colleagues, either at RAND or at universities. RAND is a nonprofit institution established in 1948 whose mission is to inform public policy decisions through research and analysis. The RAND Statistics Group, established in 1976, currently consists of doctoral and masters level statisticians whose statistical expertise is available to all RAND research. RAND statisticians are integral parts of project teams, do short-term consulting on RAND projects, and offer short courses to the research staff. RAND is a unique and exciting place to do statistical work in that it combines exposure to a variety of public policy issues with a collegiate environment akin to a small academic department.

RAND was created at the behest of the Air Force, a newly created military service at the end of World War II. Its mission was to provide objective research on national security issues. In the 1960s, RAND moved from working only on national security problems to major problems of domestic policy as well. Today, RAND researchers operate on a broad front, assisting public policy-makers at all levels, private sector leaders in several industries, and the public at large in efforts to better inform policy decisions through research. RAND works in many areas, including national defense, education and training, health care, criminal and civil justice, labor and population, science and technology, community development, international relations, and regional studies. RAND has an independent endowment, but most of its studies are supported by grants and contracts. U. S. government agencies provide the largest share of support, followed by charitable foundations, private sector firms, and other governments (state, local and foreign).

We hope that this book will be used by readers with a variety of backgrounds. To fully appreciate the case studies in the book, it would be helpful to know linear and logistic regression at the level of an advanced undergraduate or beginning graduate class. We have structured this volume so that it may be used as a supplementary text for applied statistics courses at both the advanced undergraduate and graduate levels. The book is also suitable as a supplementary text for courses in a variety of other disciplines including public policy, public health, economics, and sociology. It also may be a useful resource for courses in professional schools in business, law and medicine. We hope that this volume will also prove informative to empirical researchers and policy makers, especially those in government and at other research institutions. The introductory section of each chapter and the index can be used to identify those case studies that either apply to particular substantive policy areas, or that use specific statistical techniques. Datasets are available on our website www.rand.org/centers/stat/casebook, and allow the reader to immediately apply techniques discussed in the case study using the exercises listed at the end of each chapter.

The book is the product of the hard work and advice of many. As the book neared its completion, James Hodges reviewed the entire manuscript and made many excellent suggestions. At Springer-Verlag, we would like to especially thank our editor John Kimmel for his support, patience, and encouragement, and our production editor Antonio Orrantia for his and his staff's thorough copyediting of the manuscript. At RAND, we were assisted by the Publications Department, headed by Margaret Schumacher. In particular we'd like to thank Janet DeLand, Sally Belford, Sharon Koga, Judy Lewis, Sandy Petitjean, and Carolyn Rogers. We take responsibility for any shortcomings that remain.

Preparation of this book was supported by RAND's own funds. The RAND Statistics Group has been fortunate to receive core funding from its beginnings in 1976. We are grateful for the support of James Thomson, President and Chief Executive Officer, and Michael Rich, Executive Vice President of RAND, and especially acknowledge the encouragement of Albert Williams and Adele Palmer. We thank all the case study authors for their hard work and dedication. In addition, we thank those members of RAND project teams who may not necessarily be authors of the corresponding case study chapters. Without these RAND projects, this volume would not exist. Finally, as the current and the founding Heads of the RAND Statistics Group, we, the editors, are fortunate to have all of the RAND statisticians as our colleagues.

In this book, we hope to give you a glimpse of why we are so enthusiastic about our work as typified by the case studies in this volume.

SALLY C. MORTON AND JOHN E. ROLPH

Santa Monica, California

Contents

Understanding Relationships

Why You Should Read This Book

Sally C. Morton and John E. Rolph

Statistics is about making decisions under uncertainty. Since uncertainty characterizes many important public-policy questions, it is no surprise that answering such questions often requires innovative statistical thinking. This book of case studies tells real stories about using statistics to inform decision-making.

We begin with an example that captures the essence of the book.

Is It a Serious Fire?

In the late 1960s, the New York City Fire Department had so many false alarms that the Department's ability to respond to serious fires was being affected. Indeed, in 1968 alone, the number of fire alarms in the Bronx jumped by about 50%. On hot summer evenings, when an alarm signaling a serious fire was sounded, the nearest firehouse was often empty because its fire company was out responding to a false alarm. The delay that resulted while a fire company from another firehouse reached the scene increased property loss and heightened the potential for loss of life. It also caused workloads in the fire department to skyrocket.

As part of his effort to make New York City government more efficient, the then recently elected Mayor, John Lindsey, and RAND created the New York City-RAND Institute. The Institute undertook studies of fire protection, police protection, housing policy, welfare policy, and other critical areas identified by the city and RAND. To address New York's fire protection problems, the RAND research team developed analytic models aimed at more effective dispatching of fire companies to fire alarms, more efficient relocation policies (relocating fire companies from outside the region to temporarily vacant firehouses whose companies were fighting fires), and more effective siting of firehouses (Walker, Chaiken, and Ignall 1979).

In the course of developing and implementing these models, a number of statistical issues arose. For example, at that time, most fires were reported by pulling a street alarm box. Improved dispatching decisions recommended by our models required an estimate of the probability that the incoming alarm signaled a serious fire rather than a minor fire or false alarm. Under the improved dispatching rules, alarms with a high probability of being a serious fire would have more equipment dispatched to them (e.g., three engine (pumper truck) companies, two hook and ladder companies, and a fire chief) than what was dispatched to the other alarms (e.g., two engines, one ladder, and a chief). Estimating these probabilities was not straightforward.

One of the most interesting statistical problems that arose is what is now referred to as a small area estimation problem. That is, should the probability estimate of whether an alarm signaled a serious fire be based only on the history of the particular alarm box that was pulled, on the history of alarm boxes in the neighborhood of the alarm box, or on some combination of the two?

Borrowing strength across geography is now a classic application of Bayes and empirical Bayes methods. Empirical Bayes methods were in their infancy at the time of this study, and solving this estimation problem required extending the existing empirical Bayes methods to cover this situation (Carter and Rolph 1973, 1974). Specifically, we developed an "unequal variance" empirical Bayes (EB) shrinkage estimator so that the EB probability estimate for a particular alarm box shrinks the alarm box history estimate toward the neighborhood history estimate, with the degree of shrinkage varying with the number of alarms at the alarm box in the past three years. Our EB estimator combined the alarm box history and the neighborhood history in a way that fit plausible assumptions about fire alarm generation, including adjustments for such factors as trend, season, day of week, and time of day.

We were fortunate in that we could compare out-of-sample probability estimates using the EB estimator and the conventional direct estimator (based only on alarm box history) using an operationally realistic loss function. Our loss function was the number of mistakes—serious fires that would receive a reduced response—when the dispatching rule used the "serious fire" probability estimates from each of the two different approaches. Although it has been well known since Charles Stein's original papers (Stein 1955; James and Stein 1961) that the shrinkage approach is superior with squared error loss as the criteria, we were reassured that a realistic loss function reflecting property damage and potential loss of life also demonstrated the superiority of shrinkage estimation.

The New York City Fire Department experience was an intriguing combination of understanding a substantive problem and tailoring an appropriate statistical approach to address it. The ten chapters in this book describe more recent, but equally interesting, applications of statistical thinking to public policy problems. In describing them, we have not pulled any punches. We tell you exactly how the problem unfolded and how we tackled it, warts and all.

How the Book Is Organized

RAND has a long tradition of empirical analysis in support of research into public-policy problems. A nonprofit research institute, RAND is supported mostly by grants and contracts from the government and various foundations and is dedicated to providing high-quality relevant research to inform public-policy decision-making. RAND researchers, both in statistics and in other disciplines, have applied statistical methods to policy problems in innovative ways. The contexts have ranged from large social experiments to observational studies as part of program evaluations. Data for these studies are frequently gathered from surveys of human subjects or from various types of administrative records.

Our goal in this volume is to convey the richness of both the analytical techniques and the substantive applications to readers who wish to understand better how statistical thinking can be applied to interesting public-policy problems.

Our philosophy is to be critical yet constructive. We strive to bridge the gap between needing to indicate clearly what cannot be said and needing to gather information or use the information at hand to draw valid, but sometimes only approximate, inferences about important questions. The public-policy researcher must often advise a policy-maker who is making a decision in the face of substantial uncertainty. Rather than simply saying what cannot be known, the researcher's responsibility is to draw relevant inferences, even if heavily qualified ones, that can inform the decision.

The three sections of this book reflect the three major tasks in empirical research: collecting data, detecting effects, and understanding relationships. Although each case study includes, to a greater or lesser extent, methods from all three tasks, we have placed cases in the section that best reflects their methodological focus. Every chapter describes the public-policy problem it addresses and discusses the policy implications of the results.

Collecting Data

- Did a school-based intervention program reduce initiation and regular use of alcohol, cigarettes, and marijuana by adolescents?

- Do people with less generous health insurance plans tend to consume less medical care, and how does that affect their health status?

- How many homeless people live in Orange County, California, what part of the county do they live in, what are their demographic characteristics, and how well are they served by public programs?

The first three chapters of this book discuss collecting data in the context of answering these and other questions. In examining how to collect data, we describe the quasiexperimental evaluation of an intervention (Chapter 1), the design of a large public-policy experiment (Chapter 2), and the sampling of a hard-to-reach population (Chapter 3). Our goal is to give you a full understanding and appreciation for each case study's data: its design, source, collection, and transformation into an analytic dataset.

Detecting Effects

- Could cycles in the global temperature record mask the definitive signs of global warming?

- Controlling for other relevant factors, does race of victim or race of defendant affect whether or not a defendant convicted of a capital murder is sentenced to death?

- Does the frequency of medical malpractice claims of physicians impaired by substance abuse or psychological disorders differ from that of comparable unimpaired physicians?

The fourth, fifth, and sixth chapters of this book are concerned with detecting effects in the settings of global warming (Chapter 4), death penalty sentencing (Chapter 5), and medical malpractice (Chapter 6). In statistical terms, the core question is whether the observed signal is real or simply a result of chance. We describe the use of estimation and hypothesis testing to make statistical inferences, specifically via the application of bootstrapping, logistic regression, classification and regression trees (CART), and through the use of matching to produce comparable cases and controls. Especially relevant in the public-policy arena is the challenge of conveying to the decision-maker the uncertainty of an estimated effect and making clear what that uncertainty implies for the decision.

Understanding Relationships

- What are the potential causes of delays in repairing F-14 jet engines, and how can we focus improvement efforts most effectively?

- How can data on hospital mortality rates be used to understand which hospitals provide poor-quality medical care?

- How does the supply of eye care professionals compare to public health needs for eye care services? What is the uncertainty in this comparison?

- In terms of equity, how do current federal block grant formula funding allocations to states for substance abuse treatment compare to those based on alternative estimates of treatment need and cost?

The last four chapters focus on understanding the underlying relationships between factors in models used to address particular public-policy problems. These case studies use a variety of statistical and other techniques to unveil underlying structure: graphical tools (Chapter 7), empirical Bayes methods (Chapter 8), linear programming and bootstrap methods (Chapter 9), and synthetic estimation (Chapter 10). As with all of the chapters, these four case studies describe what the analytic results imply for public-policy decision-making.

In terms of prerequisites for all of the chapters, readers should know linear and logistic regression at an advanced undergraduate or master's level.

How the Case Studies Are Organized

Because our goal is to provide a realistic rendition of how to apply statistics in public-policy settings, our chapters do not follow the academic journal style. Instead, we describe, in detail, the research process in an empirical study. That includes: a description of data collection, data management, variable coding, exploratory analyses, blind alleys, and the other important but sometimes neglected aspects of empirical research. Successful statistical studies follow an iterative process in model formulation, model reformulation, model checking, sensitivity analyses, and the other steps necessary to give one confidence that the results from fitting a statistical model actually apply to a real policy problem. Our blow-by-blow description of how the research unfolds gives you more than just a flavor of this process.

In every case study, we emphasize how to translate a public-policy concern into researchable questions. To illustrate how to address these questions using statistical methods, we describe the study design and data collection methods, the analytic approach, and the empirical results and their policy implications. Every chapter also provides open-ended questions, extensions, and other issues that can be explored using the dataset included with the case study.

Each case study has seven main sections:

- an introduction to the policy problem, the research questions, the statistical questions, and a summary of data and methods;
- the study design, data collection, data sources, and data elements;
- the dataset creation, including file construction and variable derivation, descriptive statistics, and the results of any exploratory data analysis undertaken;
- the statistical methods and model as applicable;
- the results of the analysis, including model validation and sensitivity analysis;
- a discussion of the results, how they were used, their limitations, and their implications in terms of policy; and
- exercises, including a dataset obtainable on our website (www.rand.org/centers/stat/casebook) if applicable.

References to relevant RAND publications (which can be obtained via the RAND website: www.rand.org) are given in each chapter, and all references are presented in a comprehensive reference section at the end of the book.

Further RAND Reading

Carter, G., and Rolph, J. (1973), *New York City Fire Alarm Prediction Models: I. Box-Reported Serious Fires.* R-1214-NYC, Santa Monica, CA: RAND.

Carter, G., and Rolph, J. (1975), *New York City Fire Alarm Prediction Models: II. Alarm Rates.* R-1215-NYC, Santa Monica, CA: RAND.

Collecting Data

1

School-Based Drug Prevention: Challenges in Designing and Analyzing Social Experiments

Robert M. Bell and Phyllis L. Ellickson

Executive Summary

Many important public-policy decisions rely on evaluating the effectiveness of social interventions. However, such evaluations pose substantial statistical challenges not faced by clinical trials in trying to reach valid conclusions. This chapter describes the design and analysis strategies adopted in a longitudinal experiment to evaluate a school-based drug-prevention program called Project ALERT. The experiment, conducted at 30 junior high schools in California and Oregon, assessed whether the curriculum reduced initiation and regular use of alcohol, cigarettes, and marijuana by adolescents.

The chapter describes specific steps taken to address the following challenges: achieving full but realistic implementation of the curriculum; testing the program in diverse environments; obtaining well-matched experimental cells; obtaining reliable measures of use; adjusting for baseline differences among experimental groups; and accounting for intra-school correlation of outcomes.

1. Introduction

1A. Policy Problem

Drug use among adolescents is a major national concern. The most commonly used drugs during early adolescence are alcohol, cigarettes, and marijuana—the so-called gateway drugs. Although hard drugs get more attention from legislators and the media, each of the gateway drugs can trigger serious health, safety, or developmental problems. Thus, preventing the use of gateway drugs by adolescents is an important public health and criminal justice priority. One promising approach is school-based prevention programs, which provide a convenient way of reaching almost all adolescents. However, to choose successfully among the multitude of available programs, schools need hard evidence about which, if any, prevention strategies work.

1B. Research Questions

This case study describes and evaluates the design and analysis strategies adopted in a multisite drug-prevention experiment at 30 junior high schools in California and Oregon (Ellickson and Bell 1990a,b, 1993). This chapter draws heavily, occasionally verbatim, from previously published work by its coauthors (Ellickson and Bell 1990a, 1992). The program, called Project ALERT,[1] is based on the social influence model for prevention (Flay 1985). The model assumes that a decision to begin using alcohol, cigarettes, or other substances is primarily influenced by family, friends, and other societal forces such as advertising, whose impact is reflected in the young person's own beliefs about drugs. This experiment addressed the following questions:

- Did Project ALERT reduce initiation and regular use of alcohol, cigarettes, and marijuana by adolescents?

- How long did the effects, if any, last?

- Did results differ among groups defined by early substance use, race/ethnicity, or other factors?

1C. Statistical Questions

Experiments typically address a question such as: What is the average effect on outcome A when treatment B (as opposed to a control) is applied to population C? Two criteria for assessing experiments are internal and external validity (Campbell and Stanley 1966; Cook and Campbell 1979; Moses 1992). *Internal validity* is a technical criterion that addresses whether the experimental comparison produces unbiased estimates and valid tests of statistical significance. That is, if the experimental intervention truly has no effect, is it equally likely to perform better or worse than the control? Is the probability that the treatment is deemed statistically significant equal to the nominal level of the statistical test? Even if an experiment possesses perfect internal validity, it may miss the mark because it asks and answers the wrong question. *External validity* is whether an experiment is evaluating an appropriate outcome, treatment, and population. Assessment of external validity rests on expert judgment about the research question and conduct of the experiment.

Randomized controlled experiments are a central tool of scientific research. For example, clinical trials regularly inform the medical community about the effectiveness of alternative drugs and other treatments (Lavori, Louis, Bailar, and Polansky 1983). Evaluating the effects of social interventions, such as Project ALERT, poses substantial statistical challenges not faced by clinical trials:

- By their nature, social interventions are frequently not as easy to replicate as medical interventions, such as drug therapies. Thus, extra care must be taken to ensure that the version of the intervention in the experiment is typical of what would occur in practice.

- Some social interventions are designed to act on groups rather than individuals—requiring that groups be the unit of assignment to experimental treatments. Correlations among individuals within groups tend to make it difficult to construct similar comparison groups, resulting in greater sampling variation in the comparisons than if individuals were the units of assignment.

- If the effectiveness of an intervention may vary widely across environments, it is important to test the intervention under diverse conditions. When the intervention must be applied to groups, achieving diversity becomes more difficult than in a clinical trial.

- It may be impossible to keep participants from knowing which intervention they have received. Clinical trials of drugs typically use a procedure known as "blinding," in which control subjects are provided with a placebo to avoid any effects caused by knowledge of what treatment has been received.

- Measuring the relevant outcomes in a social intervention objectively may be more difficult than in a clinical trial.

During the 1980s, school-based programs aimed at preventing adolescent drug use proliferated. However, credible evaluations of their effectiveness were rare, in part because of the obstacles listed above. As with all such studies, the credibility of the findings depends on the rigor of the experimental design. Earlier school-based prevention studies had several weaknesses: limitations in scope (too few schools and students, too little diversity), lack of random assignment, faulty implementation of curricula, uncertainty about the accuracy of reported drug use measures, and inadequate statistical controls (Biglan and Ary 1985; Moskowitz 1989).

In this chapter, we describe the specific steps that we took to avoid these problems. The statistical questions we faced were:

- Did the curriculum receive a full but realistic implementation?

- Was the program tested in diverse environments?

- Were the experimental cells well matched?

- Was use measured reliably?

- Did the analysis adjust for baseline differences among experimental groups?

- Did the analysis account for intraschool correlation of outcomes?

1D. Summary of Data and Methods

We evaluated Project ALERT with a randomized controlled experiment using school as the unit of assignment. We recruited 30 schools from eight school districts scattered throughout California and Oregon. The 30 schools were randomly assigned to one of three experimental groups:

- In ten schools, the entire seventh-grade cohort received the Project ALERT curriculum from an adult health educator.

- In ten other treatment schools, teen leaders from neighboring high schools assisted the adult teacher.

- The ten control schools were allowed to continue any traditional drug information programs they had as long as they did not focus on resistance skills and motivation. Four schools implemented programs that focused on providing information about drugs during grades seven or eight.

Therefore, the Project ALERT curriculum was judged against the performance of traditional programs delivered in control schools.

Baseline self reports of drug use, related attitudes and behaviors, and other information were collected in seventh grade in all 30 schools, immediately before the Project ALERT curriculum was begun in the 20 treatment schools. Similar data were collected at six follow-up waves extending into the twelfth grade. We used logistic regression at the student level to analyze a series of binary outcome measures for each target substance (alcohol, cigarettes, and marijuana) as a function of treatment and baseline covariates for over 4000 students. This case study focuses on methods and results from the first 15 months of the experiment. The data collection and program delivery schedule are shown in Figure 1.1.

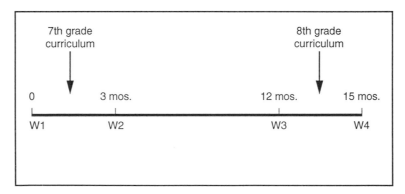

Figure 1.1. Data Collection and Program Delivery Schedule. Data used in this case study were collected in four waves (W1, W2, W3, W4). The program consisted of eight weekly lessons in seventh grade and three booster lessons in eighth grade.

2. Study Design, Data Collection, Description of Data Sources, and Description of Data Elements

2A. Curriculum

Description. The Project ALERT curriculum followed the social influence model of prevention. Prevention strategies based on this model help adolescents develop the motivation to resist pro-drug influences and the skills to translate that motivation into effective resistance. They focus on: (1) developing social norms against use and reasons not to use; (2) enhancing adolescents' awareness of the social influences at work; and (3) teaching specific techniques for resisting those influences (how to say "no"). In contrast, earlier approaches tried to prevent drug use by disseminating information and teaching general skills. Social influence programs also emphasize the effects of drug use on students' daily lives and social relationships now, rather than long-term consequences that may seem irrelevant to teenagers.

The Project ALERT curriculum uses question-and-answer techniques, role modeling, and repeated skills practice to promote student participation and learning. The curriculum was designed for seventh and eighth graders—a group that is highly vulnerable to pro-drug social influences but typically not yet regular users. All students received eight weekly lessons in seventh grade and three booster lessons when they reached eighth grade. Two program delivery methods were tested:

- classes were taught solely by an adult health educator hired for the experiment.
- a pair of older teens from a neighboring high school assisted the adult in four of the eight seventh-grade sessions.

Achieving a Full but Realistic Implementation. A prevention program can fail either because the underlying model is ineffective or because the program is implemented poorly. Unfortunately, many evaluations do not distinguish between these two causes (Schaps, DiBartolo, Moskowitz, Palley, and Churgin 1981). To avoid this failing, we worked hard to ensure that the program was faithfully implemented. Outside health educators who had the time and commitment to learn both the content and teaching process of the curriculum conducted the intervention. Training for both the adult teachers and the teen leaders stressed how important it was to faithfully follow the content and delivery style of the curriculum. At the same time, we designed curriculum activities that allowed teachers to assess and build on student knowledge and capabilities, which also allowed individual teachers to adapt the teaching process to their own styles and different classroom environments. We believe that the interactive nature of the curriculum makes it likely that other teachers can adapt it successfully for their own classrooms.

To assess whether the curriculum was delivered as designed, we monitored 41% of the 2300 classroom sessions scheduled during grades seven and eight using standardized observation forms that had been tested and refined during the program's pilot test. For each of a lesson's major activities, a monitor assessed whether its key components had been covered and how well it generated student interest and participation.

2B. School Selection

Testing the Program in Diverse Environments. Previous drug prevention studies had been criticized for focusing primarily on White, middle-class suburban communities with few minority students (Flay 1985). To ensure the external validity of the Project ALERT experiment, we recruited school districts representing a wide range of community types, socioeconomic levels, and ethnic mixes. At the same time, to ensure the internal validity of the experiment, we required that every school abide by certain conditions:

- submit to random assignment;

- forgo any existing drug-prevention curriculum with resistance skills training if assigned to a treatment condition;

- provide mixed-gender classes with a maximum of 40 students;

- follow a weekly lesson schedule; and

- accommodate our data collection requirements (including the collection of physiological samples).

We sought diversity in terms of: geographic region, community type (urban/suburban/rural), race/ethnicity composition, socioeconomic level, school size, and grade span for the middle or junior high schools. We began the recruiting process by visiting promising districts in California and Oregon, and exploring whether they were willing to meet the experimental requirements. As some districts joined the experiment and others dropped out of consideration, we contacted new districts that would complement those already included. Eventually, 11 of the districts we approached chose not to participate in the experiment because they could not meet one or more of our requirements.[2]

In the end, the experiment included three to five schools from each of eight districts, for a total of 30 schools. Because we could only afford a total sample size of 30 schools, we did not include all the potential schools in some districts.

2C. Assigning Schools to Experimental Cells

Social influence model prevention programs are designed to affect school-wide norms. Thus the curriculum should be given to all of the students in a school.[3] Consequently, schools are the natural experimental assignment unit. We divided the 30 schools equally among the three intervention cells (health educator, health educator plus teen leader, and control).

The bottom-line goal for any design is to produce experimental groups that would yield identical outcomes in the absence of any treatment. While that goal is impossible to reach in any experiment of this type, we employed three strategies to move in that direction:

- random assignment of schools,
- use of district as a blocking factor, and
- restricted randomization.

Random Assignment. Random assignment is the cornerstone of experimental design (Cochran and Cox 1957). Without randomization, there is an unanswerable threat that the experimental groups may differ systematically in unknown ways that affect the outcome. For example, had we allowed school district officials to dictate the treatment assignments (or to veto those from a random assignment), all the schools with the worst drug problems might have ended up in the two treatment cells. Randomization ensures that any unknown factors are equally likely to appear in each experimental group so that, unconditional on the actual assignment, there is no systematic difference among the experimental groups.

Blocking by District. For several reasons, we might expect schools within the same district to have similar substance use rates. Local socioeconomic status and community norms may influence substance use in ways that other measured variables could not explain. Also, district policies (e.g., how severely officials penalize substance use on campus) may influence the rate of substance use. Consequently, if all three schools from a particular district were randomly assigned to the same experimental cell, disentangling any district effect from the effect of the intervention that those schools received would be impossible. To avoid this, we used district to form approximate randomized blocks (Cochran and Cox 1957)—that is, we matched the cells as closely as possible in terms of district. In four districts that contributed three schools apiece, we required the design to include exactly one school in each treatment cell. For districts with four or five schools, each cell was constrained to be assigned exactly one or two schools. To maintain randomization, we randomly selected the one or two cells that received two schools.

Restricted Randomization. For experiments with a large number of experimental units, simple randomized assignment tends to produce experimental groups with very similar distributions of background characteristics. However, when the number of assignment units is small, for example 30, as in our case, the law of large numbers does not yet apply. Consequently, blocking and randomization alone did not ensure well-matched cells in Project ALERT. For example, even with the use of blocking, simple random assignment might easily have produced eight of ten control schools that ranked below average in family income for their districts. To maximize cell similarity, we restricted the assignments to a subset of designs containing well-matched cells and selected randomly from among those assignments. Each school in the sample had a one-third probability of being assigned to any particular cell.

Data used for matching cells included a mixture of publicly available data and some gathered specifically for this experiment. The most important data source was an 11-question survey administered to eighth-grade students at potential Project ALERT schools late in the academic year preceding baseline. This survey provided information about the mobility of the students between schools, the educational level of both parents, whether English was spoken at home, and lifetime and recent use of cigarettes and marijuana by the students. Census datafiles gave us demographic and socioeconomic status data for each school's catchment area, to produce estimates of race/ethnicity composition, median family income, educational levels of adults, and the proportion of families that included both parents. Sixth-grade reading, writing, and math achievement test scores were collected for the schools in our California sample. The state of California also supplied data on the percentage of seventh graders who possessed limited English proficiency. Each school provided data on current and past enrollment in the seventh grade.

2D. Data Collection

Trained data collectors administered questionnaires in the classroom at four waves during the program's first two years: before and after delivery of the seventh-grade curriculum (baseline and three-month follow-up), and before and after delivery of the eighth-grade booster curriculum (12- and 15-month follow-ups).

The questionnaires asked the students whether, how often, and how much they had used alcohol, cigarettes, marijuana, and other drugs; their attitudes about and exposure to substance use; perceptions about their abilities to resist pressures to use drugs; other deviant behaviors; demographic and other information.

Concerns about the Reliability of Self-Reported Substance Use. Our primary outcome measures came from student self-reports of whether, when, and how often they had used alcohol, cigarettes, and marijuana. The fact that adolescent use or purchase of each of these substances is illegal raises concern about the truthfulness and accuracy of self-reported use. Additional threats to data accuracy and reliability can arise if students have difficulty recalling past behavior or reading and understanding the questions. Such concerns threaten both external and internal validity. If adolescents systematically underreport substance use, we get a mistaken notion of the size of the problem (compromising external validity). More important, if responses in different experimental cells were subject to differing biases, that phenomenon would systematically bias estimates of treatment effects (destroying internal validity).

Steps to Enhance Data Quality. Following well-tested survey research procedures, we took several steps to address these problems (Dillman 1978). The survey instruments were carefully designed to accommodate the reading levels and experience of seventh and eighth graders. To improve response accuracy, we used response categories with objective, explicit anchors. Thus, responses indicated the number of times the students used drugs in specific time periods, rather than "sometimes" or "often." Inconsistent interpretations of subjective choices would have reduced the comparability of responses across both students and waves. To identify possible problems with wording or instruction, we pilot-tested various versions of the baseline questionnaire. These pretests allowed us to compare alternative versions for the frequency of problem indicators, such as item nonresponse, internal inconsistencies, and student questions indicating confusion, and to select the most successful items for the final instrument.

Before administering the surveys in the classroom, the data collectors described our measures for protecting data privacy and stressed the importance of telling the truth. We assured students that none of their teachers, principals, or parents would see their responses; we used numbers rather than names as identifiers; and we distributed the questionnaires in a group setting rather than in a face-to-face interview. Students had the option of refusing to participate at any time.

To minimize intentional concealment (or bragging), we collected saliva samples from the students, explaining that marijuana and tobacco use could be detected in saliva. Such procedures have been shown to improve the accuracy of self-reported tobacco use (Bauman and Dent 1982; Murray, O'Connell, Schmid, and Perry 1987). Finally, we used different staff for data collection and for program delivery to reduce the possibility that students in treatment schools might try to provide the answers that their Project ALERT teachers would like (or dislike).

3. Datafile Creation, Descriptive Statistics, and Exploratory Analysis

Survey data almost always require some processing before the beginning of useful data analysis. Among the steps we took were:

- Created binary variables corresponding to categories of nominal variables such as race/ethnicity group. We also sometimes created binary variables by aggregating responses for variables with three or more options.

- Reversed the order of values for selected survey items so that high values consistently corresponded to undesirable behavior. This step facilitated interpretation of relationships without the constant need to refer to a codebook.

- Created "scale scores" that averaged responses from multiple items intended to measure the same latent trait such as confidence to resist drug offers. The resulting variables typically relate more strongly to use or other behaviors than any one of the individual items.

- Created other derived variables that combined information from several survey items. For example, our definitions of "experimental" use of a substance combined information from questions about use in the student's lifetime, the past year, and the past month.

- Compared responses among logically related survey items to detect inconsistencies and "corrected" those where the preponderance of evidence pointed to a particular item being in error.

To determine whether the curriculum's effectiveness differed for nonusers and experimenters compared with users, we divided the students into three risk levels for each substance, defined by their baseline use. For cigarettes and alcohol, we used the three levels shown in Table 1.1.

Because students who had not tried marijuana constitute a large and heterogeneous group, we subdivided them into two risk levels: those who had not smoked cigarettes by seventh grade and those who had. The third level includes all students who had already tried marijuana.

4. Statistical Methods and Model

4A. Adjusting for Baseline Differences Among the Experimental Cells

Although randomized assignment eliminates systematic differences among experimental groups, we believe that analysts should use regression methods to rule out alternative explanations for the estimates of program effects (Cochran 1957). First, when the number of assigned units is limited, random assignment, even combined with other methods, cannot eliminate all pretreatment differences between experimental conditions. Second, some valuable predictors of outcomes do not become available until after the assignment process. Third, no matter how equivalent the pretreatment cells, postbaseline attrition can introduce bias among conditions. The potential imbalance is greatest when the number of experimental units is relatively small. In such cases, it is essential to check for preintervention

Table 1.1. Definitions of Baseline Risk Levels for Alcohol and Cigarettes

Risk Level	Baseline Use
1. Nonusers	Never tried
2. Experimenters	Tried once or twice (but not in the past month)
3. Users	Tried three or more times in the past year (or used in the past month)

equivalence and to control for multiple characteristics frequently related to drug use.

For alcohol, cigarettes, and marijuana, we analyzed a series of binary outcomes for each such as whether a student had used in the past year, in the past month, at least monthly (at least three days in the past month or 11 days in the past year), or at least weekly (six or more days in the past month). We used logistic regression to adjust estimated treatment effects for differences in baseline covariates (variables that predicted subsequent substance use) among the experimental groups. Logistic regression is an extension of linear regression designed to handle binary outcomes, where several assumptions of linear regression necessarily fail (Hosmer and Lemeshow 1989). For a binary outcome Y and vector of predictor variables X, including dummy (binary) variables indicating the experimental condition, the logistic regression model is

$$P(Y = 1 \mid X = x) = \frac{e^{\beta'x}}{1 + e^{\beta'x}} .$$

Covariates common to all the logistic regression models included dummy variables for district, dummy variables for Black and Asian (each of which tended to predict lower use), and a composite variable that equally weighted 64 baseline items. The composite variable covered peer and family use of and attitudes about alcohol, cigarettes, and marijuana, personal beliefs about those substances, and several background variables. For each specific substance, we also included intentions to use that substance, offers to use it, and a substance-specific scale of other items. When there was sufficient variation within a risk level, we included baseline use of that substance. Finally, we included other covariates that demonstrated consistent predictive power in preliminary analyses. The covariates that were used in each model are shown as rows in Table 1.2, with the table columns and entries indicating the models in which the covariates were used. For example, in the use of cigarette models, baseline use of cigarettes was used in the experimenter (baseline risk level 2; R2) and user (baseline risk level 3; R3) models but not in the nonuser (baseline risk level 1; R1) model. Baseline use of alcohol was used as a covariate for all three risk-level models, as were demographic variables on gender and race/ethnicity. To avoid knowing the impact that any covariate might have on estimated treatment effects, we excluded treatment indicators until the choice of covariates was finalized.

4B. Accounting for School as the Unit of Assignment

As noted above, we fit logistic regression models with individual students as the unit of analysis. However, since the unit of assignment is schools, estimates based on individual data must be adjusted for within-school correlation of outcomes. Such correlation causes a downward bias in standard-error estimates for school-level variables like treatment and thus excessively liberal significance tests. For linear regression, the default estimated variances for intervention ef-

Table 1.2. Covariates Included in Logistic Regression Models,
by Substance

| | Substance | | |
Covariate	Cigarettes	Alcohol	Marijuana
Baseline use			
Cigarettes	R2, R3	R1, R2	R2, R3
Alcohol	XX	R2, R3	XX
Marijuana	R3		R3
Intentions			
Same substance	XX	XX	XX
Number of offers			
Same substance	XX	XX	XX
Cigarettes		XX	
Demographics			
Gender	XX		
Black	XX	XX	XX
Asian	XX	XX	XX
District indicators	XX	XX	XX
Other variables			
Composite scale (64)	XX	XX	XX
Substance-specific scale (10–20)	XX	XX	XX
Cigarette scale (17)			XX
Friend scale (14)	XX		XX
Nonsubstance items (17)			XX
Academics (2)	XX		XX
Confidence to resist smoking			
on a date	XX		
Adult use of alcohol		XX	

NOTE: For scales, the number of items appears in parentheses after the name. XX = Covariate was used for all three risk levels for the substance. R1, R2, R3 = Covariate was used for corresponding risk level(s) for the substance.

fects need to be multiplied by a correction factor roughly equal to $1 + (m - 1)\rho$, where m is the average cluster size and ρ is the intracluster correlation (i.e., the correlation of errors for any two observations from the same cluster) (Kish 1965). Because the logistic regression model does not include error terms, we used the corresponding linear regression to estimate the intracluster correlation ρ for the models used in Project ALERT.

5. Results

5A. Fidelity of Curriculum Implementation

Monitoring of class sessions indicated that Project ALERT was indeed delivered as intended. Every scheduled class was presented, although several had to be rescheduled to accommodate special school events or unanticipated disruptions such as blizzards. The monitors recorded missed activities in 16% of the observed classes, but in half those cases, the omitted activity was the lesson wrap-up, which introduces no new material. In over 90% of the monitored classes, the 17 observers felt that the health educator and teen leaders had satisfactorily established the intended classroom environment, conveyed the intended substance, and combined substance and process. The monitors also observed that the teachers used a wide variety of styles to achieve these goals.

5B. Characteristics of the Sample Schools

In all, eight school districts ranging in size from three to nine middle schools, signed up. The resulting group of participating districts and schools encompassed a wide range of community and school environments (Tables 1.3 and 1.4). The eight districts included urban, suburban, and rural communities from five regions in California and Oregon, while the participating schools included a wide range of socioeconomic levels and ethnic and racial groups.

Among the participating seventh graders, 41% came from disrupted families (i.e., they did not live with both natural parents), and one-third had a minority background. The selection process also yielded substantial variation on other school characteristics for which no information was available at the time of district selection. For example, the percentage of students who had used cigarettes in the month prior to the baseline survey ranged from less than 10% in five schools to more than 30% in three other schools.

Table 1.3. Characteristics of the Eight Sample Districts

Characteristic	Number of Districts
Location	
Oregon	3
Northern California	3
Southern California	2
Locale type	
Large city (over 100,000)	2
Medium city (50,000–100,000)	1
Small city (under 50,000)	1
Suburb	3
Rural	1
Grade span	
6–8	2
7–8	4[a]
7–9	2

[a]One of these districts includes two schools with grades 7 to 12.

Table 1.4. Characteristics of the 30 Sample Schools

Characteristic	Number of Schools
Seventh-grade enrollment	
Under 200	5
200–299	16
300–399	6
400–499	3
Non-White (%)[a]	
0–9	6
10–19	9
20–49	6
50 or more	9
Parent with some college (%)[b]	
37–49	5
50–59	11
60–69	7
70–80	7

[a]Combined percentage of Black, Hispanic, Asian, American Indian, and multi-racial students, based on self-reports on the baseline survey.

[b]Percentage of students who reported at baseline that at least one parent had attended college for some time.

5C. Results of the Assignment Process

Table 1.5 compares the three experimental cells on several pretreatment sample characteristics measured at baseline. The assignment procedure achieved substantial comparability on the several measures displayed here that were unavailable when the assignments were made. For each of the substance use variables, the differences between cells are small compared with differences that might constitute "meaningful" treatment effects.

Use of blocking and restricted randomization substantially improved the balance across the experimental cells. For most variables, the amount of variation among cells is several times smaller than would have occurred, on average, with the use of simple random assignment.[4] An imbalance greater than expected occurred for only one variable; the percentage of parents who refused consent. Even for this variable, however, simple random assignment would have created greater imbalance about 20% of the time.

5D. Accuracy of Self-Reported Substance Use

The procedures to encourage honest reporting of substance use appear to have worked. Independent verification that the vast majority of students accurately reported recent cigarette use comes from the laboratory assessments of saliva cotinine. Using a cutoff point of 10 nanograms per milliliter (chosen to avoid mis-

Table 1.5. Baseline Survey Data by Experimental Cell

	Experimental Cell		
Item	Adult Only	Adult + Teen	Control
Mean school size	234	234	203
Parents who refused consent (%)	7	8	10
Percentage Black	11	9	11
Percentage Hispanic	12	7	12
Percentage Asian	8	9	7
One parent who attended college (%)	63	66	60
Used alcohol in lifetime (%)	74	74	73
Used cigarettes in lifetime (%)	52	52	52
Used marijuana in lifetime (%)	20	19	22
Used alcohol in past month (%)	21	24	23
Used cigarettes in past month (%)	16	16	14
Used marijuana in past month (%)	7	6	7

classifying nonsmokers who are exposed to second-hand smoke), we identified only 17 students out of more than 6500 as probable liars (i.e., they denied recent use of tobacco, but their saliva tests argued otherwise). Further, of students identified as recent tobacco users based on the laboratory tests ($n = 257$), 95% admitted to recent cigarette smoking or use of chewing tobacco.

However, the saliva cotinine test may not detect students who have used a relatively small dosage and offers no evidence about the accuracy of self-reported alcohol and marijuana use. For these reasons, we also assessed the consistency of student reports for all three substances, both within a questionnaire and over time. Fewer than 5% of the students provided incomplete or inconsistent responses within questionnaires, rates that reflect those found in other studies of self-reported drug use by adolescents (Single, Kandel, and Johnson, 1975; Barnea, Rahav, and Teichman 1987). Moreover, the rates declined after we eliminated skip patterns from drug use item batteries, suggesting that the problems largely reflected confusion and carelessness rather than deliberate misrepresentation.

Severe inconsistencies between questionnaires were also rare.[5] Although more than 40% of the students committed at least one longitudinal inconsistency over four data collection periods, over 95% of these discrepancies were minor. They involved inconsistent reporting of experimental use (which might have been long before) or errors in placing previously reported use within the appropriate 12-month period. Table 1.6 shows the frequency of retractions by wave (data collection period) and substance. At two of the three waves, they averaged less than 5% across substances; at the fourth, they averaged less than 7%. Throughout this period, there were comparatively fewer retractions for marijuana, largely because fewer students had used marijuana at each data collection period. Only 5% of the total number of discrepancies reflected reversals of pre-

*Table 1.6. Percentage of Students Who Retracted Previously
Admitted Use*

Wave	Alcohol	Cigarettes	Marijuana
2	6.0	3.8	2.1
3	7.1	5.2	2.5
4	8.3	7.5	4.2

viously admitted frequent use (at least 11 times in the past year or six times in the past month). These findings support the conclusions of earlier studies that the majority of inconsistencies are committed by students who have used marijuana infrequently (Single, Kandel, and Johnson 1975; O'Malley, Bachman, and Johnston 1983; Collins, Graham, Hansen, and Johnson 1985; Mensch and Kandel 1988).

5E. Impact of Intraschool Correlation

After controlling for intervention, district, baseline use, and other covariates, intraschool correlations were generally small. However, values for individual outcomes could not be estimated very precisely. Indeed, about 40% of the estimated values of the intraschool correlations ρ, the population intracluster correlation, were negative. Using those values would have produced "correction" factors that reduced the estimated standard error, an implausible result. Our analysis indicated that the various substance use outcomes analyzed during junior high school shared a common ρ of approximately 0.0032. The resulting multiplicative adjustment factors for standard errors were small, ranging from 1.04 to 1.11. Nevertheless, those adjustments substantially lowered the number of statistically significant program effects. Twenty-four percent of the differences that were significant at the 0.05 level before the adjustment did not breach this threshold after recalculating the t-statistics. Thus, when schools are the unit of assignment and individuals are the unit of analysis, experimental research that fails to incorporate appropriate adjustments for school effects runs the risk of sharply overstating treatment effects. This risk applies whenever the two units, assignment and analysis, differ; the criticism holds for many drug-prevention studies.

5F. Summary of Results and Conclusions from the First 15 Months

The main findings and conclusions during junior high school were (Ellickson and Bell 1990a,b):

- The program was effective at reducing marijuana use, particularly for students who had not used either cigarettes or marijuana before baseline. For students who had never used marijuana or cigarettes (risk level 1), marijuana initiation was reduced by one-third in both treatment groups. Project ALERT's effect on students in the two higher risk levels showed a consistent pattern of reductions, but the effects were smaller and less often statistically significant.

- Among those who had experimented with cigarettes at baseline, the treatment groups smoked significantly less on several measures, from occasional to serious use. Fifteen months after baseline, current use (any use in the past month) was 17–27% lower in the treatment groups than in the control group. Weekly use was one-third to one-half lower. These favorable results typically did not show up until after the students had received the three booster lessons.

- Project ALERT was not effective for baseline smokers, whose use was actually higher in the treatment schools. Fifteen months after baseline, current smoking was 15–29% higher in the treatment schools.

- Immediate reductions in drinking for all three risk levels—nonusers, experimenters, and users—eroded after the students entered the eighth grade. This suggests that the social influence approach to prevention is more likely to succeed against substances that are disapproved by society.

- The results apply to a wide variety of school environments in California and Oregon. The program was at least as effective in schools with high minority enrollments as in White, middle-class schools.

- Our findings suggest that booster lessons are important for maintaining and strengthening early program results. The eighth-grade booster curriculum appeared to provide the reinforcement needed for the emergence of significant smoking reductions and to prevent the erosion of seventh-grade program effects for marijuana.

- Program outcomes did not justify the extra time and resources involved in using teen leaders in the classroom. Contrary to our expectations, the findings yielded no clear recommendation for using older teens in the classroom. Neither method of curriculum delivery showed a dominant pattern across all three substances.

6. Discussion

Learning from the successes as well as the failures of social experiments helps the scientific community build on past experience and improve future work. What lessons emerge from our experience?

First, working directly with institutions rather than with individuals introduces design challenges. Our contact-to-success recruitment ratio was slightly more than two to one. That ratio was a function of our dual requirements: (1) to obtain a diverse collection of communities; and (2) to obtain communities and schools that would adhere to strict experimental requirements. Successfully putting together a broad test of this program entailed considerable effort and expense. Clearly, a more cost-effective approach would have been to try to select a set of diverse schools within one large political entity. The tradeoff, of course, would have been reduced external validity in terms of geographic locations and community types.

Neither the sample of schools nor the resulting sample of students can be considered a random or representative sample from California and Oregon. However, our goal was to evaluate Project ALERT's effectiveness across different school and district environments rather than to estimate use in a specific population. Just as critically, each school complied fully with experimental conditions we set forth in our screening process. Thus, the purposive nature of the sample enhanced the study's generalizability without affecting its internal validity.

Second, communities and schools will abide by experimental conditions if they understand the importance of doing so and feel that their burden has been minimized within that constraint. Such cooperation is critical because the loss of a single school after the assignments are complete threatens the credibility of the entire experiment. Once they had agreed to the requirements, the organizations that participated in Project ALERT cooperated fully with the study over several years. Setting forth clear agreements at the beginning of the study and following through on each obligation was central to developing and maintaining a cooperative relationship.

Third, it is important to balance the need for full implementation of an intervention with steps to ensure that the implementation can be replicated in the real world. The effective innovation literature highlights ownership and the ability to adapt an innovation to its particular organizational environment as key to successful implementation (Berman and McLaughlin 1978; Sarason 1982; Ellickson and Petersilia 1983). We worried that teachers might resist our requirement that schools implement the curriculum as designed and would deliver an inadequate program. During training, therefore, we repeatedly encouraged teachers to inject their own styles into the delivery process while also following the written lessons. The judgments of 17 different monitors indicate that the great majority of teachers both conveyed the curriculum's substance and created a facilitative classroom environment in which student participation was encouraged and rewarded.

Fourth, as several other studies have shown, carefully encouraging truthful and accurate reporting can yield reliable drug use self-reports (Single, Kandel, and Johnson 1975; Williams, Eng, Botvin, Hill, and Wynder 1979). We gave strict privacy guarantees, collected physiological samples before survey administration, and pilot-tested questionnaire items. The overall results proved to be very successful, but we cannot judge which of these activities was the most or least effective in improving accuracy.

Fifth, both design and analysis should address balance among cells. For field trials in which the units of assignment are large and limited in number, producing a balanced experimental design requires more than simple random assignment. While the best mix of blocking, matching, and randomization will vary from one study to another, some effort to limit the preintervention differences pays a generous reward in terms of credibility.

Even with these efforts, it is important to control for theoretically important or empirically relevant variables when estimating treatment effects. Even if pretreatment measured variables are equal, attrition can produce substantial differences across conditions over time.

Finally, we could not have achieved many of our objectives in a moderate-scale study of, say, ten schools in two or three sites. To compare the results in high- versus low-minority districts requires several districts with multiple schools per district. The additional schools also provided the flexibility needed to construct balanced experimental groups and to estimate reliably the size of correlations within schools. This is one reason why conducting experiments with schools and other institutions is often so difficult. Funding and implementing large-scale experiments is expensive, time consuming, and a lot of work. Nonetheless, well-designed and well-implemented studies provide the best information available to decision-makers. Thus, they can be as valuable to the development of public policy as clinical trials are to medical science.

7. Exercises

The dataset and accompanying documentation for the following exercises are available on our website (www.rand.org/centers/stat/casebook).

1. The Project ALERT experiment hired and trained outside teachers to deliver the curriculum. Alternatively, existing classroom teachers from the treatment schools could have been trained to give the lessons. Discuss the pros and cons of that alternative in regard to internal and external validity.

2. The dataset named "alert" on the website contains data on recent marijuana use at ninth grade (variable m_mo_9) and selected baseline predictors for a 25% sample of students with complete data. For simplicity, the dataset includes only some of the observations and variables included in the full analysis of ninth-grade outcomes (Bell, Ellickson, and Harrison 1993). Fit a logistic regression for the binary dependent variable m_mo_9 on nine independent variables: m_level2, m_level3, m_intent, black, asian, scale64, friends, hec, and tlc. Repeat this regression separately for samples defined by the three values of m_level. Note that m_level2 and m_level3 must be dropped from the model. Compare twice the log likelihood ratio for the first logistic regression with twice the sum of the log likelihoods for the three other regressions. The difference provides a chi-square statistic for testing the null hypothesis that the three sets of regression coefficients other than the intercepts are equal for the three risk levels. How many degrees of freedom does this chi-square statistic have? What is the result of the test?

3. Refit the logistic regression for the combined sample, deleting various subsets of the covariates (i.e., independent variables other than hec and tlc).

How sensitive are predicted probabilities of use to the choice of covariates? Hint: Try graphing predicted values from one model against those for another model. How sensitive are the coefficients and P-values for the hec and tlc coefficients to the choice of covariates?

Further RAND Reading

Bell, R. M., and Ellickson, P. L. (1989), *Does Pooling Saliva for Cotinine Testing Save Money Without Losing Information?*, N-3089-CHF, Santa Monica, CA: RAND.

Ellickson, P. L. (1996), *Getting and Keeping Schools and Kids for Evaluation Studies*, RP-371, Santa Monica, CA: RAND.

Ellickson, P. L. (1999), *School-Based Substance-Abuse Prevention: What Works, for Whom, and How?*, LRP-199900-01, Santa Monica, CA: RAND.

Ellickson, P. L., Bell, R. M., and McGuigan, K. A. (1993), *Preventing Adolescemt Drug Use: Long-Term Results of a Junior High Program*, RP-208, Santa Monica, CA: RAND.

Ellickson, P. L., Bell, R. M., Thomas, M. A., Robyn, A. E., and Zellman, G. (1988), *Designing and Implementing Project ALERT: A Smoking and Drug Prevention Experiment*, R-3754-CHF, Santa Monica, CA: RAND.

Ellickson, P. L., and Robyn, A. E. (1987), *Toward More Effective Drug Prevention Programs*, N-2666-CHF, Santa Monica, CA: RAND.

Notes

[1]We thank the Conrad N. Hilton Foundation for its generous support in making the development and testing of Project ALERT possible.

[2]Five declined because they already had a drug-prevention program they did not want to drop; six others felt they could not comply with other experimental requirements— random assignment of schools (one), collection of physiological samples (one), or weekly scheduling of all curriculum sessions during one semester (four).

[3]For operational reasons, it was only feasible to offer the program to a single cohort of students in each school.

[4]Although blocking by district is responsible for much of the improvement over simple randomized assignment, matching schools across cells contributed as well. That is, the imbalance for most variables was less than would have occurred on average with blocking and randomization alone.

[5]Longitudinal inconsistencies occurred when: (1) students retracted previously admitted lifetime use; (2) they admitted lifetime use, but the new admission occurred within a time period covered by previous denials; or (3) they denied use in the past year after having admitted to current use three to nine months earlier. The third type was most frequent, reflecting problems in placing use within a precise time period.

2

The Health Insurance Experiment: Design Using the Finite Selection Model

Carl N. Morris and Jennifer L. Hill

Executive Summary

The Health Insurance Experiment (HIE) was designed in the 1970s to examine how different levels and types of insurance would affect health care spending and health status. We describe the design of this large public-policy experiment, concentrating on the sample allocation. We introduce an allocation methodology, the Finite Selection Model (FSM), that was developed explicitly for the HIE and produced substantial improvements in balance and efficiency compared to simple random sampling. The concepts and techniques used in the FSM have wide applications in survey and experimental design.

1. Introduction

1A. Policy Problem

The 1960s and 1970s were the era of large public-policy experiments, including the RAND Health Insurance Experiment (HIE). The first large-scale national public-policy experiments were the Income Maintenance Experiments, the first of which was completed in 1972 as the HIE was being developed. The HIE benefited from both its scientific and political legacy.

The debate on national health insurance in the early 1960s raised numerous unanswered policy questions. For example, some advocates of free health care believed that even if all citizens were covered, the demand for health services would increase little. However, at that time the effect of government subsidies on the demand for health care could only be estimated from observational data relying on strong assumptions.

In the face of such uncertainties about the potential cost of national health insurance, the Office of Economic Opportunity (OEO) awarded a grant to RAND in 1972 to investigate the effects of free or subsidized health insurance on the demand for care through the HIE. The HIE was fielded between 1974 and 1982 and involved nearly 3000 families in six sites nationwide. In this chapter, we draw heavily on Newhouse and the Insurance Experiment Group (1993).

1B. Research Questions

The principal research questions addressed by the HIE were:

- How do variations in deductible levels and coinsurance rates in health insurance plans affect health care spending and health status?
- How does the inclusion of particular services (dental, mental health, etc.) affect cost and health status?
- How would universal health care coverage affect the supply of health care services?
- Why do people who participate in group health plans use fewer services, and what effect does that have on their health status?
- What are the practical difficulties associated with administering a plan with income-related deductibles?

1C. Statistical Questions

What prompted the government to fund a multimillion dollar experiment rather than an observational study as the best way to address these research questions? A survey of families participating in a variety of existing health insurance plans could measure spending on health care and health status. However, the conclusions drawn from such an observational study may be misleading because participant characteristics, particularly unobserved ones, presumably differ systematically across insurance plans. Further, nothing could be learned about uninsured people or about insurance plans not in existence. Therefore, differences in outcomes among the different insurance plans could not be attributed solely to differing insurance coverage. Properly designed experiments can disentangle the effects of these various influences.

Designing the HIE required using available information to make many of the design decisions, including:

- What health insurance plans should be evaluated?
- How many sites should be used?
- Where should the sites be located?
- How many families should be enrolled in each site?
- What data concerning the participants should be collected?
- How long should the families participate?
- How should families be allocated to the insurance plans?

All of these design decisions are extremely important and vary to the degree that statistical thinking is required to make them. In this chapter, we focus on the last question, presuming that the six others have already been answered. The biasedness and the efficiency of the estimates made from the experimental data rest critically on how families are assigned to plans.

1D. Summary of Data and Methods

This chapter describes the possible strategies for assigning families to the specified insurance plans and discusses how we chose among them. To do this we need to define criteria for assessing designs and describe classical strategies (simple random sampling, blocking) for performing allocations that make limited use of the preliminary participant information. The design innovation we use is the Finite Selection Model (FSM). The FSM requires as input preenrollment data on HIE participants gathered in a baseline survey of families. The survey collected a wide variety of information including health status, previous use of health care, previous health insurance, and demographic characteristics (age, family size, income, etc.). The FSM can be thought of as generalizing blocking to many continuous variables. Such a generalization is needed for the HIE allocation because about 2000 families need to be assigned to 13 plans or treatments in a way that balances across 26 variables. With blocking, the cells quickly become too sparse. We develop the necessary concepts that describe the FSM and present measures of its gains in balance and efficiency compared to traditional design methods.[1]

2. Study Design, Data Collection, Description of Data Sources, and Description of Data Elements

2A. HIE Design Constraints

The treatments, number and location of sites, number of families, types of data to be collected, and duration of the experiment were decided before the sample allocation.

Treatments. HIE treatments were 12 fee-for-service insurance plans offered to participants and a 13th HMO plan.[2] These plans spanned the range of potential plans being considered by the government so that inferences could also be made about insurance plans that were not offered to HIE participants. In order to concentrate on the experimental aspects of the HIE, we describe only the fee-for-service plans and not the HMO plan.

HIE insurance plan coverages varied primarily along two dimensions: the coinsurance rate and the maximum dollar expenditure (MDE). The coinsurance rate is the percentage of health care costs paid by the family before the MDE is met. There were four coinsurance rates: 0% (free care), 25%, 50%, or 95%. For some plans, the coinsurance rate was higher for outpatient mental and dental care. The maximum dollar expenditure is defined as the maximum total annual out-of-pocket medical expenses that could be paid by the entire family before the insurance plan took over and paid all covered costs incurred for the remainder of the year. The MDEs in HIE plans were 5%, 10%, or 15% of family income or $1000 (in 1973 dollars), whichever was smaller.

Eleven of the 12 insurance plans are denoted by 0/0, 25/5 (25), 25/5 (50), 25/10 (25), 25/10 (50), 25/15 (25), 25/15 (50), 50/15, 95/5, 95/10, 95/15. The first number in each triplet is the coinsurance rate for all care except mental and dental outpatient, the second the MDE, and the number in parentheses the coinsurance rate for mental and dental outpatient care, which differed from that for other health care only for the 25% coinsurance plans. Thus, 25/10 (50) means 25% coinsurance was paid by the family for most of their care, except 50% coinsurance for mental and dental outpatient care, and after the family's total medical spending that year reached 10% of its annual income or $1000, whichever was less, all further medical costs were free.

The twelfth plan (Ind Ded) had an individual deductible. It provided free inpatient care but applied a 95% coinsurance rate separately for each individual up to an MDE of $150 (1973 dollars) per person.

Sites and Number of Observations. The HIE was fielded in six sites: Dayton, Ohio; Seattle, Washington; Fitchburg–Leominster and nearby Franklin County in Massachusetts; and Charleston and nearby Georgetown County in South Carolina. The fixed costs of administering each site argued for few sites. However, for a given sample size, more sites provide more information because they result in more variation in health care systems and in individual characteristics. Tradeoff calculations between the number of sites and the number of observations per site led to enrolling 2000 families across six sites with approximately the same number of families (an average of 333 families) in each site plus the Group Health plan in Seattle[3] (Newhouse and Morris 1976).

The six sites were chosen purposively in an effort to represent the United States with respect to variety of health care delivery systems and health care consumers. Only sites where local health care providers, insurance agencies, and politicians would cooperate were candidates. Site selection was based on health care supply, the region of the country, city size, and several demographic variables (Table 2.1).

Data. Once the sites and eligibility criteria[4] were determined, a sample of potential households was drawn and field-workers interviewed residents to determine their eligibility. They then administered a baseline survey on characteristics relevant to the statistical design.

The survey included questions on family composition, race, gender, age, income, education level, health measures, existing health insurance, and the past medical usage (e.g., number of visits to providers), health expenditures, and health status measures for each family member. We used this pre-experimental data, available several months before family enrollment, to assign families to the treatments.

Table 2.1. Characteristics of Sites

Site	Census Region	Population of Urbanized Area of County (1970)	Primary Care Physicians per 100,000 Population (1972)[a]	Days Spent Waiting for an Appointment with a Primary Care Physician, New Patient (1973, 1974)[b]	Median Family Income (1969 $00)	Percentage Over Age 24 with less than 5 Years of Education (1970)	% Black (1970)	Intended Number of Families
Seattle, Wash.	West	1,200,000	59	4.1	11.8	1.8	3	479[c]
Dayton, Ohio	North Central	690,000	41	7.5	11.4	3.3	13	400
Charleston, S.C.	South	230,000	33	15.9	8.3	6.2	25	271
Fitchburg–Leominster, Mass.	Northeast	78,000	30	25.0	10.0	4.3	1	247
Franklin County, Mass.	Northeast	59,000	46	9.2	9.9	2.8	1	294
Georgetown County, S.C.	South	34,000	44	0	6.4	20.6	48	309
United States	—	—	46	7.1	9.6	5.5	11	—

[a] Includes general practitioners, family practitioners, internists, and pediatricians.

[b] Physicians who do not use appointment systems and take patients on a first-come, first-served basis are valued as having zero wait time. All physicians sampled in Georgetown County at the time of the survey accepted patients on this basis. For other sites, the values are negligibly affected if only physicians using appointment systems are included.

[c] An additional 1892 participants were enrolled in the Group Health Cooperative of Puget Sound.

Duration. At each site, 75% of enrolled families participated in the experiment for three years and 25% participated for five years. Several considerations went into this decision. Families needed enough time to make health behavior and health provider changes in response to the benefits provided by their insurance plan. A short enrollment period also would be inadequate for health status to change in response to the better care provided by better health coverage.

On the other hand, studies that last too long may not provide timely and policy-relevant information, may have higher levels of attrition, and are more costly. The decision to enroll some families for three years and some for five helped to balance these tensions, and having two different enrollment periods allowed a test of the hypothesis that longer exposures to an insurance plan may have a different effect than shorter exposures.

Additional Considerations. The simplified description of the HIE given above ignores other complexities such as the five subexperiments that were conducted within each site to permit testing for potential sources of bias (Newhouse et al. 1979).

2B. Experimental Design Principles

Classical Criteria. A properly controlled experiment can separate out the treatment effect from the effects of all the other observed or unobserved population characteristics. Ideally, to attribute differences in outcomes between two groups purely to the difference in treatment, the people in each group should be identical (i.e., the groups are *balanced*). With complete balance, estimates of the treatment effect will be unbiased because the groups differ only in the treatment administered.

In practice, balance must be approximated often through *randomization,* by creating treatment groups that "look alike" *on average.* Random assignment to treatment removes the possibility of ad hoc assignments by researchers, administrators, or subjects which might bias the results. However, randomization may not produce exact balance since the assignment is random. Subsection 2D of this chapter describes methods that restrict randomization to achieve greater balance.

"Replication," the use of multiple observations for each treatment combination, usually is part of a good design. In each HIE site, many families were assigned to each insurance plan. Different responses across individuals assigned to the same treatment, beyond what is attributable to differences in the individuals' measured characteristics are due to *"natural variation."* Replications permit estimation of this variation to compare with the size of treatment differences.

Optimality Definitions. Balance is not the only criterion for evaluating experimental designs. The precision of regression coefficient estimates or linear combinations of those coefficients may be more important. Specifically, assume that

$$y = \beta_0 + \beta_1 x_1 + \beta_2 x_2 + \ldots + \beta_k x_k + e$$

and that the usual ordinary least-squares (OLS) regression assumptions apply. Then the formula for the variance of the estimated regression coefficient $\hat{\beta}_1$ is

$$\text{Var}\left(\hat{\beta}_1\right) = \frac{\sigma^2}{ns_1^2\left(1 - R_1^2\right)} , \tag{2.1}$$

where σ^2 is the variance of y given x, s_1^2 is the variance of x_1, and R_1^2 is the multiple correlation coefficient of x_1 with the other covariates $x_2, ..., x_k$ (Morris and Rolph 1981, p. 343). The assignment of observations to treatment groups affects this variance because it affects the s_1^2 and the R_1^2 terms. Subsection 2D explores design criteria that minimize (2.1).

2C. Choosing a Design Method

Randomized Designs. The allocation objective in each HIE site was to assign a specified number of eligible families to each of the 12 experimental treatment groups (insurance plans). Simple random sampling (SRS) is the easiest solution, and the only sensible approach if nothing were known about the families. Even when certain family characteristics are known, SRS and the law of large numbers guarantee that in large samples approximately the same proportion of families of each type will be assigned to each group.

In the HIE, many characteristics of each family were available before the allocations were made. These included the number of prior hospitalizations and physician visits by family members, the past annual spending on health care, and measures of health status (Table 2.8). Other relevant variables were pre-experimental insurance status and income, each of which might interact with insurance plan. Our goal was to balance these variables and many others across the insurance plans.

For treatment groups averaging about 50 families, SRS cannot do the job of balancing so many variables, even approximately. Restricted randomization combats this problem by forming strata, or blocks, of similar experimental units. For example, HIE families could have been stratified into three groups on the basis of their incomes: low, medium, and high. Then all treatment groups could have been assigned the same proportion from each group or stratum.

Two main limitations of stratified sampling are that:

- continuous variables must be made discrete; and

- it can only be used for a few variables.

To illustrate the first limitation, low-income families were defined as those earning less than $9000 in 1973. Thus, families earning $3000 are equivalent to those earning $8999, while a third family earning $9000 is put in a different stratum. The second limitation comes into play if there are three income strata of approximately equal sizes, and two racial groups with one racial group representing 10% of the population. Even if income and race are independent, only one in 30 families would fall in each income group for the smaller racial group. Some of the HIE treatment groups had fewer than 30 families per site, so no additional variables beyond these two could have been used for stratification.

Optimal Allocations. Simple random sampling maximizes the amount of randomization, whereas stratified sampling, although still random, restricts randomization to eliminate the most unbalanced allocations. In the extreme, optimal designs have no randomization at all. Nonrandomized designs, however well balanced, have serious "face validity" drawbacks, since randomization is widely viewed as essential to a valid design.

Optimal Covariance Designs (OPCODE). The "orthogonality principle" is central to the theory of experimental design. The principle states that the effect of one predictor can be best estimated if the other predictors are uncorrelated with it. This can be seen from (2.1), where $R_1^2 = 0$ minimizes the variance. Thus, the covariates should be uncorrelated with the treatment indicators. Equivalently, the covariates should have the same mean for each treatment.

Orthogonality requires equal average incomes for families across insurance plans in the HIE, and similarly for all other covariates used. When the covariate is a dummy variable, for example an indicator for a racial group, averages are proportions so that all treatments must have the same proportion.

"Optimal Covariance Design" (OPCODE) is a design that perfectly balances the covariates in a linear analysis of covariance model. Consider the model with only two treatments (or, rather, a treatment group, $T = 1$, and a control group, $T = 0$),

$$y_i = \beta_0 + \tau T_i + \beta_1 x_{i1} + \ldots + \beta_k x_{ik} + e_i ,$$

where τ represents the treatment effect (with T_i the treatment assigned to individual i). The coefficients for the k covariates $x_1, \ldots, x_k$ are $\beta_1, \ldots, \beta_k$, and e_i is the random error of individual responses. The OPCODE simultaneously minimizes the variances of all treatment contrasts (e.g., of all possible differences among treatments). It minimizes the variance of all estimates of regression coefficients in this model, even for models with several treatments (Haggstrom 1976). The variance of $\hat{\tau}$, the estimate of the treatment effect from (2.1), is

$$\text{Var}(\hat{\tau}) = \frac{\sigma^2}{ns_T^2(1 - R_{T|x}^2)}$$

and $s_T^2 = p(1 - p)$, with p the fraction of individuals with $T_i = 1$. We cannot control the residual variance σ^2, s_T^2, or n at the time of allocation, assuming the treatment and control group sizes are fixed at np and $n(1 - p)$. Thus, minimizing Var $(\hat{\tau})$ requires minimizing $R_{T|x}^2$, the squared multiple correlation coefficient for predicting the treatment indicator from the covariates. Its minimum possible value of zero is achieved by making all covariates uncorrelated with T. This is equivalent to making

$$\bar{x}_{j,T=1} = \bar{x}_{j,T=0} \, , \, j = 1, ..., k.$$

The average value of each of the k covariates is the same for each group. This argument proves the orthogonality principle in this special case.

Notice what happens if the vector of predictors is enlarged to include squared and interaction terms. The orthogonality principle now requires balancing the means, the variances (because of the squared terms), and the correlations (because interactions are formed as products of a pair of covariates). Carried to its limit, using more and more functions of the predictors, OPCODE requires that the treatments be matched with respect to the entire multivariate distribution of all covariates, observed and unobserved.

When all the explanatory variables are categorical, complete balance with respect to the proportions assigned to each treatment might be achievable in several ways. In such cases, it is reasonable to randomize among all the allocations that lead to the OPCODE solution, resulting in a restricted randomization.

In practice, an exact OPCODE sample assignment in which the means of all covariates are exactly matched across all treatments rarely is achievable, even for simple models. Even when it is achievable, the OPCODE solution depends heavily on the model choice and may require omitting important squared or interaction terms or discretizing continuous variables. Optimal designs may require overly precise prospective knowledge of the models that will be fit to the data. While more robust allocations usually are desirable, the OPCODE model is a useful ideal to guide experimental planning, even though it is inappropriate for sample allocation.

Conlisk–Watts Optimal Allocation Model. Conlisk and Watts (1979) developed an optimal allocation model for use in the Income Maintenance Experiments (IME). The Conlisk–Watts (C–W) model is a linear model, like the OPCODE model, with all covariates specified as categorical variables. An algorithm finds the sample sizes from each stratum for each treatment that minimize the weighted sum of variances of the main parameters of interest. The model requires specifying both "weights" that measure the relative importances of these parameters and the relative costs of assigning individuals from each stratum to each treatment. The optimal solution is obtained as the minimum of weighted variances.

The C–W model can violate the orthogonality principle. It did in the IME because it was cheaper to assign families with higher incomes to the more generous treatments, and vice versa. This lack of balance diminished confidence in the results of the IME results.

We rejected using the C–W model to allocate families to HIE treatments because we were not confident either of the correct model specification or of the relative costs of assigning families to different insurance plans. Indeed, these costs were the main outcomes the HIE was designed to estimate. Our lack of confidence about models was justified later; the models eventually developed to fit the HIE economic data were more complicated than initially anticipated (Newhouse and the Insurance Experiment Group 1993). However, the ideas underlying the C–W model led us to develop the Finite Selection Model (FSM), the sample allocation method we used for the HIE.

2D. Tensions Between Randomized and Optimal Designs

An ideal allocation method perfectly balances the observable covariates across treatments while randomizing the unobservable error terms e_i of a linear regression model for subject i:

$$y_i = \beta_0 + \tau T_i + \beta_1 x_{i1} + \ldots + \beta_k x_{ik} + e_i \, .$$

Optimal designs focus on balancing the observed covariates, but at the risk of causing the error terms e_i to have different distributions for all the treatments. Simple random sampling randomizes the error terms but causes the covariates to differ by random amounts across treatments. Blocking and stratified sampling help to balance covariates, but only a few, and they require categorizing continuous variables so similar subjects inevitably are placed in different categories. The HIE needed a way to randomize error terms while improving the balance of many covariates; the FSM was this way.

2E. The Finite Selection Model

We developed the Finite Selection Model to assign the eligible families to the HIE treatments in each site. The FSM embraces optimal design ideas, but it also introduces a new idea, "selection order," that combines randomness with optimality. We hope that readers will find the basic ideas of the FSM simple enough for use in their own experiments and surveys.

The FSM is based on three key concepts:

- a selection order matrix,
- a selection function, and
- design assessment.

We introduce and illustrate these three considerations with a small example that assumes an experiment will be fielded to evaluate and compare three treatments. The FSM sample allocation in each of the six HIE sites was a complex version of this example. The HIE was much more complicated because the subjects were families, many more predictors were available, about 400 families had to be assigned in most sites, 12 treatments had to be assigned, and the treatment sizes were not all the same.

Example. Each of $N = 12$ subjects, six females and six males, must be assigned to one of the three treatments. Four individuals must be assigned to each treatment. Balance dictates equal chances of assignment to each treatment, so the probability that any one of the subjects is assigned to any treatment is to be 1/3. Gender and age, which are significant predictors of the outcomes, are two covariates available to help improve the balance of these assignments (Table 2.2).

The Selection Order Matrix. The FSM requires that the treatments take turns choosing from the available pool of unselected families in a random and balanced order. A "selection order matrix" (SOM) specifies this sequence of choices. If strata are needed and are defined for the subjects, the SOM also specifies the stratum from which each choice must be made. An example of a selection order matrix is listed in Table 2.3. Notice that each treatment makes four choices, two from each gender-defined stratum.

The selection order in Table 2.3 was determined in this case by randomly permuting the treatments 1, 2, and 3 so that each treatment gets one of the first three choices, two of the first six, and so on. This randomization approach is one of several possible ways to assure that no treatment has a large advantage over the others by getting more than its fair share of early selections. Use of the strata guarantees that each of the three treatments will be gender-balanced, with two males and two females each. The SOM in Table 2.3 shows treatment 2 chose first, taking a male between the ages of 20 and 60, as determined by a "selection function." The second selection for this SOM is by treatment 1, which must choose among the remaining five males according to the same selection function, and so on. At the 12th selection, treatment 2 must choose the only remaining individual, who will be male because of the stratification. At each step, the

Table 2.2. Matrix of Covariates x for the Example

ID	Female	Age
1	0	20
2	0	30
3	0	40
4	0	40
5	0	50
6	0	60
7	1	20
8	1	30
9	1	40
10	1	40
11	1	50
12	1	60

NOTE: ID = identification number; female = 1 if female, 0 if male.

selection function, explained below, determines which choice a treatment makes from the available candidates in the stratum.

The SOM for the HIE in most of the six sites had as many rows as there were families to be assigned, usually between 400 and 600. The 12 treatment groups, and also a 13th group which selected families that were not to be assigned, were ordered in the second column of the SOM. (Usually, more families than were needed were available for selection, and it was necessary to choose that "discard" group with the FSM, to balance treatment groups with the entire sample of eligible families.) These 13 groups were of differing sizes. The random selection order guaranteed that the probability that any treatment appeared in any row of the matrix was proportional to the number of families to be assigned to the treatment. A special method of blocking the selection order, called Sequentially Controlled Markovian Random Sampling, (Morris 1983), was used to be sure that the selection order was protected even against random imbalances. Finally, the HIE families were placed in 15 strata according to family size groups and three income categories. The reader can visualize the SOM used in the HIE as a large version of Table 2.3.

The Selection Function. A selection function assigns a numerical score to each of the subjects based on their covariates, subjects with higher scores being more valuable to the treatment. Subjects are assigned sequentially to treatments using the rule: choose the subject whose selection function is the maximum (ties usually are handled by randomization). The selection function value usually depends on the covariates of the individual being selected and on the covariates of individuals already selected by that treatment. It is not permitted to depend on the characteristics of any experimental unit *already assigned to other treatments*.

Table 2.3. A Possible Selection Order Matrix (SOM)

	Selection Order Matrix		Random	Age
Selection #	Treatment	Stratum	ID	Code
1	2	0	6	M60
2	1	0	5	M50
3	3	0	4	M40
4	1	1	12	F60
5	3	1	11	F50
6	2	1	10	F40
7	3	1	9	F40
8	2	1	8	F30
9	1	1	7	F20
10	2	0	3	M40
11	3	0	2	M30
12	1	0	1	M20

NOTE: "Treatment" = Treatment label. Stratum = 0 if a male is to be chosen, 1 if female. Age Code = individual selected; e.g., "M60" is 60-year-old male. Choices are for oldest age selection function (see the text).

All treatments must use the same selection function so that they make equally "informed" choices. Along with the randomness of the SOM, this condition balances the assignment of experimental units.

The simplest form of selection function is a constant and results in choosing a random individual from the specified stratum; that is, a stratified random sample. The treatment assignments are shown later in Table 2.5 with the results of other methods.

Another selection function—one that depends on the data in a simple way—values a subject according to his or her age so that the oldest available individual is chosen at each step. To simplify this presentation, ties are always resolved by choosing the individual with the highest ID number. This ID would be a random choice if the individuals were numbered at random, which we recommend and did in the HIE. With this selection function and the SOM of Table 2.3, two males of ages 20 and 50 and two females of ages 20 and 60 are the four subjects allocated to treatment 1.

Conditional Selection Functions. Both of these selection functions just mentioned are "unconditional," meaning that treatments value the subjects available for choice without considering the characteristics of the subjects already assigned to that treatment. Selection functions that are derived from an optimality criterion would make "conditional" choices, so that the best choice depends on the subjects that already have been assigned to the treatment.

A simple example of a useful conditional selection function values each subject according to its contribution to the variance of the ages of all individuals already assigned to the treatment at the time of the selection. This criterion minimizes $\text{Var}(\hat{\beta}_1)$, the variance of the estimated age regression coefficient β_1 (fitted by least-squares in a linear regression for predicting a response from age), using only the subjects already chosen for the given treatment as we saw in (2.1). It is easy to show by (2.2) for updating the variance of a sample that is increased from n to $n+1$ observations, that maximizing the variance is equivalent at each step to valuing an unselected subject more according to the absolute value of the difference between that subject's age and the average age of the n subjects already chosen by the treatment. The updating formula is

$$s_{n+1}^2 = \frac{n}{n+1} s_n^2 + \frac{n}{(n+1)^2} \left(x - \bar{x}_n\right)^2 , \qquad (2.2)$$

with $\bar{x}_n$ the mean and s_n^2 the sample variance (dividing by n, not $n-1$). Note that the randomization in the SOM still assures a degree of randomization in the conditional selection function situation.

To implement this rule, a start-up value is needed (when $n = 0$). We will assume that before any assignments have been made, the average age for a treatment is the overall average age, 40. Thus, the first choice is a subject whose age differs as much as possible from 40, with ties broken by choosing the highest ID.

The reader should follow carefully the sequence of selections made, listed under the "selection ID made" column in Table 2.4, by writing down the choices made by each treatment and still available for that selection. Those choices use this third selection function. Ties are broken by choosing the highest ID. The assignments organized by treatment are in the middle of Table 2.5.

The HIE selection function was calculated to minimize the weighted average of the variances of the estimated regression coefficients for 27 of the most important family characteristics. The weights reflected each variable's importance. Some of the largest weights were for the pre-experimental measurements of the key outcome variables: past use of medical care, health levels, and insurance coverage (Table 2.8). This provided good balance for the most important predictors of health care spending and health levels. The variances of estimates are calculated using well-known methods for analysis of covariance models. These formulas and the derivations needed to minimize computing costs—akin to (2.2)—for each selection are described in Morris (1979).

Table 2.4. Selection Order Matrix (SOM) for the Conditional Selection Function

n	Treatment	From Stratum	Available Age Range	Current Mean	Age Chosen	Selection ID Made
1	2	0	20–60	40.0	60	6
2	1	0	20–50	40.0	20	1
3	3	0	30–50	40.0	50	5
4	1	1	20–60	20.0	60	12
5	3	1	20–50	50.0	20	7
6	2	1	30–50	60.0	30	8
7	3	1	40–50	35.0	50	11
8	2	1	40–40	45.0	40	10
9	1	1	40–40	50.0	40	9
10	2	0	30–40	43.3	30	2
11	3	0	40–40	40.0	40	4
12	1	0	40–40	40.0	40	3

NOTE: "Treatment" = Treatment label; and Stratum = 0 if a male is to be chosen, 1 if female.

Table 2.5. Results of Selections as Made by the Three Selection Functions Using the Same SOM

Gender	Random Stratified				Maximum Age				Maximum Standard Deviation of Age			
	M	F	F	M	M	F	F	M	M	F	F	M
Treatment 1:	40	30	40	20	50	60	20	20	20	60	40	40
Treatment 2:	60	40	20	30	60	40	30	40	60	30	40	40
Treatment 3:	40	50	60	50	40	50	40	30	50	20	50	30

Design Assessment. Once the sample assignments are made, we could assess the statistical properties of the FSM results. In our simple example, it is informative to calculate how balanced the means and the variances of ages are across the treatments. Does the FSM actually provide better results than stratified random sampling? Table 2.6 addresses this question.

The means and standard deviations in Table 2.6 are calculated for the four ages assigned to each treatment using the results from Table 2.5. Correlations are between the ages and genders of the four individuals in each case. The OP-CODE ideal would have all means equal to 40.0, the average of the entire sample. As would be expected, the random method performs worst and the maximum standard deviation of age performs perfectly.

The standard deviations of age vary by treatment. For the second selection function they vary from 7.1 years to 17.9 years. Treatment 1, with ages of 50, 60, 20, and 20, is highly variable, which is good when making estimates for treatment 1. But treatment 3 has a small variation for its ages so that the effect of age variation can be assessed much more poorly for this treatment. Note that the third selection function again achieves by far the best balance.

The correlation between the age and the female indicator variables cannot be balanced over the three treatments very well in a sample so small, so there is little difference among the three methods in this regard. Good balance would correspond to producing correlations that are close to the population value (in this case zero) for every treatment. None of these three selection functions was designed to be concerned about correlation. A better selection function, like that used for the HIE, would also help balance the correlations.

Design assessment for the HIE was done separately for each sample selection using various measures of balance and accuracy. The selection function was specified to choose the unselected family that improved accuracy the most. Section 4 gives assessment results for the Charleston and Georgetown sites. In every

Table 2.6. Design Assessment for the Three Selection Methods

Selection Function	Treatment	Mean Age	Standard Deviation of Age	Correlation Between Age and Gender
Random	1	32.5	8.3	0.3
	2	37.5	14.8	– 0.5
	3	50.0	7.1	0.7
Maximum age	1	37.5	17.9	0.1
	2	42.5	10.9	– 0.7
	3	40.0	7.1	0.7
Maximum standard deviation of age	1	40.0	14.1	0.7
	2	40.0	12.2	– 0.4
	3	40.0	12.2	– 0.4

HIE site, the FSM provided major improvements in estimation accuracy and in the balance of the relative to stratified random sampling. Because these design assessments were obtained immediately after each sample was selected, they served as a diagnostic to be sure that nothing had gone wrong with the sample selections, whether by human error, computer error, or a very unlucky randomization.

3. Datafile Creation, Descriptive Statistics, and Exploratory Analysis

The FSM was applied separately to make sample assignments at each site over a period of about two years. The total number of families intended to be enrolled in each of the 12 treatments in each site is given in Table 2.1. An average of 333 families were meant to be enrolled in each site, for a total of 2000 families (excluding the HMO families in Seattle) with Seattle (479 intended families enrolled) and Dayton (400 intended) being somewhat larger. The sample proportions for the 12 distinct insurance plans are given in Table 2.7. More

Table 2.7. Intended and Actual Sample Allocation by Plan

Plan[a]	Optimal % for Demand Analysis	Optimal % for Health Status Analysis	Average of Columns 2 and 3	Intended Number of Families[b]	Actual Number of Families
0/0	24.2	36.2	30.2	604	635
25/5 (25)	⎧ 7.1	⎧ 6.7	3.8	76	78
25/5 (50)	⎩	⎩	3.1	62	60
25/10 (25)	⎧ 6.8	⎧ 6.4	3.6	72	76
25/10 (50)	⎩	⎩	3.0	60	67
25/15 (25)	⎧ 6.6	⎧ 6.9	3.5	70	71
25/15 (50)	⎩	⎩	2.9	58	44
50/15[c]	13.1	0	6.5	131	131
9/15	⎧	⎧	6.4	129	127
95/10	⎨ 20.3	⎨ 21.3	6.6	131	118
95/15	⎩	⎩	7.8	156	142
Individual deductible	21.9	23.1	22.5	450	456
Total fee-for-service families				2000	2006

[a]The first value is the coinsurance rate; the second value is the percentage of income limit. The figure in parentheses for the 25% coinsurance rate plans is the coinsurance rate for dental and mental health.
[b]Intended number of families equals column 4 × 2000.
[c]Includes 28 families in the 50/5 plan and 19 in the 50/10 plan in Dayton.

families were chosen in each site to allow for ineligibles. Ineligible families included those that had moved away, could not be found, or refused to enroll.

The proportions of families in each site to be assigned to each insurance plan were determined as part of the experimental design. They reflect the relative importance of each plan in estimating the regression coefficients measuring several responses of interest, especially demand for health care and health status. As Table 2.7 shows, higher proportions were needed for the extreme plans, especially for the free plan. The considerations for determining these numbers are summarized in Newhouse and the Insurance Experiment Group (1993, Appendix B).

Balance dictated that each particular treatment be assigned the same proportion of families in each site. This rule was followed closely. Thus the proportions for each plan shown in Table 2.7 were multiplied by the total number of families needed for selection in each site to determine the number $n_1,...,n_{12}$ of families to be selected for enrollment interviews.

Finally, a 13th "discard group" was created because more families than were needed were available for assignment in most sites. This 13th group had n_{13} families that could not be assigned to an insurance plan. Producing a good statistical design not only required balancing the 12 treatments with each other but balancing them with the discard group, so that all groups are similar to the entire sampled population. Thus, the numbers $n_1,...,n_{13}$ were fixed and known as input to the FSM before sample allocation in each site, the total $N = n_1 + ...+ n_{13}$ being the number of families available for assignment in the site.

In each of the six sites, information from a baseline survey of the families was available for use in allocating families to the 12 plans. From this file, 21 factors were identified as most relevant to the sample assignment, resulting in 24 variables in the regression model since two of these factors—health status and age group—were decomposed into categories (Table 2.8). Other variables were needed for the stratification part of the selection order matrix. The stratification was based principally on family size, ensuring that the same proportion of families of each size was assigned to each treatment. Further control also was exerted through stratification so that multiple family units were distributed equitably to the plans. For example, if several families lived in the same household, all were required to be assigned to the same insurance plan. Learning how insurance plans might affect families differently was one of the HIE's main goals. Therefore, the three income categories (family income below $9000, between $9000 and $14,999, and above $15,000 in 1973 dollars) also were assigned as strata in the selection order matrix, guaranteeing balance for these categories across the insurance plans at the time of the FSM assignment. Income was used in this way as a covariate in the linear model and also as a stratification variable in the FSM.

The variables in Table 2.8 were specified for the linear regression. Some variables were transformed based on our modeling experience. Total income and its nonwage income component were specified in logarithmic form, and the physician visits of children and the adults in the family were averaged separately

Table 2.8. Variables and Weights Used in the Finite Selection Model

Variable	Specification	Number of Variables	Weight
Annual physician visits			
Children (<18)	Average among family	1	100
Adults (18+)	members in age group	1	100
Self-perceived health status	Excellent, good, fair–poor	3	100
Income	Logarithmic, adjusted for family size, using two years of data[a]	1	100
Family size	Logarithmic	1	100
Age	Proportion of family members in each of four categories (0–5, 6–17, 18–44, 45+)	4	100
Education of male head	Scaled according to ability to predict income	1	100
Education of female head	Same as education of male head	1	100
Maximum wage rate	Maximum of hourly wages over all heads[b]	1	100
Pain	Proportion in family experiencing pain at least fairly often	1	80
Worry	Proportion in family with at least some health worry	1	80
Health insurance	Had health insurance at time experiment began	1	80
Number of heads of household	1, 2, . . .	1	80
Race	White or other	1	80
Sex	Proportion of females in family	1	50
AFDC recipient		1	50
Employed head	Categorical variable, indicating at least one employed head	1	30
Nonwage, nontransfer income	Logarithmic	1	30
Location	Miles east and north from a fixed point	2	30
Annual hospital admissions	Proportion in family with at least one	1	30
Constant term		1	10

[a]Adjusted for family size using an equivalence scale.

[b]Salaried workers were inputted an hourly wage based on annual earnings and hours worked, as were individuals with other forms of compensation such as commissions and bonuses.

for each of these two categories after transforming them by taking the logarithm of the number of visits for each individual plus 2. Finally, the mean of each of these 24 variables over all families was subtracted from each variable to make the constant term for each treatment interpretable as the treatment effect. That makes the constant term the most important parameter of the 25 specified for each treatment. This data matrix plus the stratum assignments for each family were all the data needed to apply the FSM.

4. Results

4A. How Well the Design Worked

The FSM was intended in the HIE to balance the covariate values of individuals in the 13 treatment groups at each of the six sites better than stratified random samples could. A stratified random sample was saved each time the FSM was used for comparison purposes. Focusing on nine treatment groups (clustering several of the smallest groups), let us consider results for the final two sites.

Charlestown Example. Across 24 variables and nine treatment groups, the differences between the group means and the overall means were reduced by 25% on average by the FSM. The variance of estimates for each of the nine treatment groups was reduced 11% in aggregate. This is equivalent to a 10% increase in sample size as compared to random sampling. The FSM reduced the variances of the treatment effects by 34%, the equivalent of a 50% increase in sample.

A more complicated measure of balance, but natural in the FSM context, is how different the variances, adjusted for sample size, are for a particular covariate across the nine groups. Ideally, all nine groups are the same (i.e., the standard deviation of these nine numbers is 0). Relative to stratified random sampling, these 24 standard deviations were reduced 50% by the FSM, providing much better balance than a stratified random sample. This variability across the nine groups was reduced by 90% for the treatment effects

Georgetown Example. The comparison of FSM to stratified random sampling in the Georgetown, S.C., site is even more favorable. The means for the nine treatment groups averaged 40% closer to the grand mean for each variable. The other comparisons are harder to assess because the stratified random sample did not assign any welfare families to one of the smaller groups (technically, the variance for estimating the welfare effect in that treatment group with the random sample would be infinite, making all global averages of variances infinite). Even excluding that case, overall gains by the FSM exceeded a 15% reduction in variances compared with the random sample. The variance reduction for the nine treatment effects was 38% relative to the random sample.

Refusal may affect the balance in any design. Even if a perfectly balanced allocation had been feasible, some families inevitably would drop out and diminish the balance. The overall refusal rate was about 13%. The FSM still provided substantial gains in the presence of refusals.

These two examples typified the gains provided by the FSM in the other sites. In all cases, relative to stratified random sampling, there were noticeable reductions in the variances of estimates for treatment effects and for covariate (income, age, and other covariates) effects. Improvements in balance by the FSM were even greater.

4B. HIE Results

The HIE analyzed different response variables and summaries of some main analyses follow.

Effects on Medical Care Use. Table 2.9 shows annual per capita use of medical services for five categories of plans. The table gives simple ANOVA estimates from data collected during the experiment (not data available to the FSM).

Families with less generous coverage tend to use fewer health services and spend less money on health care. All of the χ^2 tests except that for inpatient expenditures indicate heterogeneity across plans. All of the t-tests of the hypotheses of equal outcomes between the free and the 95% MDE group are statistically significant.

Effects on Health Status. Several health status measures were recorded for each participant at the end of the experiment. These include respiratory, circulatory, musculoskeletal, gastrointestinal, and endocrine measures as well as tests on vision and hearing and an analysis of blood and urine samples. Comparisons between the cost-sharing plans and the free plans reveal only one statistically significant result. There were higher levels of dyspepsia among free-plan participants across the 27 variables observed (Newhouse and the Insurance Experiment Group, 1993, pp.198–199).

The Finite Selection Model was an integral component of the Health Insurance Experiment's design. Its key features include a random selection order matrix (SOM), a linear model with parameters to be estimated as accurately as possible, a selection function derived from the model, and a design assessment. Part of the design assessment required calculation of a "precision-balance" matrix. This is the matrix of variances (relative to stratified random sampling) for the estimates of the parameters of interest, as discussed in Section 4. This matrix showed substantial improvements in overall precision due to the FSM in each HIE site.

5. Discussion

5A. Advantages and Limitations

Any complex statistical method such as the FSM has advantages and limitations. Here are some limitations.

- The FSM did not completely determine the assignment of families to treatments in the HIE. Family changes and moves occurred after FSM selections that made the actual assignments more random. Several months lapsed between the time the data were collected describing the families and when the families were contacted for assignment. During that time

Table 2.9. Annual Use of Medical Services per Capita by Plan (Standard Errors in Parentheses)[a]

Plan	Likelihood of any Use (%)	Outpatient Expenditures (1991 $)	Face-to-Face Visits	One or more Admissions (%)	Total Expenditures (1991 $)	Total Admissions	Inpatient Expenditure (1991 $)	Number of Person-Years
Free	86.8	446	4.55	10.3	982	0.128	536	6822
	(0.8)	(14)	(0.17)	(0.45)	(50.7)	(0.0070)	(42)	
25%	78.7	341	3.33	8.4	831	0.105	489	4065
	(1.4)	(20)	(0.19)	(0.61)	(69.2)	(0.0070)	(56)	
50%	77.2	294	3.03	7.2	884	0.092	590	1,401
	(2.3)	(22)	(0.22)	(0.77)	(189.1)	(0.0166)	(182)	
95%	67.7	266	2.73	7.9	679	0.099	413	3727
	(1.8)	(16)	(0.18)	(0.55)	(58.7)	(0.0078)	(49)	
Individual deductible	72.3	308	3.02	9.6	797	0.115	489	4175
	(1.5)	(16)	(0.17)	(0.55)	(60.3)	(0.0076)	(55)	
χ^2 (4)[b]	144.7	85.3	68.8	19.5	15.9	11.7	4.1	
P-value	2.8×10^{-30}	1.3×10^{-17}	4.1×10^{-14}	0.0006	0.003	0.02	n.s.	
P-value for free vs. 95% contrast[c]	1.6×10^{-22}	2.0×10^{-17}	1.0×10^{-13}	0.00037	0.000051	0.0028	0.027	
Noise index[d]	0.009	0.032	0.037	0.044	0.052	0.055	0.078	

[a]The values in the table are sample means by plan. All standard errors are corrected for intertemporal and intrafamily correlation using an approach due to Huber; see Newhouse and the Insurance Experiment Group (1993). Dollars are expressed in 1991 dollars. Visits are face-to-face contacts with M.D., D.O., or other health providers and exclude visits for only radiology, anesthesiology, or pathology services. All data exclude dental services and outpatient psychotherapy services. The sample includes children born into the study except for the year of birth and excludes partial years except for deaths.

[b]Testing null hypothesis of no difference among plans.

[c]P-value comes from one-tail t-test.

[d]Value shown is coefficient of variation in free-care plan.

some families moved out of the area. Others were ineligible for the study or changed their composition. Some eligible families refused enrollment (about 13%). These factors together resulted in about a 25% loss in sample. Even though these losses were found to be random with respect to treatment assignment, the resulting balance among plans dropped from the original sample assignment. However, the outcome still was a much more balanced sample assignment than would have occurred had stratified random sampling been used instead of the FSM.

- The FSM is harder to use than simple random sampling, and it takes more time to implement. However, for an expensive experiment, including many that are less costly than the HIE, the benefits of the FSM will more than justify the effort.

- We cannot point to off-the-shelf software that readers can use to implement the FSM calculations. The special software developed at RAND to implement the FSM, although it has been used at RAND for the design of several other experiments and surveys, is too cumbersome to be made widely available. That version of the FSM actually used is much more complicated than described here. Modifications were needed to handle the constraints that all HIE individuals and families in a household be assigned to the same treatment; to make assignments for some families in some sites before all families were available; and to assign special subexperiments (Newhouse and the Insurance Experiment Group 1993) designed to learn about the possible artifacts of the HIE data collection. However, a SAS program code, with examples of the use of the FSM is available (Steffy 1984).

To summarize, the main advantage is that the FSM provides a better experiment without risk of doing worse even if poor covariates are chosen. The FSM can use more variables than other random allocation methods. Still, as with any statistical method, how much is gained depends on the skill of the analysts.

5B. Implications for Analysis

The choice of the design affects the analysis. When the design provides more balance than a simple random sample, accuracy improves. However, if the analysis is the same as for a simple random sample and thus ignores the design, then the calculated standard errors will be larger than the true standard errors. The true accuracy will be greater than for random sampling, but the result might be reported as less accurate (Fisher, 1953, pp. 62–63). The simplest way to account for this problem is to include the design variables as covariates in the analyses after the FSM has been used. That was not always done for HIE analyses. For example, the means presented in Table 2.9 actually have smaller standard errors than those listed.

5C. Policy Implications: Relevance of Using the FSM

An experiment with better balance among key variables not only is more informative but has the appearance of providing more reliable results and has better "face validity." Policy-makers, critics, and scientists are more likely to trust such results, which makes the information more useful and more likely to be used for policy. The results of the HIE were used, and continue to be used, in the debate about national health insurance. In particular, the HIE results are part of a computer model currently used by the government to predict the costs of proposed health insurance plans. The inability to make such predictions for various plans in the 1970s kept policy-makers from agreeing even on the costs of alternative plans and eventually led to the Health Insurance Experiment. Health insurance policy-making after the Health Insurance Experiment has been much better informed.

6. Exercises

1. (a) Construct a group of ten distinct integers for which there is no way to allocate them into two equal-sized groups X_1 and X_2 so that $\overline{X}_1 = \overline{X}_2$, the "OPCODE" solution, is achieved.

   (b) Construct a group of ten distinct integers for which there is only one way to divide them into two equal-sized groups X_1 and X_2 such that $\overline{X}_1 = \overline{X}_2$. (Note that this actually implies *two* allocations, depending on the assignment of the labels, "1" or "2," to each group).

   (c) Suppose that (20, 20, 40, 40, 40, 40, 60, 60) represent ages of eight participants in an experiment. Suppose further that you were trying to fit the model:

$$\text{income} = \beta_0 + \beta_1\,(\text{age}) + \beta_2(\text{age}^2)$$

   within each of two groups. Find an allocation meeting the criterion $\overline{X}_1 = \overline{X}_2$ that would be particularly problematic for this model. (Hint: What kind of allocation would you need in order to efficiently fit a linear term? A quadratic term?) How would your answer change if the numbers were (20, 25, 40, 40, 40, 40, 55, 60)?

2. Prove formula (2.2)

$$S_{n+1}^2 = \frac{n}{n+1}S_n^2 + \frac{n}{(n+1)^2}(x - \overline{x}_n)^2\,,$$

   where $S_n^2 = n^{-1}\sum_{i=1}^{n}(x_i - \overline{x})^2$.

3. Extending the example in Section 2 and allowing X_1 to denote the vector of ages, suppose we also have information on annual incomes (in thousands of dollars) for the experimental participants, $X_2 = (20, 40, 50, 40, 50, 40, 20, 30, 20, 50, 20, 40)^T$.

(a) Create a selection order matrix for assigning the participants to two groups using a random selection order that seems fair.

(b) Let $Z_{ji} = (X_{ji} - \overline{X}_j)/S_j$, for $j = 1,2$, where X_{ji} is the value of the jth variable for subject i who is being considered for assignment to a particular treatment group, and the sample mean ($\overline{X}_j$) and standard deviation (S_j) are over only the subjects already assigned to that group plus the current subject (i) under consideration. Use the selection criterion

$$\max_i(Z_{1i}^2 + Z_{2i}^2)$$

and your selection order matrix from part (a) to allocate subjects to treatment groups A and B. (Hint: The formula in Exercise 2 should be helpful.)

(c) Why is this a useful criterion?

(d) In what situation might this criterion be problematic? (Hint: Think about the correlation between the two variables.)

(e) Summarize outcomes in your allocation vs. the outcomes under a simple random sampling approach by calculating

$$\frac{(\overline{X}_{jg} - \overline{X}_j)^2}{S_j^2}$$

for each treatment group, $g = A,B$ and each variable, $j = 1,2$. Here $\overline{X}_j$ represents the grand mean for variable j across both groups and S_j^2 represents the sample variance for variable j across both treatment groups.

Further RAND Reading

Newhouse, J. P., and the Insurance Experiment Group (1993), *Free for All? Lessons from the RAND Health Insurance Experiment*, Cambridge, MA: Harvard University Press.

Notes

[1]We are grateful to the editors for helpful suggestions and clarifying questions. The second author acknowledges the support of an NSF grant, DMS-97-05156.

[2]The 13th plan, operating only in the Seattle site, involved membership in the Group Health Cooperative of Puget Sound. This kind of health maintenance organization (HMO) care was new at the time and was not uniformly available across the country. Because previous studies had shown that individuals who participated in HMOs tended to be more healthy than those using fee-for-service insurance, the HIE included this treatment in order to compare a random sample of the general population assigned to a group health setting with a random sample of families who were in an HMO by their own choice.

[3]The decision regarding number of observations per treatment is described in more detail in Section 3 of this chapter.

[4]Ineligible categories included the elderly (62 or older), those with annual incomes exceeding $25,000 (approximately equivalent to $77,000 in 1991 dollars), disabled veterans, military personnel, individuals who were institutionalized, and the homeless.

3

Counting the Homeless: Sampling Difficult Populations

Allan F. Abrahamse

Executive Summary

"The size of the homeless population is probably the most highly charged issue in the debate surrounding homelessness because it ultimately focuses on political claims for public resources and attention. The estimates range from 250,000 to 350,000 . . . to more than 3 million, or around 1 percent of the American population. . . . "

Baum and Burnes (1993)

Estimates of the number of homeless persons in the United States can differ because of differences in definitions of who is a homeless person, differences in techniques used to count them, and differences in reasons for being interested in this number. Politics probably accounts for the fact that the estimates at the high end are at least an order of magnitude higher than estimates at the low end. For example, the estimate of 3,000,000 homeless was first announced by activist Mitch Snyder in 1980, who later admitted that "these numbers are in fact meaningless." For a full discussion of these political dimensions, we encourage the reader to consult Baum and Burnes (1993), from which the above quotation has been taken.

As would be expected, estimates at the local level differ as much as those at the national level. In 1988, a letter to the Orange County Edition of the Los Angeles Times said "up to 10,000 men, women and children . . . wander Orange County streets, parks and abandoned buildings, trying to find someplace to lay their hungry, weary, frightened bodies" (Los Angeles Times, August 7, 1988). In sharp contrast, just one year earlier, RAND had conducted a survey of the homeless population of Orange County and concluded that there were only about 1000 homeless persons in the county on any given night, of whom only about 300 spent the night "on the street"—as opposed to spending the night in a shelter.

This chapter discusses how we reached this count of the street population. In 1986, the California State Legislature asked RAND to conduct an independent review of programs designed to address the needs of mentally disordered homeless persons. This study had three components: (1) a survey of the homeless population in three counties designed to provide a count of the number of homeless persons and a profile of their characteristics; (2) case studies designed to provide a picture of how services funded by the legislature were being implemented; and (3) interviews with heads of service agencies to identify the characteristics of services being provided.

We conducted our survey of Orange County's homeless population on several nights in September, 1987. The survey was based on a fairly small sample of census blocks but designed to provide evidence that the number of homeless was nowhere near the upper range suggested by some of the higher national estimates. Another part of our study, not described here, counted about 500–600 homeless persons in shelters, thus bringing our total estimate to around 1000 homeless persons.

1. Introduction

1A. Policy Problem

Most people believe that the number of homeless persons has increased during the last 20 years or so. But it is difficult to turn such an impression into a quantitative fact. Homeless persons are elusive. They are hard to find; they move around frequently; they do not have phones or mailboxes; they do not belong to organizations; they do not subscribe to magazines; and they do not regularly go to particular places such as employment or a fixed residential address. In short, they have few if any of the characteristics that survey researchers use to contact members of a population.

Nevertheless, an accurate estimate of the number of homeless persons is important in order to allocate resources aimed at serving their needs, coordinating care among community service agencies, encouraging rehabilitation, and providing protection. This chapter describes our attempt to produce a scientifically sound estimate of the number of homeless persons in Orange County, California.

1B. Research Questions

About one in every four homeless persons has experienced mental disorders such as schizophrenia, clinical depression, or bipolar disorder (Lehman and Cordray 1994). California's Mental Health Services Act of 1985[1] mandated a number of services for the mentally disabled homeless and required an "Independent Performance Review" of these programs. In 1987, RAND was asked to conduct this review. The major research questions addressed by this study were:

- How many homeless persons are there, where do they live, and what are their demographic characteristics?

- Which programs provide services to the seriously mentally ill population, and what type of programs are they?
- Which homeless people are served by these programs?
- How well do these programs achieve their objectives?

Of these four questions, this chapter deals only with the first part of the first question; we will describe how we estimated the number of homeless persons on the streets of Orange County. For the rest of the questions, we urge the reader to consult Vernez, Burnam, McGlynn, Trude, and Mittman (1988).

1C. Statistical Questions

The statistical questions we addressed in this study were:

- How should the sample be designed?
- How should we analyze the results?

Homeless persons do not have permanent addresses or phone numbers. In fact, they have very few of the features that survey researchers are accustomed to using to locate and contact members of a target population. However, if we walk around enough in the right places, we can find them, so to count homeless persons, we do not sample people. Instead, we sample places in which homeless people can be found. Specifically, we draw a sample of census blocks, count the number of homeless persons in each sampled block, and extrapolate the result to the entire county. Most of the statistical thinking lies in the design of the sample. The extrapolation of the sample count to a county-wide total is relatively straightforward.

1D. Summary of Data and Methods

Homeless persons cannot be counted in the same way one might count, say, consumers interested in buying a particular product. Our survey followed closely an approach pioneered by Rossi (Rossi, Fisher, and Willis, 1986; Rossi, 1989): we counted the number of homeless persons in a sample of census blocks[2] and inferred the count for the entire county.

Orange County has about 4000 census blocks, and we could afford to visit only a very small fraction of them. Most blocks have no homeless persons on them. As a result, a small simple random sample of blocks, in which every block has an equal probability of being sampled, might well contain no homeless persons at all. We therefore asked local experts to tell us where homeless persons were more likely to be found, and we stratified the blocks so that blocks where many homeless persons were thought to be located had high probabilities of being sampled. Specifically, our sampling design followed six broad steps:

- Experts (policemen, local city officials, persons involved in homeless programs, and others), ranked census tracts according to how many homeless persons were thought to be found there.

- We selected a sample of tracts, oversampling those that contained more homeless persons.

- The same experts ranked census blocks within the sampled tracts according to the number of homeless in the blocks.

- We selected a sample of blocks.

- Interviewers visited the sampled blocks and counted all the homeless persons they could find in each block.

- Counts from the sampled blocks were extrapolated to the entire county.

2. Study Design, Data Collection, Description of Data Sources, and Description of Data Elements

As mentioned above, we counted the number of homeless persons in a sample of census blocks and extrapolated this count to the county. Our budget constrained the number of blocks we could afford to visit. Whether we surveyed a block that was empty of homeless persons or one that contained dozens, as some did, the cost of sending an interviewer to that block was about the same. In designing our survey, therefore, we needed to decide how to allocate a fixed amount of effort in the most efficient manner.

Sampling Methods. Our survey of homeless persons is a three-stage stratified cluster sample. In the first stage, we selected a stratified sample of census tracts (clusters)[3] according to how prevalent the census tracts expected the homeless to be.

In the second stage, within each sampled tract we asked our experts to stratify the blocks, also according to the prevalence of homeless people. We used this stratification to draw a sample of blocks.

On the nights of the survey, we sent interviewers, accompanied by an off-duty policeman, to the sampled census blocks. The interviewers were instructed to look in all places—sidewalks, doorways, abandoned buildings, underpasses, etc.—in each sampled block where homeless persons might be found. Each person encountered was to be approached, offered a small amount of money, and asked questions to determine if that person was really homeless on that night. In this third stage of sampling, some of those who were homeless were then asked to participate in a longer interview for which they were also paid, but we will not discuss this additional stage in this chapter.

Sample Design Overview. A simple random sample of blocks—that is, a sample in which every block has the same probability of selection—would have worked well enough as long as all blocks contained "about" the same number of homeless persons. Since most blocks have no homeless persons, some blocks have a small number, and a few blocks have a great many, a *stratified* sample is more efficient than a random sample, as it provides an estimator with a smaller variance given the same sample size.

A stratified sample is a sample that first divides the target population into a fixed number of mutually disjoint groups (each group is called a *stratum*; collectively they are called *strata*). Then, a sample, perhaps a simple random sample, is drawn from each stratum. If the purpose of the exercise is to estimate the size of a population, an estimate is made of the size of each stratum, and then these strata estimates are summed to obtain an estimate of the total population size.

In our situation, some census blocks contained many homeless persons, whereas some blocks contained only a few or none at all. We designed a stratified sample that placed the blocks with many homeless persons in one stratum and then *oversampled* this stratum—that is, we selected these blocks with a higher probability than we would have used with a straight simple random sample.

In addition, as we shall see below, there were reasons besides variance reduction for stratifying a sample. Fortunately, in our case, these reasons harmonized with our goal of reducing the variance of our estimator, but this situation does not always happen. Populations must sometimes be stratified in order to obtain more precise information about certain subpopulations (e.g., racial and ethnic groups), and such a stratification may increase the variance of the estimator. This important topic is beyond the scope of the present chapter.

To design a stratified random sample that oversampled the "higher homeless" blocks, we asked "experts" (police, social workers, and others) to identify block groups with large numbers of homeless persons. However, the total number of blocks was over 4000, too many for us to ask our experts to evaluate every one. Moreover, one of the major costs of counting homeless persons in a block is the cost of getting to that block in the first place. We decided to reduce this cost by first selecting a sample of census tracts and then selecting a sample of blocks within each sampled tract. That way, once an interviewer had arrived at a tract, more than one block could be visited without incurring high travel costs. After some thought, we decided we would attempt to survey 12 tracts, and as many blocks in each of these 12 tracts as we could manage to visit.

We conducted our sampling in stages. First, we asked experts to estimate the number of homeless persons in each tract, and we used these estimates to stratify the census tracts into four groups:

- tracts with many homeless;
- tracts with "some" homeless;
- tracts with "a few" homeless; and
- tracts with no homeless.

We then drew a sample of tracts, oversampling the tracts with "many" and "some" homeless and dropping the tracts with no homeless from the sample altogether. We returned to our experts with this sample and asked them to estimate the number of homeless in each block in each sampled tract. From this information, we stratified the blocks in the sampled tracts into three strata:

- blocks with many homeless;
- blocks with "some" homeless; and
- blocks with no homeless.

We then drew a sample of blocks, in effect oversampling blocks with many homeless and ignoring blocks with none.

If our experts knew everything perfectly, of course, there would have been no need for the rest of the survey. We did not think they knew everything perfectly; indeed, the experts were quite sure they did not know everything. Each expert was very familiar with one or more communities, and each knew places where he or she had seen lots of homeless persons night after night, places where homeless persons had been seen once in a while, and places where homeless persons had never been seen. None of the experts had ever stopped to actually count the number of homeless persons in any particular place, but they were willing to give us a guess. These guesses helped us to improve our sample design.

It is highly unlikely that our procedure overlooked any place in Orange County that contained many homeless persons. Our experts—policemen, social workers, and homeless advocates—were professionally alert to the problems of homeless persons and knew the places they frequented. Setting statistical theory aside, had we failed to visit a few well-known places in the county (e.g., a campground specifically set aside for homeless persons), our results would have failed to satisfy those who knew about these places, no matter how technically good our design. Our experts alerted us to such places.

Our failure to sample those tracts in which the experts said no homeless persons would be found was a risk we were forced to take given the economic constraints we faced. Our final estimate may be a biased estimate, differing from the true number of homeless persons by the number of homeless persons in all the blocks where the experts told us there were no homeless persons at all. We could have produced an unbiased estimate by assigning a positive probability to all the blocks, but this estimate would have had a higher standard deviation. In our judgment, our (possibly) biased estimator with a smaller standard deviation is more accurate.

As it turned out, we had a hard time finding homeless persons in the tracts we actually sampled, and generally our counts fell below the expert guesses. We think this supports the contention that the tracts the experts thought were empty really did contain very few homeless persons, if any at all.

Sample Design Details. To decide on which tracts to select, we first asked local experts in Orange County to estimate the number of homeless in each of the county's 418 census tracts. Of these tracts, our experts identified only 50 that they thought would contain any homeless at all. One of these tracts contained a public campground that was thought to contain over 100 homeless persons on any particular night. Many of the other tracts were thought to contain only one or two homeless. We decided to confine our sample to these 50 tracts.

In ignoring the tracts that our experts thought were empty of homeless persons, we committed a coverage error—that is, because our survey had probability zero of selecting certain places, we failed to cover the entire target universe. Such an error introduces a bias into our estimate equal to the number of homeless persons in the tracts that the experts thought were empty. We hoped that our visits to the sampled tracts with the fewest number of expected homeless persons would give us some idea about the ability of the experts to rule out tracts that were empty of homeless persons. We also assumed that the sampling error would be much larger than the bias. Our expert estimates are shown in Table 3.1.

Under the assumption that the expert estimates were correct, we found that a simple random sample of 12 tracts would produce an estimate of total number having a standard deviation of about 230. But, because of the large relative differences among the number of homeless persons in these tracts, it was clear that a stratified sample that oversampled the larger tracts would produce a much more precise estimate. After some experimentation, we adopted the following sampling scheme:

- Pick the five "largest" tracts with probability 1 ("High Stratum").
- Pick four tracts at random from the next 14 ("Middle Stratum").
- Pick three tracts at random from the remaining 31 ("Low Stratum").

The estimator based on this scheme had an estimated standard deviation (based on the expert estimates) of about 24—one-tenth the standard deviation of a simple random sample—so it represents a very large improvement.

The scheme probably does not represent the "optimal" sampling plan—that is, the one with the lowest possible standard error of the estimator. Possibly, if we had used four or more strata, or allocated 12 tracts among three strata in some other way, we could have obtained a more efficient estimator. But we need to keep in mind that any estimate of sampling efficiency depends strongly on the expert counts, and these counts cannot be regarded as very accurate—if they were, we would not need a sample. We invite readers to improve on our design (see Exercise 4).

We used a random number generator to select the seven tracts to be sampled from the second and third strata of our design. Table 3.1 marks with an asterisk the tracts selected into the sample.

Using our tract sample, we returned to our experts and obtained estimates of the number of homeless within each block of each sampled tract. The experts thought some of the blocks would be empty of homeless and provided estimates for the other blocks in the sampled tracts. In some cases, they could not provide estimates for individual blocks but instead pointed to a group of blocks and estimated the homeless in that group. We apportioned this estimate equally among the blocks.

Table 3.1. Tract Sample Design

Tract	Expert Estimate	Tract	Expert Estimate
Tracts with "many" homeless		*Tracts with "a few" homeless*	
219.07	125*	748.04	3
626.05	40*	760.00	3
745.01	20*	883.01	3
748.02	20*	992.11	3
873.00	20*	993.02	3
		993.03	3
Tracts with "some" homeless		996.01	3*
750.02	15	996.02	3
744.01	10	997.01	3
874.01	10	997.03	3
887.02	8	999.01	3*
626.07	5	626.17	2
626.19	5	626.20	2
865.01	5	627.00	2*
865.02	5*	628.00	2
866.01	5*	635.00	2
867.01	5*	636.03	2
872.00	5	866.02	2
421.02	4	998.01	2
745.02	4	999.04	2
761.03	4*	1102.03	2
		12.00	1
		19.03	1
		995.05	1
		1100.10	1
		1101.04	1
		1101.09	1
		1101.10	1
		1101.11	1
		1101.12	1
		1101.13	1

NOTE: Standard error for simple random sample = 230.40. Standard error for stratified sample = 23.69.
*Means tract that was sampled.

Consistent with our earlier decision to avoid tracts that the experts thought would be empty, we decided not to visit blocks that experts thought would be empty. The remaining blocks fell roughly into two classes: (1) blocks with lots of homeless; and (2) blocks with only a few homeless.

We really did not know how many blocks our interviewers could cover in a given night. We definitely did not want them to run out of tasks once they got to a sampled tract, so we adopted the following general scheme. We asked our interviewers to visit:

- at least one block in every sampled tract,
- and *every* block thought to contain many homeless persons, and
- as many of the remaining blocks in each tract as time allowed

To implement this scheme, we gave the interviewers a list of all blocks in each sampled tract. We placed all blocks identified by our experts as containing "many" homeless at the top of the list, and we sorted the other blocks in random order. The first block in each list, and every block identified as containing many homeless, was marked "high-priority block"; the rest were marked "low-priority block." Table 3.2 lists these blocks that were given to the interviewers. Interviewers were instructed to visit every high-priority block and as many low-priority blocks as time allowed, *in the order that these blocks were listed*. This last point is very important: if it were left to the interviewers to choose which blocks to visit, we could not be sure that every block visited had equal probability of being visited, nor that the blocks were independently selected. For example, an interviewer, once finished with a block and left to choose the next block, might choose the next nearest block for the next visit, leaving a sample that is clustered around the first block selected. On the other hand, an interviewer who might be aware that such a clustered sample would pose a problem might select the block that is furthest away, leaving a sample that is not clustered enough. The field is no place to make sampling decisions. Interviewing is a hard job, and interviewers should not be required to make decisions that can be made before the work begins.

Final counts from a low-priority block were used in the analysis only if the interviewer completed the survey of that block. If an interviewer started counting homeless persons in a block but ran out of time to complete that count, the partial count was discarded and the block was marked as not having been visited at all. If we had not done this, results from partially counted blocks would really have been partial sample counts from that block, but we had no information, nor any way to obtain information, that would allow us to estimate reliably the complete count had there been time to make it.

Fieldwork. Interviewers went to Orange County during the week of September 15, 1987. Each interviewer was accompanied by an escort, most of whom were nonuniformed off-duty police officers. Interviewers and escorts worked collaboratively to search areas such as stairwells, parked cars, abandoned houses, behind bushes, and anywhere else people might hide. When a sleeping person was found in such places, the escort gently awakened that person and immediately explained that we wanted to conduct a brief interview for which we would pay a small sum of money. During the interview, the escort stood aside, out of hearing, and looked around the block for other possibly homeless persons. At the close of the interview, each respondent was given a paper containing RAND's telephone number and instructions on how to call (collect) to obtain or

Table 3.2. Block Sample Design

Tract	Block	Expert Estimate	Priority	Tract	Block	Expert Estimate	Priority
Tracts with "many" homeless				*Tracts with "some" homeless*			
219.07	905	125	High	761.03	112	4	High
626.05	227	10	High		107	1	High
	337	10	High		102	1	Low
	330	3	Low		103	1	Low
	332	3	Low		118	1	Low
	123	2	Low		211	1	Low
	203	2	Low	866.01	301	1	Low
	225	2	Low		312	1	Low
	228	2	Low		401	1	Low
	329	2	Low		402	1	Low
	113	1	Low		407	1	Low
	114	1	Low	867.01	114	1.25	Low
	118	1	Low		212	1.25	Low
	208	1	Low		213	1.25	Low
745.01	108	20	High		307	1.25	Low
748.02	111	9	High	*Tracts with "a few" homeless*			
	107	4	Low	627.00	213	0.33	High
	104	2	Low		214	0.33	Low
	138	2	Low		333	0.33	Low
	112	1	Low		513	0.17	Low
	113	1	Low		515	0.17	Low
	146	1	Low		516	0.17	Low
873.00	418	9	High		518	0.17	Low
	305	0.69	Low		538	0.17	Low
	306	0.69	Low		539	0.17	Low
	307	0.69	Low	996.01	232	0.5	High
	308	0.69	Low		205	0.5	Low
	309	0.69	Low		214	0.5	Low
	310	0.69	Low		215	0.5	Low
	405	0.69	Low		216	0.5	Low
	406	0.69	Low		218	0.5	Low
	407	0.69	Low	999.01	128	1.5	High
	408	0.69	Low		127	1.5	Low
	409	0.69	Low				
	410	0.69	Low				
	411	0.69	Low				
	105	0.25	Low				
	106	0.25	Low				
	115	0.25	Low				
	116	0.25	Low				

give additional information about the study. The paper also contained a referral list of shelters, drop-in centers, and other resources in the city for homeless persons.

For each block, our interviewers recorded two numbers. First, they recorded the number of "verified homeless"—the number of people seen in the block who were approached and asked some questions that verified that they were homeless according to the project definition of that term. Second, they recorded some "possibly homeless"—a number of people seen on the street who "looked" homeless[4] but who refused to answer questions to verify homeless status and so could not be actually verified. A number of people were also seen on the street who were judged as "not homeless" and were not interviewed. Results of the fieldwork are displayed in Table 3.3.

3. Datafile Creation, Descriptive Statistics, and Exploratory Analysis

Our survey produced a simple dataset, and we analyzed it with a spreadsheet package. Little exploratory analysis was required.

4. Statistical Methods and Model

The textbook question for designing a sample is "how big should my sample be?" There's only one answer: "it should be as big as you can afford." The real question is "how should I allocate my fixed resources to obtain the best answer?"

This is not the place for an extended discussion of sampling theory. Almost any textbook on survey sampling will provide the reader with an adequate introduction to this deep subject (Kish 1965; Cochran 1977; Thompson 1992). However, a brief overview of a few topics will prove useful.

Suppose we have a population of N numbers, $X_1, X_2, \ldots X_N$, and we want to estimate the sum

$$T = \sum_{k=1}^{N} X_k$$

of these numbers by drawing a sample of size M. The simplest approach is to draw a *simple random sample without replacement*; that is, we draw an independent sample of size M without replacement in which each unit X_k has an equal probability $p = M/N$ of being selected. Whatever the sum of the numbers in this sample is, we divide it by M and multiply it by N to estimate T.

We can analyze the properties of this estimator as follows. Let I_k be an indicator function equal to 1 if unit k falls into our sample and equal to 0 if it does not. Our estimator X of T can be described by the expression

Table 3.3. Survey Results

Tract	Block	Expert Estimate	Priority	RAND's Count Verified	RAND's Count Not Verified
		Tracts with "many" homeless			
219.07	905	125	High	54	6
626.05	227	10	High	3	0
	337	10	High	10	8
	330	3	Low	18	2
	123	2	Low	0	0
	113	1	Low	0	0
	114	1	Low	0	2
	118	1	Low	0	0
	208	1	Low	0	1
745.01	108	20	High	1	0
748.02	111	9	High	44	11
	107	4	Low	0	0
	104	2	Low	15	0
	138	2	Low	0	0
	112	1	Low	0	1
	113	1	Low	37	0
	146	1	Low	2	0
873.00	418	9	High	0	1
	308	0.69	Low	1	0
	405	0.69	Low	0	0
	408	0.69	Low	0	0
	410	0.69	Low	0	0
	115	0.25	Low	0	0
	116	0.25	Low	0	0
		Tracts with "some" homeless			
761.03	112	4	High	1	0
865.02	107	1	High	0	0
	102	1	Low	0	0
	103	1	Low	0	0
866.01	312	1	High	0	0
	301	1	Low	0	0
	401	1	Low	0	0
	402	1	Low	0	0
	407	1	Low	0	0
867.01	213	1.25	High	0	0
	114	1.25	Low	0	0
	212	1.25	Low	0	0
	307	1.25	Low	0	0
		Tracts with "a few" homeless			
627.00	213	0.3	High	1	0
996.01	232	0.5	High	0	1
	205	0.5	Low	0	0
	214	0.5	Low	0	0
	215	0.5	Low	0	0
	216	0.5	Low	0	0
	218	0.5	Low	0	0
999.01	128	1.5	High	0	0
	127	1.5	Low	0	0

$$X = \frac{N}{M} \sum_{k=1}^{N} X_k I_k .$$

It is easy to verify (Exercise 2) that this estimator is unbiased—that is, its expectation is equal to T—and that its variance is $N^2(1-p)^2 \sigma^2/M$, where σ^2 is the population variance $E(X_k - \mu)^2/N$, and $\mu = T/N$, the population mean.

Finally, let us consider the general estimator

$$X = \sum_{k=1}^{N} w_k X_k I_k ,$$

where the sequence w_k is any set of numbers, and p_k is the probability that X_k is in the sample. The expected value of X is

$$\sum_{k=1}^{N} w_k X_k p_k .$$

Plainly, $E(X) = T$ if $w_k = 1/p_k$, so to obtain an unbiased estimate of the total, each element in the sample should be divided by the probability that it is in the sample.

In Table 3.4, we display the 1990 population of 20 states, listed in descending order of population. If we were to draw a simple random sample of six states to estimate the population of all 20 in the table, the standard deviation of that estimate would be about 45 million.

Population varies widely among these 20 states. The sampling error can be reduced substantially by designing our sample so that some of the more populous states are certain to be in the sample. To illustrate this point, and with no assurance that what we are about to do is the most efficient approach, we do the following:

- We stratify the 20 states into three groups consisting of the three largest states, the 12 middle states, and the five remaining smallest states.

- We draw a simple random sample of two states from each group and use that sample to estimate the population of the group.

- We add the three estimates together to estimate the population of all 20 states.

The three population estimates, one from each group of states, are mutually independent, so the variance of our total estimate is the sum of the variance of the three estimators. We calculate the variance of each estimator using the formula above, and we see (see bottom line of Table 3.4) that our new estimator has a considerably smaller standard error.

Table 3.4. Population of 20 States

Stratum	Sample Size	State	Actual Population
1	2	California	29,760,016
		Florida	12,937,926
		Illinois	11,430,602
2	2	Georgia	6,478,216
		Indiana	5,544,159
		Maryland	4,781,468
		Louisiana	4,219,973
		Alabama	4,040,587
		Kentucky	3,685,296
		Arizona	3,665,228
		Colorado	3,294,394
		Connecticut	3,287,116
		Iowa	2,776,755
3	2	Maine	1,227,928
		Hawaii	1,108,229
		Idaho	1,006,749
		Delaware	666,168
		Total	105,289,152
	Standard errors	{ Simple random	45,196,023
		{ Stratified	15,730,271

5. Results

Using the counts of verified homeless, we estimated there are 316 homeless on the streets of Orange County on any given night. If we add the additional counts of "possibly homeless," this estimate rises to 365.

These estimates were obtained by multiplying each block count by the inverse of the probability that the block appeared in our sample. A block appeared in our sample if:

- its tract fell into the sample, or
- it was a high-priority tract or was one of the blocks the interviewer found time to visit.

Details of this complete calculation can be seen in Table 3.5. We will discuss the first line, and we invite you to check the calculations yourself. Block 905 of tract 219.07 was a forest campground, and it was known that very many home-

Table 3.5. Population of 20 States

Tract	Block	Expert Est.	Priority	Survey Counts		Tract Prob.	Block Prob.	Sample Prob.	Final Estimates	
				Veri- fied	Not Veri- fied				Veri- fied	Total
Tracts with "many" homeless										
219.07	905	125	High	54	6	1	39/119	0.32773	165	183
626.05	227	10	High	3	0	1	1	1.00000	3	3
	337	10	High	10	8	1	1	1.00000	10	18
	330	3	Low	18	2	1	6/11	0.54545	33	37
	114	1	Low	0	2	1	6/11	0.54545	0	4
	208	1	Low	0	1	1	6/11	0.54545	0	2
745.01	108	20	High	1	0	1	1	1.00000	1	1
748.02	111	9	High	44	1	1	1	1.00000	44	45
	138	2	Low	15	0	1	1	1.00000	15	15
	112	1	Low	0	1	1	1	1.00000	0	1
	113	1	Low	37	0	1	1	1.00000	37	37
	146	1	Low	2	0	1	1	1.00000	2	2
873.00	418	9	High	0	1	1	1	1.00000	0	1
	410	0.69	Low	1	0	1	6/17	0.35294	3	3
Tracts with "some" homeless										
761.03	112	4	High	1	0	2/7	1	0.28571	4	4
Tracts with "a few" homeless										
996.01	232	0.5	High	0	1	3/31	1	0.09677	0	10
								Total	316	365

less persons could be found there on any given night. This block was selected with probability one, but when the interviewers arrived they discovered there were 119 campsites, too many to visit all in one night. They drew a sample of 39 of the campsites and visited those.

In this sample of 39 campsites, our interviewers counted 54 persons who were certainly homeless. Each campsite had probability 39/119 of being selected, so we estimate there were 54/(39/119) = 165 persons in the campground altogether. Since the campground itself was selected with probability one, this campground adds 165 homeless persons to the total for the county. As it turns out, this one place accounted for more than half the homeless persons found during the survey.

In some tracts, all blocks were visited. In others, only a subset of the blocks were visited, but since the blocks were presented to the interviewers in a random order, we treated the set of visited blocks as a simple random sample of all blocks and assigned a sampling probability equal to the number of blocks visited divided by the number of blocks offered.

Our estimate of homeless persons was completed by multiplying each block count by the inverse of the selection probability of the corresponding tract and then by the inverse of the selection probability of the block itself. Table 3.5 shows the details of this final estimate.[5]

6. Discussion

The principal policy implication of our estimate of the number of homeless persons on the streets of Orange County was to rule out some rather huge estimates made by homeless advocates. Estimates of homeless in the nation ranged as high as 7,000,000 persons: Orange County, with about 1% of the nation's population, might have 70,000 of these (U. S. Bureau of the Census 1995). Our estimate is nowhere near this number, nor could it come close even in the presence of a large sampling error.

The standard deviation of the estimated total number of homeless was about 24. We decided that sampling error was far smaller than errors introduced by our inability to determine who was actually homeless while we were conducting interviews—because of this uncertainty our estimate ranged from 316 to 365—more than twice the estimate's standard error. Therefore, our report paid little attention to sampling error. In another phase of the project, we counted the number of homeless persons sleeping in shelters; we found almost twice as many and concluded finally that on any given night there were about 1000 homeless persons in Orange County altogether.

Finally, we note that most of the visited "low-priority blocks"—blocks that experts thought would contain very few homeless persons—contained no homeless persons at all. We took this fact as evidence that the "zero blocks"—blocks that experts thought would contain no homeless—probably really were empty of homeless persons. These blocks were not sampled, so this indirect evidence that they were empty was welcome.

1990 Census. On or about March 20, 1990, the Census Bureau conducted a national "Shelter and Street Night" (S-Night) operation designed to count homeless persons housed in shelters and on the street. For the street count, homeless persons were counted on the street and in open public locations that had been previously indicated by city and community officials as "places where the homeless congregate at night." Enumerators did not ask if a person was "homeless"; if a person was seen at one of these "places where the homeless congregate," he or she was counted as homeless. Thus, the number of homeless the Census enumerators counted corresponded roughly to our upper bound estimate that included confirmed homeless persons plus persons seen and thought to be homeless but whose status could not be confirmed.

It must be regarded as coincidental that the Census Bureau counted 371 homeless persons, only six more than our upper bound estimate of 365 persons made about three years earlier. However, the census estimate confirms the most important implication: on any given night the streets of Orange County are "home" to only a few hundred persons, not ten thousand.

Policy Implications. When our report was released in 1988, it received relatively wide attention in Orange County. Several newspaper articles described the findings. As mentioned above, our count was more or less consistent with that of the census of 1990.

But in December of 1993, a letter in the Orange County Edition of the Los Angeles Times mentions "between 12,000 and 15,000 homeless people living on the streets of our beautiful county" (Los Angeles Times, December 5, 1993). Two weeks later, an editorial in the same paper begins "The streets are rarely kind to the estimated 10,000 Orange County men, women and children who have no homes" (Los Angeles Times, December 28, 1993). Can there have been a tenfold increase in the number of homeless persons since our 1987 study? Probably not.

In spite of careful efforts by many qualified researchers, estimates of the number of homeless persons that reach a wide audience still appear to be driven largely by political motives. As Baum and Burnes stated in 1993, ". . . neither the (homeless) movement nor much of the voluminous research and analysis has helped to explain the real causes of homelessness in the 1980s, and as a consequence, both have failed to inform the development of solutions that have any genuine chance of ameliorating the problem" (Baum and Burnes 1993).

Limitations. Our main finding is that the size of Orange County's homeless street population is closer to 400 than to 4000, but there are limitations to our estimates that need to be recognized.

Our survey was conducted during a single week in the fall of 1987. It seems plausible to suspect that homelessness is seasonal, although perhaps less so in a place like Orange County where the winters are mild compared to, say, Chicago or New York. But a count taken at another season might have been different (perhaps higher in mid-winter, or lower in mid-summer).

As mentioned before, we did not even visit certain places thought to be empty of homeless persons; if our experts were wrong about these places, then our estimate is also.

We never published an estimate of the sampling error of our estimate. This neglect stemmed largely from a perception that errors in our estimate were dominated by things other than sampling (e.g., determining who among the persons seen in the street were indeed homeless).

7. Exercises

1. Let $I_1, I_2, \ldots, I_N$ be a sequence of indicator functions such that $\Sigma I_k = M$, $E(I_k) = M/N = p$, and $\text{Cov}(I_i, I_j)$ is the same for every $i \neq j$. Show that $\text{Cov}(I_i, I_j) = -p(1-p)/N(N-1)$.

2. For any sequence X_1, X_2 ,..., X_N, let $X = (N/M)\Sigma X_k I_k$. Show $Var(X) = N^2(1-p)\sigma^2/M$, where σ^2 is the population variance

$$\Sigma(X_k - \mu)^2/(N-1),$$

and $\mu = T/N$ the population mean. (Hint: $Var(X) = Cov(X, X)$, and use the result of Exercise 1.)

3. Generalize Exercise 2 to the case where M is a geometric random variable (i.e., $Prob(M = m) = (1-\lambda)^{m-1}\lambda$). (Assume the sampling fraction is essentially zero and eliminate the "1 − p" term.)

4. Verify the standard deviations reported in Table 3.1.

5. Suppose an estimator X of a count μ_1 has the expected value μ_2 and variance σ^2. Show that $E[(X - \mu_1)^2] = (\mu_1 - \mu_2)^2 + \sigma^2$. Use this expression to discuss the question: Is an unbiased estimator *always* better than a biased one?

6. Using the expert counts in Table 3.2, develop a more efficient sampling scheme than the one shown there.

7. It is reasonable to assume that the experts can only estimate counts with an accuracy of about 25% in each tract. Use a spreadsheet to develop a simulation model that compares the sampling scheme you develop in Exercise 4 to that of Table 3.2 under different values for expert counts.

Further RAND Reading

Vernez, G., Burnam, M. A., McGlynn, E. A., Trude, S., and Mittman, B. S. (1988), *Review of California's Program for the Homeless Mentally Disabled,* R-3631-DCMH, Santa Monica, CA: RAND.

Berry, S. H., Duan, N., and Kanouse, D. E. (1990), *Developing a Probability Sample of Prostitutes: Sample Design for the RAND Study of HIV Infection and Risk Behaviors in Prostitutes,* N-3190-NICHD, Santa Monica, CA: RAND.

Gallagher, T. C., Andersen, R., Koegel, P., and Gelberg, L. (1998), *Determinants of Regular Source of Care Among Homeless Adults in Los Angeles,* LRP-199708-02, Santa Monica, CA: RAND.

Marshall, G. N., Burnam, M. A., Koegel, P., Sullivan, J. G., and Benjamin, B. (1996), *Objective Life Circumstances and Life Satisfaction: Results from the Course of Homelessness Study,* RP-520, Santa Monica, CA: RAND.

Notes

[1]California State Legislature, Assembly Bill No. 2541, Chapter 1286, 1985 Regular Sessions, *Deering's* California Codes, No. 7, 1985, pp. 103–121. The bill was more commonly known as the Bronzan–Monjonnier Act.

[2]Census blocks are small areas bounded on all sides by visible features such as streets, roads, streams, and railroad tracks and by invisible boundaries such as city, town, township, and county limits, property lines, and short imaginary extensions of streets and roads [Census].

[3]Census tracts are small, relatively permanent statistical subdivisions of a county... [They] usually have between 2500 and 8000 persons and, when first delineated, are designed to be homogeneous with respect to population characteristics, economic status, and living conditions [Census]. Any block is entirely contained within a single tract.

[4]Not everybody who "looks" homeless *is* homeless. In the course of this study, interviewers encountered several individuals who "looked" homeless but in fact had a place they called home.

[5]Sharp-eyed readers may note that the upper estimate in this book is ten persons higher than that reported in Vernez, Burnam, McGlynn, Trude, and Mittman (1988). In preparing this chapter, the author discovered a typo in Table E.4 of RAND's report that led to an overestimate.

Detecting Effects

4

Periodicity in the Global Mean Temperature Series?

John L. Adams, James K. Hammitt, and James S. Hodges

Executive Summary

Global climate change presents a complex set of policy-analysis challenges. The potential damage to the environment from carbon dioxide emissions is uncertain and difficult to quantify. The costs of preventing climate change are difficult to predict in a dynamic world economy. The timescale of the potential climate changes is also uncertain and possibly quite long. Which nations would suffer the largest damages from climate change is unknown. In a world where international agreement is often impossible to achieve on relatively simple matters, the challenge of developing a strategy to prevent global warming is daunting.

One of the pieces of the global climate change policy puzzle is the possibility of empirical early detection of the change. Most of the analysis predicting global warming comes from basic physical arguments and computer simulations. These results lack the convincing immediacy of a real observable trend in the global temperature record. But a trend in the global temperature record will be slow to become convincing due to the natural variability of the series. Many analyses have been done searching for this trend as well as other features of the temperature record, among them cycles. Cycles are a particular concern since they could mask the trend, delaying detection. This chapter addresses one issue in the cycle detection problem: Could apparent cycles in the series found by others simply be random noise?

1. Introduction

1A. The Policy Problem

Many researchers, policy analysts, and environmentally oriented citizens are concerned about global warming. There are good physical reasons to believe that the CO_2 emitted from burning fossil fuels could create a greenhouse effect. For

75

some, the basic physics of what we think CO_2 should do is compelling enough. Unfortunately, talk of a new ice age a few years ago damaged the physical science community's credibility for affecting public policy with basic physical arguments.

Figure 4.1 presents the Southern Night Marine Air Temperature (SNMAT) series. This is one of the temperature series that analysts have examined when looking for evidence of global warming. While we will examine other temperature series, this series will be our primary example. It shows more than a 0.5 degree Celsius temperature increase since the early 1900s. This has been a period of rapidly increasing fossil fuel burning.

There are many potential negative consequences of global warming, including changes in weather patterns and sea level rise. It is unlikely that a temperature change would be uniform (Kattenberg et al. 1996) and the potential economic consequences are large (Watson, Zinyowere, and Moss 1996). An increase in temperature in the Great Plains could disrupt one of the world's most productive agriculture regions. Corresponding changes in rainfall patterns could be similarly disruptive. Historically cold regions (e.g., Siberia) might not be able to pick up the slack without centuries of topsoil development. Sea level rise from polar ice melting could submerge many coastal areas, including some of the world's largest cities and even entire island nations.

Even granting that there is a persistent increase in global temperature, what is the cause? Causes are either natural or anthropogenic (man-made). The longer

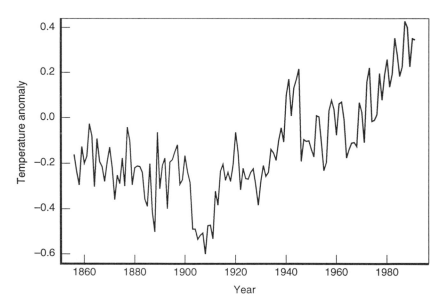

Figure 4.1. Global temperature series are traditionally plotted as "anomalies." Anomalies are obtained by subtracting the mean temperature from 1951 to 1975 from the series.

climate record (thousands of years) has extended periods of both higher- and lower-temperature regimes (Nicholls et al. 1996). If the apparent recent increases in temperature are natural variation, we must cope with them. If, on the other hand, the temperature increases are anthropogenic, we may be able to act to prevent further increases or roll them back.

How could we slow down an anthropogenic temperature increase? Decreasing CO_2 emissions would be very costly, which makes global climate change a unique problem. High near-term costs to obtain benefits 100 years in the future is an unprecedented public-policy challenge.

Since climate change abatement costs are so large and potentially disruptive, definitive proof of climate change may be needed to persuade society to act. The search for a definitive signal in the recent global temperature record is what motivates the analysis in this chapter. The specific policy question we address is:

- Could cycles in the global temperature record mask the definitive signs of global warming?

Figure 4.2 illustrates the question. It depicts a hypothetical trend imposed on a 22.7-year cycle for the post-1980 period. Both the linear trend and cycle are plausible fits to the actual historical series. The feature of concern is the "roll over" of the cycle toward the end of the historical series (i.e., a cycle turning down will mask the trend during the 1990s). To add insult to injury, the subsequent upswing of the cycle would amplify the trend.

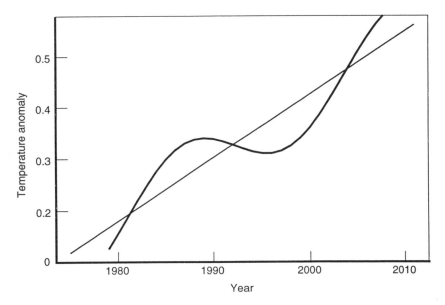

Figure 4.2. The hypothetical trend line is a regression extrapolation from the last ten years of the series. The amplitude of the sine function is determined via regression methods.

Researchers have identified a number of possible periodic fluctuations in the global temperature record. Oscillations with periods of two to seven years (Jones 1988), five to six years (Ghil and Vautard 1991), 16 years (Ghil and Vautard 1991), 21 to 22 years (Newell, Newell, Hsiung, and Wu 1989; Ghil and Vautard 1991), 65 to 70 years (Schlesinger and Ramankutty 1994a), and 80 to 90 years (Friis-Christensen and Lassen 1991) have been reported. The two-to-seven and five-to-six year periodicities have been associated with the El Nino/southern oscillation (ENSO) years (Jones 1988; Ghil and Vautard 1991), but the sources of the "bidecadal" (16 to 22 years) and longer periodicities are more speculative (Elsner and Tsonis 1991; Allen, Read, and Smith 1992a; Tsonis and Elsner 1992, Allen, Read, and Smith 1992b; Elsner and Tsonis 1994; Schlesinger and Ramankutty 1994b). Possible changes in solar radiance have been suggested (Newell, Newell, Hsiung, and Wu 1989; Friis-Christensen and Lassen 1991). We focus on the bidecadal oscillations. The shorter-term oscillations are plausibly associated with ENSO. The oscillations with periods of 60 or more years cannot be effectively evaluated since available data series have a length of only 140 years. In contrast, the bidecadal oscillations can be evaluated and may significantly obscure our ability to detect a general upward trend in mean temperature (Ghil and Vautard 1991).

1B. Research Questions

Our main research question is: Are there cycles in the global temperature series that could cause us to mistake them for trends? This can be broken down into several subquestions:

- Are there cycles of significant amplitude in the historical record?
- Are the cycles of a frequency (5–30 years) that might increase the difficulty in making policy decisions?
- How confident are we that the cycles exist?

1C. Statistical Questions

Searching for cycles in time series almost inevitably means mining the data. Frequently time series analysts look at many potential cycles in the same analysis. We were unsure whether earlier analyses had properly adjusted for multiple testing that typifies such data mining. Our key questions are:

- At what frequencies are there likely cycles in the series?
- How can we assess the statistical significance of these cycles?

The statistical issues we confront are classic. The difference is that we address them in a somewhat unusual and, for most readers, unfamiliar setting. They are:

- a classical multiple comparisons problem;

- a challenge in the interpretation of a hypothesis test; and
- a difficult and somewhat obscure statistical methodology to master.

1D. Summary of Data and Methods

Our initial interest in this topic was motivated by our skepticism of the statistical significance of results in papers by Ghil and Vautard (1991) and Newell, Newell, Hsiung, and Wu (1989). These papers focused on two different global temperature time series. These series were based on direct measurements of air and ocean temperature from the mid-19th century to the present. There are several different series of this type available. They differ in their geographic coverage (northern hemisphere vs. southern hemisphere and land vs. sea) and in their measurement methods (night marine air temperature vs. sea surface temperature.) We decided to explore all the commonly recognized series.

Our biggest contribution is developing a Monte Carlo/bootstrap hypothesis test to assess the statistical significance of the cycles.

2. Study Design, Data Collection, Description of Data Sources, and Description of Data Elements

Since this is necessarily an observational study, design and data collection decisions consist largely of the choice of historical data series. There are other global temperature series that we could have analyzed. Longer time series based on tree rings are available, as are other indirectly derived series (Briffa et al. 1990; Scuderi 1993; Nicholls et al. 1996). We focus on the direct measurements because of their currency in the global warming debate.

Even within the direct series, there are important measurement issues. In the early portions of the series, marine measurements were conducted by hauling a bucket of water up to the deck of a boat and measuring the temperature with a thermometer. The water could cool due to evaporation before and during the thermometer reading and due to conduction of heat through the bucket (with differences between canvas, wood, and metal buckets). Also, the water could be warmed while the bucket was on a hot deck. For these reasons, night measures are preferred to day measures. The fundamental problem is that we do not know very accurately the conditions that apply to the different observations (Nicholls et al. 1996). Later measurements were conducted by the presumably more accurate method of measuring the intake temperature of cooling water for the ship's engines. The geographic coverage of the measurements has varied over time depending on the popularity of various ocean routes. Moreover, the comparability of land measurements over time has also changed (Jones, Wigley, and Wright 1986; Nicholls et al. 1996). Measurement sites have moved from urban centers to airports, and the microclimate of growing urban areas has affected temperatures near measurement sites.

3. Datafile Creation, Descriptive Statistics and Exploratory Analysis

File creation was not difficult since we analyzed previously used series. When we started this work, we did need to order some of the data on magnetic tape. In the interim, the explosion of data sources on the World Wide Web has made data access much easier. Even more current versions of the data series are available at the following Web sites:

- http://www.giss.nasa.gov/,

- http://www.cru.uea.ac.uk/t, and

- http:// cdiac/esd/ornl/gov/.

First, we looked at some plots of various global temperature series as shown in Figure 4.3. We examined global and hemispheric temperature-anomaly series of Hansen and Lebedeff (1986, 1988) (land), Jones Wigley, and Wright (1986), and Jones, Wigley, and Briffa (1993) (land and sea), night marine air tempera-

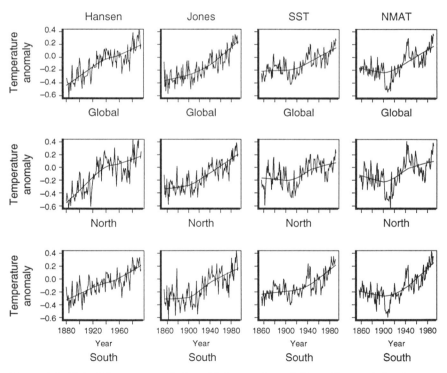

Figure 4.3. Global Temperature Series with Lowess Smooth Lines. Hansen is land series, Jones is land and sea, SST is sea surface temperature, and NMAT is night marine air temperature. The top panel is the global series built up from north and south series in the lower panels. See the text for further details.

ture (NMAT) (Bottomley, Folland, Hsiung, Newell, and Parker 1989), and sea surface temperature (SST) (Jones 1993). The notation we use for each is similar. For example, the global night marine air temperature is NMAT, the Southern Series is SNMAT, and the Northern Series is NNMAT.

The smooth lines were produced by lowess (Cleveland 1981), a local regression smoothing technique. Lowess fits a series of regressions, one per data point here, on points surrounding the data point, more heavily weighting nearer points. The series are not independent. The global series are built up from the land/sea and north/south series. Even different authors' series use some common data.

This simple descriptive analysis has generated considerable discussion in the literature on these series. Note that the general upward trend is evident in all of them. This trend is a primary cause of all of the policy concern. Also note the flattening or dip between 1900 and 1920 in several of the series. Recognition that aerosols associated with fossil fuel and biomass burning lead to global cooling has led to improved correlation between observed trends and models of temperature change (Penner, Dickinson, and O'Neill 1992; Santer, Wigley, Barnett, and Anyamba 1996.)

4. Statistical Methods and Model

4A. A Brief Introduction to Frequency Domain Analysis

The natural statistical techniques to apply to this problem are those of frequency domain time series. Even statisticians familiar with more traditional time domain time series methods tend to be uncomfortable with these methods. For such readers, we briefly describe these methods. All of the material in this section is covered in more detail in Bloomfield (1976).

The primary tool of frequency domain analysis is the periodogram. It uses a discrete data version of the well-known Fourier decomposition to transform the time series into a collection of sines and cosines:

$$f(t) \approx \frac{a_0}{2} + \sum_{r=1}^{k} a_r \cos(rt) + b_r \sin(rt) \ ,$$

where a_0, a_r, and b_r are fit by minimizing the approximation error. If k is infinite, this formula is exact for continuous functions. If your data are sampled at regular intervals, you can get a perfect fit if k is equal to the number of data points. Each sine and cosine pair for any k are orthogonal to the pair for any other k. This property makes it useful to think of this approximation as a regression of $f(t)$ onto the orthogonal pairs of sines and cosines. If you did this regression, you would get the a_r and b_r that are produced by frequency domain techniques such as the fast Fourier transform (FFT).

It is useful to remember Euler's formula from trigonometry class:

$$a_r \cos(rt) + b_r \sin(rt) = A_r \cos(rt + \phi_r) \, ,$$

where

$$A_r = \sqrt{a_r^2 + b_r^2}$$

and

$$\phi_r = \tan^{-1}\left(\frac{-b_r}{a_r}\right) .$$

A_r is the peak height of the oscillation, and ϕ_r is the distance from the origin where the cycle first peaks. The frequency r is the number of cycles completed in one time unit. These formulas make it clear that the sine and cosine pairs can be expressed as single cosines by shifting the origin (phase). This formulation is useful because it makes it easy to express the "power" in a particular frequency component of the series. The power at frequency r is $NA_r^2/2$, where N is the length of the series. The plot of these powers against r is the periodogram. The sum of these powers is equal to the variance of the original series.

The application of the Fourier method to data analysis is not as straightforward as one might hope. The assumptions underlying the Fourier decomposition are that the pattern in your data repeats over and over as in a sine wave. This assumption necessitates some preprocessing of data before applying the periodogram. The first step is to remove any mean structure from the data using a regression or moving average. By mean structure, we mean any trend or pattern that is not a repetitive, cyclic pattern. The periodogram can then be applied to the residuals from the mean estimation process. The second step is "tapering" the data. If the series of residuals begins and ends at different values, the method assumes that the data repeat over and over, with that difference appearing in every replication. Data tapering multiplies the data by a function that smoothes the beginning and end of the series to the same value. This process leaves the middle 90% of the data series unchanged but helps prevent artificial features from clouding the analysis.

To help develop a sense of how these methods work, we present simulated series with their periodograms and their expected (theoretical) periodograms. The first series in Figure 4.4 is 100 uncorrelated, standard normal values, or "white noise." The periodogram of this series in Figure 4.4 is very jagged. The superimposed straight line is the theoretical periodogram for a white noise series. The great variability of the observed periodogram is an important lesson. As the length of the original series gets larger, the periodogram does not get less jagged. Instead of using more data to get better-behaved estimates, the periodogram just estimates more frequencies. This makes it difficult to separate real peaks from random chance.

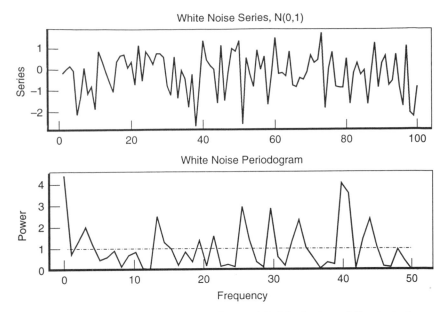

Figure 4.4. White Noise Series with Periodogram Fit. The horizontal line in the bottom panel is the theoretical periodogram for a white noise series.

Figure 4.5 shows a sine wave series of ten cycles in the 100 observations. Note the single spike in the periodogram at a frequency of 10. This is the classic example. It is traditional to plot the periodogram vs. frequency but it would be just as valid to plot it vs. wavelength (λ or wavelength $=1/f$). For example, the frequency of 10 could be referenced by a wavelength of 10 (100/10). In the climate series analysis, we will often refer to the wavelength in years. The climate series is a little more than 100 years in length, and our primary interest is in wavelengths near 20 years.

Figure 4.6 shows a series that is the sum of a ten-cycle series and a 20 cycle series with half the amplitude. Note the two peaks in the periodogram in Figure 4.6, one for each frequency. These correspond to wavelengths of 10 and 5.

Finally, the series in Figure 4.7 is a simulated "$1/f$" series. This series has a continuous periodogram, like white noise, but the periodogram in Figure 4.7 is proportional to the reciprocal of the frequency. The smooth line superimposed is the theoretical $1/f$ spectrum.

If you are having trouble understanding how the periodogram works, you are in good company. Much of the literature on frequency domain time series is motivated by the electrical engineering literature, which tends to be more mathematical than applied. Also, it tends to address problems with extremely long data series exhibiting strong periodic behavior, well summarized by a few peaks in a periodogram, as in a radio signal. For our purposes, think of the periodogram as a "black box" which turns a time series into its constituent frequencies. These examples convey the flavor of this process.

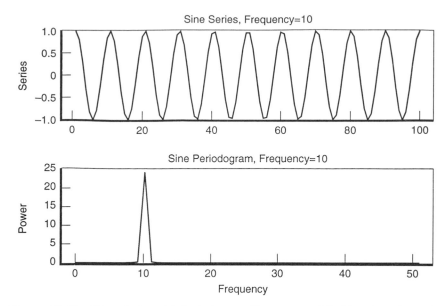

Figure 4.5. Sine Wave Series with Periodogram (Frequency = 10). Note the spike in the periodogram at the frequency of the sine wave.

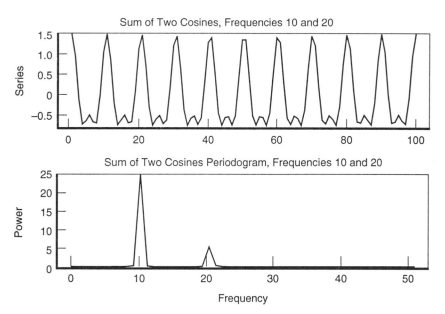

Figure 4.6. Sum of Two Sine Wave Series with Periodogram (Frequencies = 10 and 20). Note the spikes in the periodogram at the two frequencies in the sum.

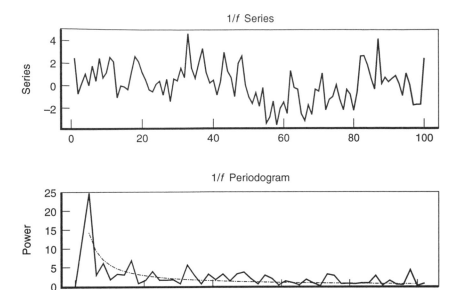

Figure 4.7. Simulated 1/f Series with its Periodogram. The smooth curve is the theoretical 1/f spectrum.

4B. A Review of Hypothesis Testing and Multiple Testing

One of our messages is that no matter how obscure the particular method, the grand themes of statistics still apply: What are the assumptions? How do the assumptions affect the conclusions? How do I adjust for multiple comparisons? All of the usual statistical issues are here. Our conclusions from these time series differ from those of previous authors because of our relaxed assumptions and our adjustment for multiple tests. To understand these differences, a brief discussion of hypothesis testing is in order.

In traditional hypothesis testing (Hogg and Craig 1995) there is a null hypothesis (H_0) and an alternative hypothesis. The null hypothesis is usually "no effect." The alternative hypothesis is usually some specific departure of interest from the null hypothesis. A classic example is: $H_0: X \sim N(0,1)$, $H_a: X \sim N(\mu,1)$ with $\mu \neq 0$. These hypotheses motivate the usual Z-test.

It is well known but not discussed nearly enough that all tests have maintained assumptions. In the Z-test above, the maintained assumptions are the normality assumption, the independence assumption, and the known and equal variance assumption. The key point is that when we reject the null hypothesis, we are either rejecting H_0, rejecting the maintained assumptions, or both. Thus, we can reject the null hypothesis with high probability even if the center of the data's distribution is, in fact, zero. For example, if the data are actually Cauchy-distributed with center zero and scale one, even for a sample of size 1000 the Z-test will reject the hypothesis $\mu = 0$ about 95% of the time, as can be easily verified by simulation. The reason the Cauchy distribution does this is because in samples of size 1000 it almost always produces a gigantic outlier that sends the mean to a huge value, thus rejecting the null. One of the goals in our analysis is to do everything we can to limit the effect of the maintained assumptions on our conclusions. Toward this goal, we develop a method that lets the data select the maintained assumptions as much as possible.

Another testing problem we face in this analysis is multiple testing. This problem frequently rears its ugly head in other settings—in medical and biological research as well as most social sciences. In the medical setting, a study may collect a large list of potential explanatory variables to predict an outcome. The explanatory variables may be demographics and baseline descriptors of health status and disease progression. The outcome could be death or disease. If each of the explanatory factors were tested for its effect on the outcome, we might get a "false positive" by chance if we had enough explanatory variables. Indeed, the traditional 5% significance test can be expected to yield one false positive in every 20 explanatory variables with no relationship to the outcome.

Multiple testing is a significant issue in an analysis based on periodograms. The problem is that a periodogram has half as many frequencies as there were data points in the original time series. This means that a 100-year annual time series has 50 potential significance tests. If these were done on a white noise series at the 5% level, 2.5 false positives would be expected. The most popular technique for adjusting for multiple comparisons is the Bonferroni method. This method takes the 5% significance and divides it over the number of tests performed, so an overall 5% error rate would be maintained if five tests were done at the 1% level.

4C. The Bootstrap and Bootstrap Hypothesis Testing

The bootstrap is a relatively recent addition to the statistical tool kit. For an easy introduction, see Efron and Gong (1983). For a textbook at the graduate student level, see Efron and Tibshirani (1993). The bootstrap is based on the elegantly simple idea that the variability in a statistical estimator can be simulated by repeatedly resampling from the original data and seeing how much the estimator changes from replication to replication.

Emerging in the wake of the booming applications of the bootstrap is a related idea, the bootstrap hypothesis test. The idea is to use the data to simulate the distribution of a statistic under the null hypothesis. The observed statistic can then be compared to this null distribution and its significance assessed. The challenge of the bootstrap hypothesis test is to change the raw data so that it conforms to the null hypothesis without changing other features of the data.

For example, consider a bootstrap hypothesis test of the situation above— $H_0{:}\mu=0$ versus $H_a{:}\ \mu\neq0$. To perform a bootstrap hypothesis test, subtract the mean from the data (so $\mu=0$) and draw repeated samples from the adjusted data. The original mean would then be compared to this null distribution. Figure 4.8

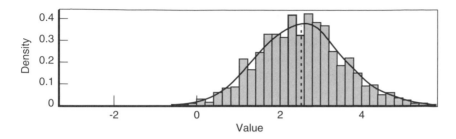

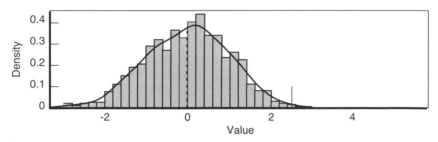

Figure 4.8. Bootstrap Hypothesis Tests. The upper panel shows 100 bootstrap means. The lower panel shows the same distribution shifted to a mean of zero. The vertical line above 2 in the lower panel is the mean of the original data.

shows how the histogram of values would be shifted. The top histogram is the means of 100 bootstrap samples from a population with $\mu=2$. The bottom histogram is the same distribution shifted to have mean zero. We can either test whether most of the upper distribution is above zero (interpreting the bootstrap confidence interval as a test) or compare the mean of the observed distribution to the critical value of the shifted distribution below. Note that no assumptions about normality or equal variances need to be made. The distribution used is whatever was the distribution of the observed data. This is how we minimize the effect of the maintained hypotheses, as we discussed in the hypothesis testing section.

In our temperature series analysis, the bootstrap is more complicated than this simple case. We discuss the details in the next section.

5. Results

It is a cliché that statistical modeling is the art of separating data into two parts: truth and noise. In typical applications, this amounts to separating data into a mean model and error. Frequency domain time series takes this view one step further and divides the data into three parts: trend (low frequency), cycles (middle frequency), and noise (high frequency.) We use this view to build a null hypothesis that is tuned to the data for our problem and leads naturally to a bootstrap hypothesis test.

5A. *Applying the Method*

We developed a simple algorithm that generates simulated replicas of the temperature series:

- Lowess the data, and save the residuals. This takes out the trend.
- Fit an Autoregressive Moving Average (ARMA) model and use it to filter the residuals from the first step. This takes out the high frequencies.
- Resample from the filtered residuals. This scrambles the middle frequencies.
- Use the fitted ARMA model to put the high frequencies back.
- Add the fitted trend back in.

This process generates a simulated global temperature series that has high and low frequencies similar to the original data. However, like the bootstrap hypothesis test for the mean that we discussed above, which has its mean removed, this series has its middle frequencies removed.

We compute the bootstrap independently for each series discussed in Section 1. First, we smooth the series using robust locally weighted regression (lowess) with smoothing fraction 0.4 to suppress the lowest frequency peaks. Analyses using alternative smoothing fractions or a fitted linear trend yield similar results. We compute the residuals from the smooth, their autocovariances at lags 1 and 2, and, from these, the covariance matrix Σ reflecting only these two lags of autocovariance. We premultiply the residual vector by $\Sigma^{-1/2}$ (defined by $\Sigma^{-1/2}\Sigma\Sigma^{-1/2} = I$) to obtain transformed residuals with no autocorrelation at lags 1 and 2. The bootstrap consists of 1000 repetitions of the following:

- Construct a pseudo-residual series by drawing a simple random sample with replacement from the transformed residuals;
- Premultiply it by $\Sigma^{1/2}$ to insert the high-frequency structure;
- Add it to the smooth; and
- Calculate the periodogram as discussed above.

The rationale is to remove the low frequencies from the data with the smooth, capture the high frequencies in $\Sigma^{-1/2}$, and obliterate the middle frequencies by sampling from the transformed residuals. This simulates a null distribution as much like the actual data as possible but without structure in the middle frequencies, for which we are testing. The selection of two lags of autocovariance is somewhat arbitrary, but the results are not sensitive to other choices.

As an example, we will use the Southern Night Marine Air Temperature Series (SNMAT). A virtue of this bootstrap method is its automatic selection of a null spectrum that is tuned to the data. Traditional significance testing in time series requires a priori selection of a null spectrum, typically uniform (white noise) or inversely proportional to frequency, neither of which describe SNMAT. Figure 4.9 presents the possible null spectra as well as the implicit null spectrum

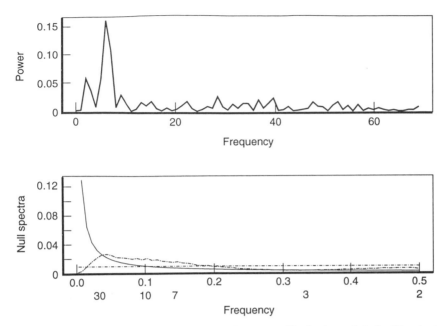

Figure 4.9. The Power and Null Spectra vs. Frequency. The horizontal dashed line (---) in the lower panel corresponds to the white noise null spectrum, and the solid line (—) corresponds to the 1/f null spectrum. The dashed line that peaks near 30 years is the bootstrap null spectrum.

from our method. Had we assumed a white noise or 1/f null spectrum, the dashed lines in Figure 4.9 would be horizontal or proportional to the period, respectively. Figure 4.9 plots the pointwise median of the bootstrap null distribution along with the white noise and 1/f spectra. Note that the bootstrap differs from the 1/f as well as the white noise spectrum. Note also that the bootstrap picks up the amplitude damping effects of the lowess on the low-frequency end of the spectrum.

5B. Conclusions

Figure 4.10 presents the periodogram for the SNMAT with the 5% and 1% critical values from the bootstrap hypothesis test superimposed. We used the 1% value as a five-test Bonferroni adjusted test. This five-test adjustment is based on the generous assumption that if analysts were mining the series at least they were restricting their attention to periods in the bidecadal range. The prominent peak at 22.7 years at the left of the spectrum would have been statistically significant if the frequency had been prespecified. However, since the peak was not prespecified, it is more appropriate to compare the peak to the higher 1% critical value. From this comparison, we conclude that the peak is not statistically significant. We do not attempt to interpret the peak at longer than 30 years at the far

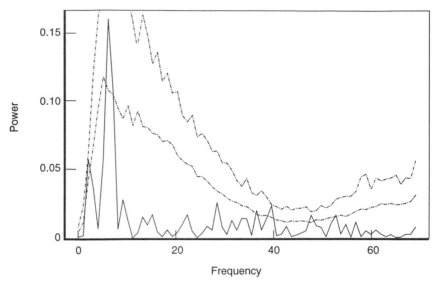

Figure 4.10. Periodogram for SNMAT Series. The upper dotted lines correspond to 5% and 1% critical values from the bootstrap hypothesis test.

left. It is difficult to take seriously a frequency of that length in a series this short. Note that there are several peaks in the two-to-seven-year range that would be significant at the 5% level and one peak that nearly touches the 1% level. This is the range of El Nino/southern oscillation (ENSO) frequencies and should be considered prespecified since there is ample observed evidence of ENSO from other measurements.

We conclude that the evidence for a 22.7-year cycle in the SNMAT is weak. It could easily be explained away as an accident of multiple testing. But what about the other series? Figure 4.11 presents the periodograms for all of the series. We cover these in the discussion below.

6. Discussion

Figure 4.11 shows that many of the prominent ENSO-related peaks are significant if treated as prespecified, and several remain significant if selected from among five prespecified peaks. In contrast, none of the bidecadal peaks are significant if adjustment is made for selection, although four are significant in some southern hemisphere series if viewed as prespecified: 14.2 years (Southern Hansen, p-value = .014), 19.4 years (SNMAT, .048 and SSST, .014), and 22.7 years (SNMAT, .011). Again, we ignore any peaks in the greater than 30-year region.

Even looking at the series as a group, the evidence for any bidecadal cycles seems weak. In some sense, the SNMAT series is the strongest case for a

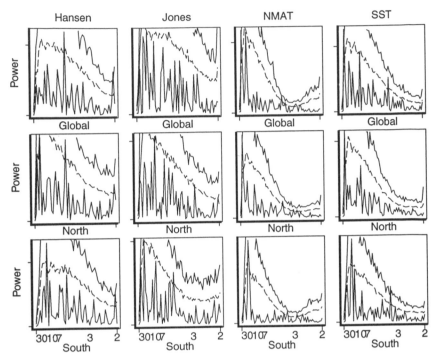

Figure 4.11. Periodograms of the Global Temperate Series with 1% and 5% Critical Values Superimposed. See Figure 4.3 for a description of the series.

bidecadal cycle since there is one clean peak with a lot of visual impact. But in the end, no series has compelling proof of a bidecadal oscillation.

We have shown that the cycles are probably not statistically significant. Does this mean they are not there? Of course not! We should not make the mistake of interpreting failure to reject a null hypothesis as acceptance of the null hypothesis. However, an argument for bidecadal cycles would need to be based on additional data or an explicit and compelling physical model.

Some open statistical questions remain. For simple cases, how to do the bootstrap hypothesis test is obvious. For example, a test of means just requires shifting the mean of the simulated distribution. For complicated cases, like ours, how to simulate from the null is less obvious. What we did was sensible but by no means the only possibility.

Whether or not this is the right hypothesis test, there is a case to be made for something called, for the lack of a better name, data informed Monte Carlo. Postulate a null distribution; so much the better if it is informed by data. If we simulate from it, we can frequently get things that look like what you think is interesting even if they are not features of our null distribution. Even if we do not replicate the sampling process, a key bootstrap requirement, we have destroyed any confidence in your results. The idea is to postulate an alternative model that generates the same observables. If this can be done, it undermines confidence in the original model. This method may be better suited to criticism than estimation.

7. Exercises

1. What is the effect on the conclusions of changing the smoothing fraction?

2. What is the effect of using more elaborate—for example higher-order autoregressive (AR)—models for the high-frequency noise?

3. Another popular frequency domain technique is cosinor analysis. Instead of the Fourier transform, cosinor analysis regresses a time series on the sine and cosine series directly. How would you use this technique and bootstrap it for this problem?

4. A popular method of combining information from medical studies is meta-analysis. How would you combine evidence across these series?

5. Note that some of these series share data. How would you bootstrap from them simultaneously to preserve this structure?

6. (Theory) The use of lowess, a nonlinear smoother, makes working out the exact properties of this procedure difficult. Can you replace lowess with a linear smoother and work out the asymptotics of this bootstrap test? (Warning: This is a dissertation-sized question.)

7. How would you design a simulation study to evaluate the small sample properties of this test? (Just when you thought you had a big enough computer, the simulation evaluation of a bootstrap procedure crops up.)

8. In Section 6, we made our lives easier and were generous by Bonferronizing only across five hypothetical peaks. How would you use the bootstrap to evaluate a procedure that selected the largest peak in the periodogram?

Further RAND Reading

Hammitt, J. K., Lempert, R. J., and Schlesinger, M. E. (1992), *A Sequential-Decision Strategy for Abating Climate Change,* RP-138, Santa Monica, CA: RAND.

Hammitt, J. K., Jain, A. K., Adams, J. L., and Wuebbles, D. J. (1996), "A Welfare-Based Index for Assessing Environmental Effects of Greenhouse-Gas Emissions," *Nature,* 381, 301–303.

Lempert, R. J., Schlesinger, M. E., and Bankes, S. C. (1996), *When We Don't Know the Costs or the Benefits: Adaptive Strategies for Abating Climate Change,* RP-557, Santa Monica, CA: RAND.

5

Racial Bias in Death Sentencing: Assessing the Statistical Evidence

Sally C. Morton and John E. Rolph

Executive Summary

Using data for California defendants whose convictions for murder required sentences of either death or life without the possibility of parole, we compare how well logistic regression and tree models predict who was sentenced to the death penalty. For each method, we assess the degree to which cases with White victims receive the death penalty compared to those without White victims controlling for other relevant case characteristics.

We discuss the pros and cons of logistic regression and tree models in this setting. On statistical grounds, logistic regression is attractive because it can efficiently incorporate a large number of variables, it is widely available in statistical software packages, its linear structure is well understood, and a variety of model diagnostics are available. However, logistic regression is oriented toward modeling main effects, with complex interactions among explanatory variables being of secondary interest, and a priori, one would expect that interactions are just as important as main effects in explaining death penalty sentencing and charging.

For states with a death penalty statute, sentencing law requires that the death penalty be imposed in neither an arbitrary nor a discriminatory way. Statistical studies of sentencing outcomes in capital cases can shed light on whether the sentences meted out exhibit either an arbitrary or discriminatory pattern.

1. Introduction

In states that have death penalty statutes, defendants can be sentenced to death only if they are found guilty of a murder that involves one or more statutorily defined conditions (such as murdering more than one person). These are called "special circumstances" in California. The process through which a person is sentenced to the death penalty has many steps. Putting aside police investigation and arrest, the major steps leading to a death sentence consist of being charged with a capital offense, being found guilty of murder with special circumstances at trial, and finally, at a separate penalty trial, being given the death sentence rather than life without the possibility of parole.

At any stage of this process, there is the possibility that decisions may be made in a racially biased way, either based on the defendant's racial group or the victim's racial group. Assessing whether racial bias is present in the decisions *in a particular case* can be done by scrutinizing the steps in the judicial process that occurred *in that case*. Alternatively, a defendant may attempt to prove racial bias by investigating whether there is a pattern in which defendants receive the death penalty that is related to race. If so, the defendant can argue that he has been a victim of the racial bias that is present in the system.

There are a variety of specific questions that can be asked about possible patterns of racial differences. First, at what stage of the judicial process should one look—charging, guilty verdicts, sentencing verdicts, or some combination? Second, should one investigate differences in outcomes categorized by race of defendant, race of victim, or both?

In this chapter, we describe an empirical investigation of racial differences in the sentencing outcomes in capital cases in California. We concentrate on detecting race-of-victim patterns in sentencing but also address possible race-of-defendant patterns.

Sentencing Law. The U.S. Supreme Court has ruled that in making death penalty decisions, "the sentencer [should] not be precluded from considering, as a mitigating factor, any aspect of the defendant's character or record and any of the circumstances of the offense that the defendant proffers as a basis for a sentence less than death" (*Lockett v. Ohio,* U.S. 586, 604 (1978)). In *Zant v. Stephens* the Court ruled that nonstatutory aggravating and mitigating circumstances may be considered in imposing the death penalty (462 U.S. 862, 906, n.1 (1983)). See also *McCleskey v. Kemp,* 481 U.S. 279 (1987); and *Eddings v. Oklahoma,* 455 U.S. 104 (1982).

The California Penal Code states that: "In the proceedings on the question of penalty, evidence may be presented by both the people and defendant as to any matter relevant to aggravation, mitigation, and the sentence including but not limited to, the nature and circumstances of the present offense" (Cal. Penal Code par. 190.3 (West 1991)). To sum up the rules: first, the existence of certain statutorily defined conditions, referred to as "special circumstances" in the remainder of this chapter, makes imposition of the death penalty possible, but not mandatory *(Woodson v. North Carolina,* 428 U.S. 280 (1976)); second, the jury, in the exercise of its discretion, is required to weigh the unique aspects of each case.

Previous Research on Racial Bias in Sentencing. Empirical research on death penalty sentencing laws has focused primarily on arbitrariness and on discrimination. Arbitrariness occurs when similarly situated offenders receive different sentences. Thus, the more accurately sentences can be predicted from case characteristics, the weaker the empirical evidence of arbitrariness. While this chapter is an empirical study of discrimination, we implicitly address arbitrariness when we assess the predictive accuracy of our models.

Since it is impossible to know, let alone measure, all the factors that might influence sentencing decisions in a particular case, any statistical attempt to predict sentencing outcomes will necessarily be less than 100% accurate. To the extent that departures from perfect prediction are systematically related to victim or defendant race, there is the possibility that race affects the penalty decision. Such considerations have motivated studies of the relationship between sentencing decisions and legally cognizable case characteristics, as well as whether differences between actual sentences and predicted sentences are related to defendant or victim race (General Accounting Office 1990). In order to develop empirical evidence on the question of whether there is a systematic pattern of juries meting out death sentences in a discriminatory way, one must control for some set of case characteristics. Otherwise, disparities in death-sentencing rates between racial groups may be due to differences in legally cognizable case characteristics. How well one controls for relevant case characteristics when comparing differences between racial groups in death-sentencing rates is the key to assessing the empirical evidence of possible racial discrimination in sentencing.

Two key race-of-victim studies of this kind are described in Baldus, Pulaski, and Woodworth (1983), Baldus, Woodworth, and Pulaski (1990), and Barnett (1985). Baldus et al. (1983, 1990) did not find strong statistical evidence that race of victim was related to sentencing decisions in Georgia. However, they did find race-of-victim disparities in death-sentencing rates for cases that did not clearly call out for the death sentence. For the 23% of defendants whose predicted probability (using a logistic regression model based on a set of nonracial case characteristics) of being sentenced to death was in the 22–75% range, the death penalty rate for White victim cases was 11–12 percentage points higher than for the Black victim cases. Barnett's (1985) reanalysis of the same Georgia data using a different method yielded consistent results—virtually all the race-of-victim disparity arose from just 5% of the defendants who have middling predicted probabilities of receiving a death sentence. More recently, Baldus was the Special Master for the New Jersey Supreme Court's proportionality review (Baldus 1991; Baldus and Woodworth 1993) in which he used logistic regression methods to assess the possible arbitrariness and/or racial bias in New Jersey death sentences. Most recently, Baldus and Woodworth published a study on prosecutorial and jury decision-making in Philadelphia death penalty cases (Baldus, Woodworth, Zuckerman, Weiner, and Broffit, 1998). Their conclusions were that both race-of-victim and race-of-defendant disparities remained after adjusting for defendant culpability using logistic regression.

1A. Policy Problem

A typical situation that spurs a charge of racial bias is when charging, verdicts, or sentencing outcomes vary substantially by the race of defendant or the race of victim. The question of interest is: If two cases are identical in all their relevant nonracial characteristics, is there a systematic difference in the outcome that is related to race? Since no two cases are clones, analyses of past cases that adjust for nonracial differences in cases are commonly used to draw conclusions about the presence or absence of racial bias in the criminal justice process.

We analyzed the data in a study of race-of-victim bias in sentencing in California (Klein and Rolph 1991).[1] This study covered 496 homicide defendants in California who were found guilty of murder with "special circumstances." Defendants were classified as having killed a White victim if at least one of the victims was White. Killers of White victims were more often sentenced to death than were killers of non-White victims (33% vs. 23%, respectively). Does this difference persist after adjusting for *relevant* differences in the case characteristics?

To conclude that there is racial bias in the system of death penalty sentencing in California, a statistical analysis must *adequately control for* all of the aggravating and mitigating circumstances that can legitimately influence a penalty phase jury's decision to impose the death penalty. This "equivalency" assumption is needed to conclude that, *all else equal,* the killer of a White victim is more likely to be sentenced to death than a defendant who did not kill a White victim.

In this chapter, in the context of possible race-of-victim bias in sentencing decisions, we explore statistical methods for making cases comparable and the difficulties in interpretation. We discuss the selection of variables that may appropriately influence sentencing decisions, the degree to which our models capture complex relationships among variables, and more broadly how to assess the adequacy of the data and a statistical model for drawing conclusions about whether or not racial bias is present.

1B. Research Questions

Specifically, our research questions are:

- Controlling for all other relevant factors, are defendants convicted of murder with special circumstances sentenced to death in white-victim cases more often than those in non-White-victim cases?

- Controlling for all other relevant factors, are defendants convicted of murder with special circumstances sentenced to death more often if they are non-White than if they are White?

- Controlling for all other relevant factors, is there an interaction of victim race and defendant race in death penalty sentencing decisions?

1C. Statistical Questions

There are two predominant statistical methods used for adjusting for differences in cases when investigating the possible effects of race on sentencing decisions. The most prevalent method is logistic regression (e.g., Baldus, Wood-worth, and Pulaski 1990; Klein, Petersilia, and Turner, 1990). Tree models were used in Klein and Rolph (1991), and it is the dataset from that study that we use in this chapter.

On statistical grounds, logistic regression is attractive because it can efficiently incorporate a large number of variables and is widely available in statistical software packages. Using linear combinations to capture the relationships between variables is both its strength and weakness. On the one hand, the linear structure is well understood and a variety of model diagnostics are available. On the other, it is oriented toward capturing main effects and so is relatively less effective in identifying complex interactions among explanatory variables when predicting sentencing or charging decisions. A priori, it would seem that interactions are just as important as main effects in explaining death penalty sentencing and charging.

Tree models put main effects and interactions on the same footing and have been gaining popularity in recent years. Tree models use recursive partitioning to create classification rules. Their potential advantages in death penalty analyses include being easier to interpret than linear models; treating missing values in a more satisfactory way; and capturing nonadditive behavior better since the standard linear structure does not allow interactions unless they are prespecified in a particular multiplicative form. This latter point may be summarized as saying that tree-based models do not impose a linear form on how the explanatory variables are combined.

Prior to Klein and Rolph (1991), tree models had one precursor in death penalty racial bias research in Barnett (1985). Barnett reanalyzed the data from Baldus, Pulaski, and Woodworth (1983) using a subjective method of grouping cases with similar characteristics with some success. By contrast, we will automate the process by fitting trees using a recursive partitioning algorithm.

In our study of death penalty sentencing decisions in California, we fit the data using both logistic regression and tree models and, in the process, address two statistical questions:

- What are the pros and cons of using logistic regression versus tree models for this application? In particular, does the efficiency of the linear structure and readily available diagnostics for logistic regression outweigh the easier interpretability and cross-validation that tree models afford?

- What are good modeling strategies for each method that are defensible and interpretable?

1D. Data and Methods

We used logistic regression and tree models to analyze cases selected from the California Bureau of Criminal Statistics (BCS) database as discussed in more detail below.

2. Study Design, Data Collection, Description of Data Sources, and Description of Data Elements

Data Collection. In 1984 the California Bureau of Criminal Statistics (BCS) created a list of the 542 California offenders who had committed a homicide after August 10, 1977, the date that California's death penalty law took effect. BCS did this by obtaining a list of all offenders who were under a sentence of death or life without the possibility of parole (LWOPP) as of March 1, 1984. Offenders who had their sentences overturned by this date were not included.

BCS searched the Automated Homicide File (AHF) to find information on each of the offender's victims. The AHF records contain police data about victims and their suspected assailants' names, which were used to match victim records to the offender list. We cannot be certain that all victims were included in the AHF, nor that all matches were correct, though every effort was made to correct matching errors. If BCS was unable to find a match for an offender in the AHF, it asked the Department of Corrections to search its files for the names of that offender's victims so that BCS could match AHF data based on victim name(s) in those cases.

Analysis Sample. In this manner, the BCS merged the original offender list with the AHF files to create an offender/victim level dataset. For cases that had more than one victim, the data from the various AHF victim files were aggregated into victim variables as described below. The sample size of this merged dataset was 496 offender/victim(s) pairs, a loss of 8% of the original 542 offender list. Ten offenders in the original list were found not to have committed a homicide, and victim information for 36 offenders could not be found in the AHF. Comparing the offenders lost to analysis revealed some differences: only 15% of the excluded offenders received the death penalty, while 29% of those included in the analysis file did; 33% of the excluded offenders were White, while 43% of the included offenders were.

Nine of the 496 (2%) remaining offenders were women. Due to the smallness of this subgroup and the possibility that women are treated differently from men in the criminal justice system, we did not analyze female offenders. Thus, our final analysis sample had 487 offenders.

Our only potentially missing data were on victim characteristics, and, as reported above, we dropped these cases from the analysis datafile. Thus, our analysis did not have to deal with missing data.

3. Datafile Creation, Descriptive Statistics, and Exploratory Analysis

Variable Construction Limitations. BCS constructed both victim and offender variables using the AHF, offender criminal records, and the Department of Corrections data. Several points should be kept in mind:

- The AHF record for a crime was entered shortly after the victim's death, which occurred before sentencing. Thus, BCS coded the "special circumstances" believed to be present based on the data available rather than on trial records.

- Of the 487 cases, 17% had no coded "precipitating events," 75% had one coded event, and the remaining 8% had two or three coded events.

- For cases with more than one victim, a case was considered a "White victim" case if the case had at least one White victim. A similar definition was used for "female victim."

- Whether the offender was just an accomplice could not be determined from the AHF.

- Of the 487 cases, 35% had no relationship between the victim and the offender coded, 44% had one relationship coded, 17% had two relationships coded, and the remaining 4% had three or more relationships coded.

Variable Definitions. Table 5.1 shows the BCS constructed variables that we considered as possible explanatory factors. We dropped several variables from consideration that had almost all cases taking one value or were highly correlated with other potential explanatory variables (e.g., the number of prior convictions). All variables in Table 5.1 are dichotomous dummy variables; for example, OFWHITE=1 if the offender's ethnicity was White and OFWHITE=0 if not. Table 5.1 shows the prevalence of each variable in the analysis sample. For example, 43% of the offenders are White (OFWHITE).

Variable Reduction. We reduced the set of variables shown in Table 5.1 in the following ways:

- To get easily interpretable variables and to focus our attention on the potentially largest racial effects found in past studies, we dropped all race and ethnicity variables (OFBLACK, OFHISP, VIBLACK, VIHISP) except those for the White offender (OFWHITE) and White victim (VIWHITE).

- In the remaining variable domains, we aggregated variables that had low prevalence and substantive reasons for aggregation. To "aggregate" variables, we set the new indicator variable equal to one if any of the component indicator variables equaled one—that is, if any of the component conditions were true. We aggregated:

  – VILOVER and VIWIFE into VILVWF;

  – VICAR, VIHIWAY, and VISTREET into VICRHIST;

  – VIOBUS and VISTORE into VIBSST;

  – VIROBBER and VIBURGLE into VIROBBUR; and

  – VIRAPE and VIOTHSEX into VISEX.

  (See Table 5.1 for variable definitions.)

Table 5.1. Candidate Variables and Their Prevalence

Variable	Description	Proportion
	Offender Characteristics	
OFWHITE[a]	White offender	43%
OFBLACK	Black offender	38%
OFHISP	Hispanic offender	16%
OFYOUNG[a]	Offender under 20	13%
OFOLD[a]	Offender over 30	23%
OFEARLY	First arrest as a juvenile	38%
OFNOPRIS[a]	Prior criminal record, but no prison	50%
OFPRIS[a]	Prior prison record	30%
	Victim Characteristics	
VIWHITE[a]	White victim	67%
VIBLACK	Black victim	15%
VIHISP	Hispanic victim	15%
VIFEMALE[a]	Female victim	39%
VIYOUNG[a]	Victim under 20	19%
VIOLD	Victim over 49	24%
TWOVICTS[a]	Exactly two victims	19%
MANYVICT[a]	More than two victims	6%
	Victim/Offender Relationship	
VIWIFE	Killed wife	3%
VILOVER	Killed a lover	1%
VILVWF	Killed wife or lover	4%
VIOTHFAM	Killed other family member	4%
VIFRIEND	Killed a friend	16%
VICOP	Killed a cop	3%
VIACQUAI	Killed an acquaintance	21%
VISTRANG	Killed a stranger	43%
VIALLACQ[a]	All victims were acquaintances	42%
VIALLSTR2	All victims were strangers	1%
VISTRANG2	Some victims were strangers	20%
	Special Circumstances	
SCINTENT[a]	Intentional for personal gain	3%
SCWITNES[a]	Avoid arrest/victim an officer	4%
SCATRTOR[a]	Atrocity or torture	3%
SCINWAIT[a]	Intentional while laying in wait	2%
SCNOTSEX[a]	While engaged in nonsex crime	69%
SCOTHER[a]	Other special circumstance	5%
SCPRIOR[a]	Prior murder conviction	2%
SCMULT[a]	More than one murder conviction	25%

Table 5.1. (continued)

Variable	Description	Proportion
	Location of the Crime	
VIBAR[a]	In a bar	3%
VIOHOME	In offender's home	2%
VIVHOME	In victim's home	33%
VIRURAL[a]	In rural area	12%
VICAR	In a car	5%
VIHIWAY	On a highway	1%
VISTREET	On a street	10%
VICRHIST	In a car, on a highway or street	16%
VIOBUS	In other business	11%
VISTORE	In a store, etc.	7%
VIBSST[a]	In a store or other business	18%
	Weapon Used	
VIGUN	Used gun	59%
VIROPES	Used ropes	8%
VIPERSON[a]	Used hands, etc.	5%
VIOTHOBJ	Used other object	29%
	Precipitating Event	
VIRAPE	Rape involved	13%
VIOTHSEX	Other sex involved	3%
VISEX[a]	Rape or other sex involved	15%
VIARGUE[a]	Argument involved	7%
VIROBBER	Robbery involved	53%
VIBURGLE	Burglary involved	6%
VIROBBUR[a]	Robbery or burglary involved	58%
VIDRUGS	Drugs involved	3%
VIMONEY	Money involved	1%

[a]Denotes that the variable was considered as a candidate for the logistic regression.

- In the victim/offender variable domains, we constructed three new variables:

  - VIALLSTR2, which equals one if all the victims are strangers; that is, VISTRANG equals one and VIWIFE, VILOVER, VIOTHFAM, VIFRIEND, and VIACQUAI (the nonstranger variables) are all equal to zero;

  - VIALLACQ, which equals one if VISTRANG equals zero and at least one of the nonstranger variables is equal to one; and

  - VISTRANG2, which equals one if the case has multiple victims, VISTRANG equals one, and at least one of the nonstranger variables equals one.

As discussed previously, 37% of the cases have no victim/offender relationship coded and so have VIALLSTR2, VIALLACQ, and VISTRANG2 all equal to zero for these cases. As a result of this variable construction, we dropped the victim descriptor variables VIFRIEND (friend) and VIOTHFAM (family member) from further consideration. We continued to consider the victim variables VILVWF (wife or lover) and VICOP (cop) as candidates because the literature suggests that these victim–offender relationships may have an effect on sentencing decisions.

This variable reduction left 41 candidate variables for consideration as predictors in our multivariate models.

Descriptive Statistics. Table 5.2 shows the proportions of offenders who received a sentence of death categorized by the races of the victim(s) and the offender. A sentence of death was much more likely in a White victim case than in a non-White victim case (33% versus 23%), while a sentence of death was somewhat more likely in a White offender case than in a non-White offender case (32% versus 27%, not shown). Whites who killed Whites were more likely to receive a death sentence than non-Whites who killed Whites, and the reverse was true in non-White victim cases.

4. Statistical Methods and Model

We chose the form of our final logistic regression and tree models using a similar process. In each case, we first specified candidate explanatory variables and then selected the final variables, including possible interactions, for the final model using intermediate fits to make decisions. Our model specification processes for the two methods differed primarily in two ways. For logistic regression, we considered possible main effects and then possible interactions, while for trees the fitting algorithm considered candidate main effects and interactions simultaneously. For fitting tree models, we used a formal cross-validation measure to avoid overfitting, while for logistic regression we did not.

Table 5.2. Descriptive Statistics Showing the Relationship Between Victim and Offender Race, and Sentencing Outcome

Victim's Race	Offender's Race	Number of Offenders	Percentage Sentenced to Death
White	White	186	34%
	Non-White	138	31%
	All	324	33%
Non-White	White	24	21%
	Non-White	139	24%
	All	163	23%
All	All	487	30%

Logistic Regression Modeling. Since the sentencing outcome is either death or life without possibility of parole (LWOPP), the fitted probability of a death sentence, p(x), is

$$p(x) = \frac{e^{b'x}}{1 + e^{b'x}} , \tag{5.1}$$

where x is the column vector of explanatory variables and b is the column vector of the corresponding regression coefficients fit by maximum likelihood to the 487 cases. A few lines of algebra reveal that (5.1) can be rewritten in odds ratio form as

$$\frac{p(x)}{1 - p(x)} = e^{b'x} . \tag{5.2}$$

The odds ratio form has the convenient interpretation that e^{b_i} is the multiplicative factor by which the fitted odds of a sentence of "Death" rather than "LWOPP" change when explanatory variable x_i changes from the value "0" to the value "1." Thus, in Table 5.3, the fitted odds of a death sentence are increased by more than 50% [exp(0.5078) = 1.662] if the victim is female (VIFEMALE=1) as compared to when the victim is male (VIFEMALE=0), assuming all other explanatory variables are unchanged. See Hosmer and Lemeshow (1989) for an excellent reference on logistic regression.

To reduce the size of our model specification task, we screened out any of the 41 candidate predictors that had only a small bivariate relationship with the sentencing outcome. We did this by dropping variables with a chi-squared statistic value of less than one (corresponding to a p-value of 0.32). This strategy is a common approach used in both logistic and linear regression to reduce the set of candidate variables before modeling. The result was 27 variables remaining, which are footnoted in Table 5.1.

We fit a logistic regression model with all 27 variables included. All analysis in this chapter was performed using the statistical package S-PLUS (Mathsoft Inc. 1997). This model suggested two further variable reductions. First, even though it was significant, we dropped the variable OFNOPRIS (=1 if prior criminal record, but no prison) to simplify the interpretation of the variable OFPRIS (=1 if prior prison record). With this new variable specification, we could compare outcomes for defendants with a prison record to those without. Second, we collapsed the two variables indicating the crime had more than one victim (TWOVICTS and MANYVICT) into a single variable MORETONE (= 1 if the crime had more than one victim).

After this preliminary form of variable selection, we identified two interactions of substantive importance from the literature: between offender and victim race (OFWHITE and VIWHITE) and between victim gender and the victim being young (VIFEMALE and VIYOUNG).

Table 5.3. Final Logistic Regression Model with Race Variables Included

Variable	Odds Ratio	95% Confidence Interval
Offender and Victim Characteristics		
OFWHITE	0.56	(0.17, 1.87)
VIWHITE	1.16	(0.63, 2.15)
(OFWHITE) (VIWHITE)[a]	1.93	(0.51, 7.31)
OFYOUNG	0.40	(0.17, 0.92)
OFPRIS	1.89	(1.14, 3.11)
VIFEMALE	1.66	(0.92, 3.00)
VIYOUNG	2.96	(1.28, 6.80)
(VIFEMALE) (VIYOUNG)[a]	0.43	(0.14, 1.33)
Victim–Offender Relationship		
VIALLACQ	0.55	(0.28, 1.08)
Special Circumstances		
SCINTENT	6.57	(1.76, 24.56)
SCWITNES	8.70	(2.59, 29.21)
SCATRTOR	28.34	(4.29, 187.26)
SCINWAIT	2.61	(0.49, 13.93)
SCNOTSEX	1.69	(0.88, 3.26)
SCSEXCRI	1.60	(0.76, 3.35)
SCOTHER[b]	0.01	(0.00, 2249.64)
SCPRIOR	2.89	(0.67, 12.59)
SCMULT	3.90	(2.13, 7.16)
Location of Crime		
VIBAR	0.35	(0.04, 3.01)
VIRURAL	2.23	(1.14, 4.38)
Weapon Used		
VIPERSON	1.82	(0.66, 5.01)
Precipitating Event		
VIARGUE	0.18	(0.04, 0.73)

[a]These are interaction variables.

[b]This variable separates out a set of 23 cases getting LWOPP sentences. See the text.

To perform further variable selection, we applied backwards elimination (Hosmer and Lemeshow 1989) to the full model described above. In backwards elimination, we exclude a variable at each step from the model until further elimination is not warranted. The statistic used to evaluate each alternative model is the Akaike Information Criterion (AIC), which depends on both the model fit and the number of degrees of freedom used in the model, thereby balancing fit with model parsimony. When considering whether to exclude a particular variable, we calculate the AIC for the associated model defined as the present model excluding the variable being considered. The variable excluded at each step is the one that decreases the AIC the most compared to the present model. If no new model has a smaller AIC than the present model, the present model is the final selection. Note that the AIC may result in the final model containing variables that are not individually statistically significant. See Chambers and Hastie (1992) and Weisberg (1985) for further discussion of this process and alternative statistics for model selection. Since our primary goal was assessing any "effect" of victim and/or offender race, we forced these variables and their interaction to stay in the model. Five variables (OFOLD, MORETONE, VIBSST, VISEX, and VIROBBUR) were dropped during the automatic selection.

Table 5.3 gives the resulting fitted model. In addition, we fit a logistic regression without any race effects; see Table 5.4. The tables give the odds ratios and

Table 5.4. Final Logistic Regression Model Without Race Variables Included

Variable	Odds Ratio	95% Confidence Interval
Offender and Victim Characteristics		
OFYOUNG	0.40	(0.17, 0.94)
OFPRIS	1.83	(1.11, 2.99)
VIFEMALE	1.72	(0.96, 3.08)
VIYOUNG	2.90	(1.27, 6.64)
(VIFEMALE) (VIYOUNG)[a]	0.44	(0.14, 1.34)
Victim–Offender Relationship		
VIALLACQ	0.57	(0.30, 1.10)
Special Circumstances		
SCINTENT	6.92	(1.90, 25.19)
SCWITNES	8.79	(2.65, 29.22)
SCATRTOR	29.36	(4.46, 193.53)
SCINWAIT	2.73	(0.51, 14.61)
SCNOTSEX	1.72	(0.89, 3.31)
SCSEXCRI	1.64	(0.79, 3.41)
SCOTHER	0.01	(0.00, 1486.08)
SCPRIOR	3.14	(0.73, 13.54)
SCMULT	3.82	(2.09, 6.98)
Location of Crime		
VIBAR	0.36	(0.04, 3.07)
VIRURAL	2.29	(1.18, 4.46)
Weapon Used		
VIPERSON	1.90	(0.70, 5.16)
Precipitating Event		
VIARGUE	0.18	(0.04, 0.74)

[a]This is an interaction variable.
[b]This variable separates out a set of 23 cases getting LWOPP sentences. See the text.

corresponding 95% confidence intervals. Not surprisingly, the fitted coefficients for the nonrace variables in the two tables are very similar since the race variables contribute little to the fit. We note that all 23 offenders who had an other special circumstance (SCOTHER=1) received a sentence of LWOPP. For this reason, the logistic regression does not converge and the fitted coefficient moves toward a minus infinity with each iteration. S-PLUS removes the observations that have SCOTHER=1, fits the model on the remaining observations, and reports a large negative value for the SCOTHER coefficient and hence an odds ratio near zero.

Tree Modeling. The algorithm applied to produce the tree model was binary recursive partitioning, whose most well-known implementation in the statistical literature is "CART" (classification and regression trees) as discussed in detail in Breiman, Friedman, Olshen, and Stone (1984). We used the algorithm implemented by Clark and Pregibon (1992) in S-PLUS.

The first binary split of the dataset takes place at the "root" of the tree, consisting of all members of the sample. Binary splits corresponding to each covariate are considered, and the one that produces the two most homogeneous subsets in terms of the offender's sentence is chosen. By "most homogeneous," we mean the split that produces the maximum decrease in the deviance.

Using the notation of Clark and Pregibon (1992), the maximum likelihood estimate in a particular node of the probability p_D that an offender receives the death penalty is the proportion of offenders in that node who are observed to receive the death penalty, and similarly for the estimate of the probability p_L that an offender receives LWOPP. The deviance of that node is defined as

$$D = 2y_D \log(p_D) - 2y_L \log(p_L) , \qquad (5.3)$$

where y_D is the number of offenders in the node who receive the death penalty and y_L is the number who receive LWOPP. D is minus twice the log likelihood of the node under a binomial model.

The deviance of a split equals the sum of the deviances of the resulting two nodes. This sum is compared to the parent node's deviance, and the "optimal" split, which produces the greatest decrease in deviance, is chosen. The two resulting nodes are themselves split, and successive splits occur at each level, forming branches and subsequent nodes of the tree. Splitting is continued until further disaggregation does not contribute to the model's fit.

To understand the robustness of a tree model, an analyst can examine at each node for each candidate predictor the decrease in deviance that results from each possible split on that predictor. The "local optimal" split for that particular predictor is the one that maximizes the decrease in deviance. Comparing these maximum decreases in deviance across all predictors, especially with respect to that obtained by the "globally optimal" split, allows one to determine whether the optimal splitting variable at that particular node has any close competitors. If another predictor could produce nearly the same decrease in deviance as the optimal splitting predictor, then inference based on the splitting variable choice should be tempered. One should consider the alternative tree(s), if possible. See Exercise 2.

To facilitate the interpretation of the tree model, we used slightly different variable coding in the tree model setting as compared to logistic regression. We constructed a new variable NUMVICTS that equaled the number of victims and had levels one, two, or many. In the logistic regression setting, the number of victims was coded as two indicator variables, TWOVICTS and MANYVICT, since indicator variables are easier to interpret in terms of odds ratios. We also constructed a new variable RELTN to represent the victim/offender relationship, taking on the four values unknown, all strangers, all acquaintances, or both strangers and acquaintances. The tree model algorithm allows any combination of a polytomous variable's levels to be considered as a split.

One key difference between tree models and logistic regression is that the former automatically consider a nonadditive covariate structure. Logistic regression does not allow interactions between covariates unless they are prespecified. Tree models do not impose a linear form on how the explanatory variables are combined, thereby putting main effects and interactions on an equal footing.

The key challenge for tree model building is to determine the appropriately sized tree. As discussed above, the tree is grown very large initially, and then the lower nodes are pruned back in order to ensure that the resulting model is stable. This approach balances the goal of producing a simple model (a small tree) against overfitting the data. Both the CART and S-PLUS implementations employ cross-validation to estimate the predictive accuracy of trees of a particular size.

Our Tree Model Specification. To make our tree models comparable to our logistic regression models, we also restricted ourselves to the 487 male offenders. As just explained, a crucial decision in tree models is the number of terminal nodes. S-PLUS will display a cross-validated deviance plot to inform this decision. Figure 5.1 gives the deviance plot for trees of sizes 1 to 65 terminal nodes fit to our data using the explanatory variables listed in Table 5.1. Tree sizes whose deviances were relative minima in the graph are candidates of choice. There are three trees with 8, 11, and 16 terminal nodes. (While the single-node tree has a low deviance, its lack of structure makes it uninteresting.) Figures 5.2, 5.3, and 5.4 depict the structures of these three trees.

5. Results

We turn first to the predictive performance of logistic regression versus tree models in modeling capital sentencing outcomes. Then we assess the statistical evidence of racial discrimination in capital sentencing.

Logistic Regression. The final fitted logistic regression in Table 5.3 has 22 coefficients, two of which are interactions. The signs of the variables generally

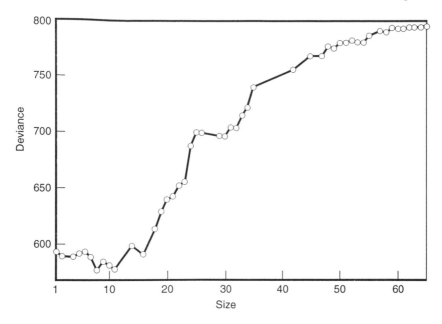

Figure 5.1. Cross-validated Deviance Plot for Trees of Sizes 1 to 65 Terminal Nodes. The horizontal variable "size" is the number of terminal nodes, and the vertical variable "deviance" is the cross-validated deviance value as defined by (5.3). Tree sizes with relative minima are the three trees with 8, 11, and 16 terminal nodes.

make intuitive sense. The fitted odds of a death sentence increase by at least a factor of 2 when the victim is young (which is stronger for female victims) and for each of several special circumstances that are present:

- intentional for personal gain;
- avoid arrest/victim an officer;
- atrocity or torture;
- prior murder conviction; or
- more than one murder conviction.

The fitted odds decrease by at least half if:

- the offender is young;
- other special circumstances are present; or
- an argument was a precipitating event.

Neither race of victim, race of defendant or their interaction is statistically significant (since the 95% confidence intervals for the odds ratios include one).

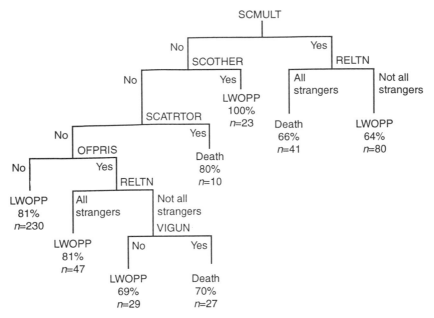

Figure 5.2. Tree with Eight Terminal Nodes. The name of the splitting variable is given at each split, and the values on the left and right branches determine how the data are split. For example, at the root node, the splitting variable is SCMULT. Those cases with more than one murder conviction (SCMULT="yes") go to the right, and all other cases go to the left. At each of the eight terminal nodes, the predicted outcome, the percentage of cases in the terminal node observed to have that outcome, and the number of cases in the terminal node are given. For example, in the right-most terminal node in the tree, the predicted outcome is life without the possibility of parole ("LWOPP"); 64% of the 80 cases belonging to that node received that sentence.

Trees. Scrutinizing the 8-terminal-node tree in Figure 5.2 also confirms one's intuition about explanatory variables. The largest terminal node on the far left consists of 47% of the cases (230), with 19% receiving the death sentence (making it an LWOPP node). The recursive algorithm gets to this node by choosing SCMULT = 0 (only one murder conviction), SCOTHER = 0 (not other special circumstances), SCATRTOR = 0 (not atrocity or torture), and OFPRIS = 0 (no prior prison record). The node with the highest death-sentencing rate of 80% has ten cases and is located in the middle of the figure. It is reached by the successive splits SCMULT = 0 (only one murder conviction), SCOTHER = 0 (not other special circumstances), and SCATRTOR = 1 (atrocity or torture). The 8-node tree uses six variables.

The 11-node tree in Figure 5.3 introduces three additional splits on SCIN-TENT (special circumstance: intentional for personal gain), VIBSST (location in a store or other business), and VIARGUE (argument precipitated the crime). Interestingly, each of these variables breaks off less than 20% of a large node in the 8-node tree.

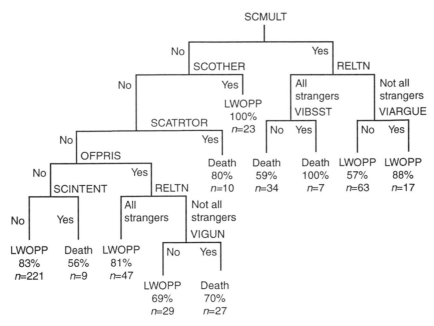

Figure 5.3. Tree with 11 Terminal Nodes. The name of the splitting variable is given at each split, and the values on the left and right branches determine how the data are split. For example, at the root node, the splitting variable is SCMULT. Those cases with more than one murder conviction (SCMULT="yes") go to the right, and all other cases go to the left. At each of the 11 terminal nodes, the predicted outcome, the percentage of cases in the terminal node observed to have that outcome, and the number of cases in the terminal node are given. For example, in the right-most terminal node in the tree, the predicted outcome is life without the possibility of parole ("LWOPP"), 88% of the 17 cases belonging to that node received that sentence.

The 16-node tree in Figure 5.4 breaks the largest node of 221 cases in the 11-node tree into six terminal nodes using the variables VIYOUNG (victim under 20), SCSEXCRI (engaged in sex crime), VIROBBUR (robbery or burglary involved), VISEX (rape or other sex involved), and OFEARLY (first arrest as a juvenile).

None of the race variables are present in any of the three cross-validated trees presented here. They appear in the unpruned tree (not shown), but both the race-of-victim and the race-of-defendant variables are split about equally on increasing versus decreasing the proportion of death sentences.

Logistic Regression Versus Trees. We compare the performance of our tree models by requiring each model to match the margins of the observed data—predict 144 death sentences and 343 LWOPP sentences. For logistic regression models, cases are ranked in order of the predicted probability of a death sentence, with the highest 144 classified as "predicted death" and the remaining 343 as "predicted LWOPP." In the case of ties, the cases are allocated to the prediction category proportionately. Thus, if three cases with the same logit value are

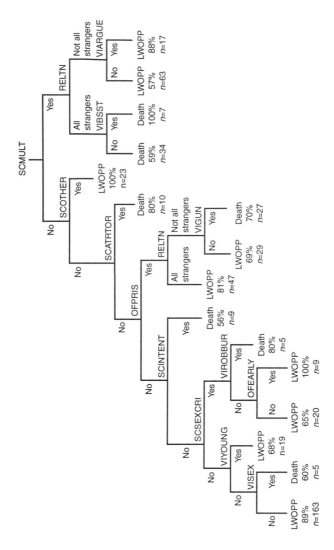

Figure 5.4. Tree with 16 Terminal Nodes. The name of the splitting variable is given at each split, and the values on the left and right branches determine how the data are split. For example, at the root node, the splitting variable is SCMULT. Those cases with more than one murder conviction (SCMULT="yes") go to the right, and all other cases go to the left. At each of the 16 terminal nodes, the predicted outcome, the percent of cases in the terminal node observed to have that outcome, and the number of cases in the terminal node are given. For example, in the leftmost terminal node in the tree, the predicted outcome is life without the possibility of parole ("LWOPP"); 89% of the 163 cases belonging to that node received that sentence.

tied for ranks 144, 145, and 146, each would count 1/3 as a predicted death. For tree models, the same procedure is followed, meaning that the terminal nodes are ranked in order of the proportion of their cases receiving the death sentences. Again, in the case of ties, cases are allocated proportionately to the prediction categories of death and LWOPP.

Table 5.5 displays the accuracy of the predictions for the two final logistic regression models (Tables 5.3 and 5.4) and the three tree models we settled on (8, 11, and 16 terminal nodes). Both the 11- and 16-node tree models do as good or better job of prediction than any of the logistic regression models in spite of the fact that they use fewer variables. The three tree models use 6, 9, and 14 variables, respectively. The two logistic regressions use 22 and 19 variables, respectively, including interactions, which corresponds to 20 and 18 variables, without interactions. It is also worth noting that the logistic regressions undoubtedly have some overfitting present—some of the variables are picking up noise. Thus, for this application, the tree modeling approach with its agnostic lack of preference of main effects versus interactions seems preferable to logistic regression.

Table 5.5 Accuracy of the Different Models

Actual	Predicted Death	Predicted LWOPP	Percentage Classified Correctly
Logistic Regression			
Observed death	82	62	57%
Observed LWOPP	62	281	82%
Logistic Regression Without Race			
Observed death	83	61	58%
Observed LWOPP	61	282	82%
8-Node Tree			
Observed death	78.8	66.1	55%
Observed LWOPP	66.1	276.9	81%
11-Node Tree			
Observed death	83.4	60.6	58%
Observed LWOPP	60.6	282.4	82%
16-Node Tree			
Observed death	86.1	57.9	60%
Observed LWOPP	57.9	285.1	83%
Total	144	343	487

NOTE: Predictions for all models are constrained to equal the observed death-sentencing rate (i..e., to predict 144 death sentences and 343 LWOPP sentences).

6. Discussion

Explanatory Variables in the Two Approaches. Interestingly, the explanatory variables used in the logit regression and the tree do not totally agree. Table 5.6 lists the variables present in the two logistic regression models and the three trees. The logistic regression without race has 18 variables, while the 8-, 11-, and 16-node trees have 6, 8, and 14 variables, respectively, reflecting the interactions present in all the trees.

The six variables in common between the 11-node tree and the 18-variable logistic regression are "boxed" in the table: OFPRIS (prior prison record), SCINTENT (intentional for personal gain), SCATROR (atrocity or torture), SCOTHER (other special circumstance), VIBSST (location: store or business), and SCMULT (more than one murder). Only VIGUN (gun used) and RELTN (offender and victim related) are in the tree and not in the regression as indicated with a superscript "b." Recall that these two models have comparable accuracy.

S-PLUS has a "burling" function that allows one to look at other candidate variables at each node—competitors to the variable actually chosen for the split. We define "close competitors" as those whose deviance contribution is at least 80% of the splitting variable chosen in the 11-node tree. With the exception of NUMVICTS (the number of victims), all close competitors are included as explanatory variables in the logistic regression. The close competitors are footnoted in Table 5.6. We encourage the reader to compare this approach with the variable importance and surrogate splitting ideas presented in Breiman, Friedman, Olshen, and Stone (1984).

Assessing Racial Disparities in Sentencing. Neither the logistic regression nor the tree modeling approach produces evidence of systematic race-of-victim or race-of-defendant disparities in capital sentencing after controlling for other variables. A comparison of the two logistic regression models, one with and one without race variables, reveals no statistically significant differences. For the 8-, 11-, and 16-node trees, race variables do not appear at all. In the 20-node tree (not shown), whose deviance is above that of the 8-, 11-, and 16-node trees (Figure 5.1), race of victim (VIWHITE) splits to produce two terminal nodes well down the tree consisting of six non-White victim cases and ten White victim cases having 17% and 70% death-sentencing rates. Thus, there the direction of the race-of-victim disparity is positive but small.

Proving that death sentences are handed out in a racially discriminatory manner requires either persuasive statistical evidence or actually observing racial discrimination in the judicial process. Our analyses of California data using two different methods of controlling for nonracial differences in cases reveal, at most, only small racial disparities in death-penalty rates. While this does not prove the absence of discrimination, it also falls well short of the statistical evidence needed to prove racial discrimination.

Table 5.6 Variables in Different Models

Logistic Regression Variables (22)	8-Node Tree Variables (6)	11-Node Tree Variables (8)	16-Node Tree Variables (14)
Offender and Victim Characteristics			
OFWHITE			
VIWHITE			
(OFWHITE) (VIWHITE)[a]			
OFYOUNG			
			OFEARLY
OFPRIS	OFPRIS	OFPRIS	OFPRIS
VIFEMALE			
VIYOUNG[c]			VIYOUNG
(VIFEMALE) (VIYOUNG)[a]			
Victim–Offender Relationship			
VIALLACQ			
	RELTN	RELTN[b]	RELTN
Special Circumstances			
SCINTENT		SCINTENT	SCINTENT
SCWITNES			
SCATRTOR	SCATRTOR	SCATRTOR	SCATRTOR
SCINWAIT			
SCNOTSEX[c]			
SCSEXCRI			SCSEXCRI
SCOTHER	SCOTHER	SCOTHER	SCOTHER
SCPRIOR			
SCMULT	SCMULT	SCMULT	SCMULT
Location of Crime			
VIBAR			
VIRURAL			
VIBSST		VIBSST	VIBSST
Weapon Used			
	VIGUN	VIGUN[b]	VIGUN
VIPERSON			
Precipitating Event			
VISEX[c]			VISEX
VIARGUE			VIARGUE
VIROBBUR[c]			VIROBBUR

NOTE: "Boxed" variables appear in both the 11-node tree and the logistic regression.

[a]These are interaction variables.

[b]These variables are in the 11-node tree but not in the logistics regression.

[c]These variables are close competitors in the 11-node tree (80% deviance of the chosen split). NUMVICTS is also a close competitor.

7. Exercises

The dataset and accompanying documentation for the following exercises are available on our website (www.rand.org/centers/stat/casebook).

1. Ask for the best eight-variable logistic regression model learning from the tree model.

2. Use the competing variables from Table 5.6 to construct a tree model with 11 terminal nodes and compare the prediction accuracy to the best 11-node tree model we fit.

3. Consider an application and dataset for which you have already fit a logistic regression model. Fit a tree model for this dataset. Compare the variables selected in the two models. For example, you may wish to utilize the "burling" function provided in S-PLUS to examine candidate variables at the tree nodes. Propose reasons for any differences between the models. Which modeling approach, in your opinion, is more appropriate for this application?

Further RAND Reading

Klein, S. P. (1991), *Racial Disparities in Sentencing Decisions,* P-7742, Santa Monica, CA: RAND.

Klein, S., Petersilia, J., and Turner, S. (1990), "Race and Imprisonment Decisions in California," *Science,* 247, 812–816.

Note

[1]This chapter extends Klein and Rolph (1991) by adding the logistic regression analysis and a comparison of it to tree models. We thank Stephen P. Klein for his work on the original study, without which this chapter could not have been written.

6

Malpractice and the Impaired Physician: An Application of Matching

Kimberly A. McGuigan and John E. Rolph

Executive Summary

Is one at relatively greater risk of getting negligent medical care if one's physician is impaired by substance abuse or psychological problems? We address this long-standing concern through a retrospective comparative analysis of medical malpractice claims of impaired physicians and comparable physicians who are not impaired. Using 13 years of claims data from the primary medical malpractice insurer in a large state, we linked insurance records and records of the state's Impaired Physician Program in order to match impaired physicians to nonimpaired physicians on their demographic and practice pattern characteristics. Using three successively narrower definitions of malpractice claims, we compare claims frequencies of impaired physicians to their matched controls.

Compared to their matched controls, impaired physicians have 25% more claims filed, 100% more claims in which peer review or indemnity payment has confirmed medical negligence, and 59% more claims in which the insurer paid a settlement or court verdict. These differences persist to varying degrees across the three different types of impairment (alcohol, drug, or psychological). Severity of impairment matters, but interestingly, the group of physicians with a medium impairment level has consistently higher relative claims rates of all types than either the low-impairment group or the severely impaired group.

While there are substantial and statistically significant disparities in claims rates between impaired physicians and their matched controls, this does not translate into an especially high overall risk to patients since impaired physicians, as defined in this study, comprise less than 2% of practicing physicians. However, our results can help justify policies aimed at identifying impaired physicians and their problem behaviors, and then doing something about them.

1. Introduction

Does a physician who is impaired by substance abuse or a psychological disorder incur an increased risk of treating patients in a medically negligent way?

While a priori one may assume that impairment would lead to a greater risk of iatrogenic injury (injury that results from medical intervention) and other adverse medical outcomes due to negligence, no one has yet analyzed this relationship. Practicing physicians suffering from substance abuse problems or other behavioral impairments have long been a concern of the medical profession (Osler 1892; Brewster 1986).

Impairment may arise from drug dependency, alcohol abuse, or psychological disorders. Approximately 3–8% of physicians and 5% of medical students report some period of time in which they experienced drug dependence (McAuliffe et al. 1986; Hughes et al. 1992), with 1.5% estimated to be experiencing dependence at any point in time (Scheiber 1983). Among those who do not report any period of dependence, 4% of physicians and 16.5% of medical students reported rates of substance use at levels high enough to be considered at risk for drug abuse (McAuliffe et al. 1986). The lifetime rate of alcohol abuse in one state was estimated to be about 4% each for practicing physicians and medical students, with 2% of physicians and 3% of medical students admitting a current drinking problem (McAuliffe et al. 1991). The prevalence of psychological disorders among physicians is unknown. The reported rate of psychological disorders varies among impaired physicians ranging from only 6% of Georgia's Impaired Physician Program enrollees (Talbott, Gallegos, Wilson, and Porter 1987) to 22% of enrollees of the Impaired Physician Program in Oregon (Shore 1987). This latter figure is consistent with a 1973 American Medical Association estimate that, among all physicians identified by state medical boards as impaired, about one-fifth are reported as having psychological impairments (Scheiber 1983).[1]

1A. Policy Problem

The performance of impaired physicians is of continuing public-policy interest to a variety of organizations. Practicing clinicians with any impairment problem are cause for concern since impairment can potentially contribute to errors in judgment or performance while delivering patient care. But does physician impairment really lead to lower quality of care? While state-sponsored impaired physician programs have been operating since the early 1980s, this question has not been addressed. In this chapter, we describe how we compare indicators of medical errors, specifically malpractice claims, of impaired and nonimpaired physicians.

1B. Research Questions

We linked data from one state's largest medical malpractice insurer to data from that state's Impaired Physicians Program. "Impaired physicians programs" are programs set up by a state's medical society, usually for the purpose of treating physicians with alcohol, drug, or psychological impairments. Using this datafile, we analyzed whether impaired physicians have higher rates of malpractice claims than comparable nonimpaired physicians. We used three different definitions of malpractice claims. We also broke out claims rates by type of impairment (alcohol abuse, drug dependency, psychological disorder) and severity of impairment. Our three key questions are:

- How do the demographics of impaired physicians compare to the general population of physicians? That is, are there systematic differences between impaired physicians and nonimpaired physicians in their distribution of age, sex, type of medical specialty, or practice pattern?

- Does the frequency of medical malpractice claims of impaired physicians differ from that of *comparable* unimpaired physicians, and, if so, how large is this difference? Specifically, we compared frequencies for three successively narrower definitions of claims:

  — All claims. These are legal claims filed by patients or their attorneys against the physician and his/her insurer that allege medical negligence. This category includes both meritorious claims (where there is evidence that physician negligence has occurred) or nonmeritorious claims (no evidence of physician wrongdoing).

  — Negligence claims. These are claims where an indemnity payment through a court verdict or settlement has occurred or the peer review process has confirmed that negligence has occurred.

  — Paid claims. These are claims that have resulted in an indemnity payment. That is, the insurer paid money as a result of a court verdict or a settlement.

- Finally, does the pattern of malpractice (all claims, negligence claims, or paid claims) differ by type or severity of impairment? For example, do physicians with alcohol abuse problems exhibit different claims histories than those with psychological problems?

The answers to these questions can inform the design of policies to deal with the problem of impaired physicians. If impaired physicians have a disproportionately high rate of malpractice claims, additional attention to this group may have a relatively large payoff in reducing injuries. For example, second opinions from a highly qualified physician might be required for high-risk procedures performed by impaired physicians. Impaired physicians might be barred from engaging in certain clinical activities. Random sampling of impaired physicians' records could be carried out in a systematic fashion to identify areas of their practices that need attention. Further, what policies make sense might vary depending on whether the negligence is concentrated in a specific subgroup of impaired physicians (e.g., alcoholism).

Note that the outcome measures in this study—malpractice claims—can be difficult to interpret. Medical malpractice represents the extreme end of the quality-of-care spectrum. Yet, malpractice claims are only an indirect indicator of quality of care. Claims reported to insurers are only a small fraction of the cases in which an adverse event accompanied by negligence occurs (Harvard Medical Practice Study 1990). Also, a large fraction (about 70%) of the malpractice claims analyzed in this study did not show evidence of negligence. A particular strength in our study is that we can identify those claims where negligence has been established either through the tort system or by peer review.

1C. Statistical Questions

Since this is an observational study, we expect to see differences between the impaired and nonimpaired physician groups in factors that may relate to malpractice claims rates. Such factors are potential confounding variables. If we do not control for confounding variables, we cannot conclude that differences in malpractice claims rates between the impaired and nonimpaired groups are caused by impairment. In our data, we were fortunate to have measurements on a large number of potential confounding variables. These include physician age, sex, training, and practice pattern descriptors, such as volume of office patients and surgical load. Also, time of exposure—that is, the amount of time that the physician is covered by the insurer—differs across physicians. Our primary statistical question is thus:

* How should we control for the differences in relevant characteristics between impaired and nonimpaired physicians to make a valid comparison of their malpractice claims histories?

We used a case-control design to control for any systematic differences in these factors by creating matched sets of one or more nonimpaired physicians ("controls") whose characteristics are very similar to the impaired physician ("case"). We could then simply compare appropriately weighted averages of outcome variables of impaired and nonimpaired physicians. Also, we used individual physician-year of coverage as a frequency weight in the analysis. This is consistent with assuming that an underlying Poisson process generates individual physician claims.

1D. Summary of Data and Methods

We linked three databases to produce the data analysis file. The three databases consisted of: (i) 13 years of claims histories and physician (policyholder) characteristics for the largest medical malpractice insurer in a particular state; (ii) a file giving extensive information for each hospital in the state; and (iii) the files of the Impaired Physician Program for the state, including the type and severity of the impairment. Combining physician specialty, demographic, personal practice pattern, and hospital environment data enabled us to select a set of comparable "control" physicians for every impaired physician identified.

We used matching or case-control methods to control for potential confounding variables that might otherwise account for any differences in malpractice rates among impaired and nonimpaired physicians. This approach allowed us to isolate the effect of impairment on the malpractice claim outcomes. Matching is particularly appropriate in observational studies such as ours when a relatively small group of subjects are exposed to a "treatment" (impairment) and a much larger group of "control" subjects are not exposed. A notable advantage of matching over regression, the common alternative as a bias-reducing method, is that matching does not use a specific function to link the outcome measure to the explanatory factors. We had 168 impaired physicians and could choose from 11,945 nonimpaired physicians as potential controls. Matching also has excellent robustness properties (Anderson et al. 1980; Rosenbaum and Rubin 1985; Rosenbaum 1995).

2. Study Design, Data Collection, Description of Data Sources, and Description of Data Elements

2A. Study Design

As just described, our design was a case control. The matching for this study was performed as depicted in Figure 6.1.

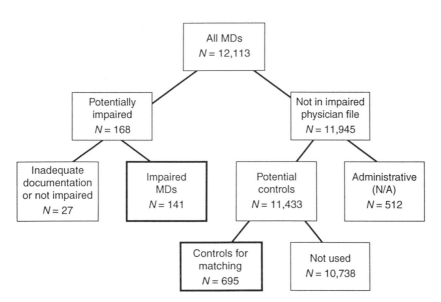

Figure 6.1. Schematic Flowchart from Original Database to Impaired and Matched Controls. This flowchart, along with the description below, demonstrates how the analysis sample of 141 impaired physicians and 695 matched nonimpaired physicians was identified.

First, we eliminated from consideration as controls the 512 nonimpaired physicians who were in specialties in which there were no impaired physicians, as they obviously would not match any of the impaired cases. We also eliminated 27 of the "potentially impaired" physicians because of inadequate documentation or because closer examination of their records suggested that they did not meet the definition of impairment. The matching procedure is described in more detail in Subsection 4A in this chapter. Briefly, we ran a logistic regression analysis using an indicator of impairment as the outcome variable and physician and hospital characteristics as the explanatory variables. Predicted values from this regression are called *propensity scores* (Rosenbaum and Rubin 1983, 1984, 1985; Rosenbaum 1995). Finally, after grouping physicians into six categories according to their propensity scores, we exact-matched impaired and nonimpaired physicians using the propensity score categories as well as on other variables we decided were particularly important to control for. The result was 695 matched nonimpaired controls to the 141 impaired physicians.

2B. Data Collection and Description of Data Sources

Data for this study are compiled from three sources:

- Malpractice claims data, practice pattern information, and demographic data from a particular state's largest malpractice insurer. This file includes physician demographic information from a 1986 insurer survey and physician claims histories by policy number for the 1977–1990 history of the company. The identity of the insurer is not revealed, at its request.

- Data for physicians with substance abuse or psychological impairment enrolled in the state-sponsored Impaired Physicians Program, including information regarding type of impairment and time period of impairment. All cases referred to the Impaired Physicians Program were reviewed by the medical director and staff to determine whether the case meets the criteria to be classified as impaired. Physicians in this Impaired Physicians Program entered through the following routes:

  — 20% self-referrals;

  — 50% referred by colleagues;

  — 10% family referrals; and

  — 20% from the state Board of Registration, hospital credentials committee, and other.

- Characteristics of hospitals in the state, including location, patient mix, and available facilities. Hospital data were collected as part of another study (Melnick, Mann, and Serrato 1988). See Kravitz, Rolph, and McGuigan (1991) and Rolph, Kravitz, and McGuigan (1991) for a complete description of these data. Most of the hospital-based variables for individual physicians were characteristics of the primary hospital at which the physician had staff privileges.

2C. Description of Data

Physicians. Subjects included all physicians who were policyholders of the state's primary medical malpractice insurer and were covered as full- or part-time practicing physicians during any period between 1977 (the founding year of the company) and 1990. Data items included underwriting details (time of coverage with the company, physician specialty), physician practice pattern characteristics, claims information (date of event, date claim was filed, basis for claim), peer review evaluation of claim, and claim disposition (closed with payment, closed without payment, open).

Impaired Physicians. Information recorded for impaired physicians included impairment type (alcohol, other substance abuse, psychological impairment, or a combination), severity of impairment (7-point scale), and timing (impairment onset, entry into program, control of impairment, exit from program).

Hospital Data. Hospital characteristics in this file included location (rural, urban), size, type (nonprofit, for profit, government owned), presence of intensive care and high-technology units, payer mix (Medicare, Medicaid, private insurance, self-pay), and hospital case mix (a measure of the severity of cases seen in the hospital).

3. Datafile Creation, Descriptive Statistics, and Exploratory Analysis

3A. Datafile Creation

Linking Impairment Data to Physician Claims. Impaired physicians were identified through the use of a "blind protocol" linkage in which the insurer supplied the state's Impaired Physicians Program with a list of names and policy numbers of all policyholders. The Impaired Physicians Program director then supplied us with policy numbers only for physicians in the program. We used these policy numbers to identify the records of impaired physicians in the insurer's file. Thus, confidentiality of the identity of impaired physicians was maintained by the Impaired Physicians Program.

Linking Hospital Characteristics to Physicians. Hospital characteristics were linked to physicians by using the physicians' primary hospital affiliations, based on self-reported proportion of workload at each of (up to) five hospitals.

3B. Exploratory Data Analyses

As Table 6.1 shows, impaired physicians are similar to nonimpaired physicians in age, hours of practice per week, number of office patients per week, and

Table 6.1. Physician Characteristics: Impaired Versus All Nonimpaired

Characteristics	Impaired (std. dev.)	All Nonimpaireds (std. dev.)
Age at midpoint of coverage	45.5	45.3
Sex (% male)	97.2%	88.8%
Board certified (or board eligible and <35 years old)	60.0%	66.0%
Privileges at flagship hospital	5.3%	6.4%
Residency at flagship hospital	16.3%	24.6%
Average hours practice/week	43.5	43.2
Average office patients/week	57.7	58.6
Average major surgeries/week	1.7	1.2
Average years of fulltime coverage	6.9	7.0

NOTE: Tabled entry is mean for that characteristic. For indicator variables, this is a percentage.

number of years of full-time coverage with the insurer. However, the impaired group reported almost half again as many major surgeries a week (1.7 vs. 1.2) and has fewer female physicians (2.8% vs. 11.2%). Impaired physicians are about 10% less likely to be board certified than their brethren, about one-sixth less likely to have privileges at flagship teaching hospitals, and about one-third less likely to have done their residency training at a flagship hospital.

It is well known that a variety of physician characteristics are correlated with malpractice claims (Rolph, Kravitz, and McGuigan 1991; Sloan et al. 1993; Gibbons, Hedeker, Charles, and Frisch 1994). Thus, to study whether there is a causal link between physician impairment and propensity to generate malpractice claims, we must control for the relevant differences in characteristics between physicians who are impaired and those who are not.

4. Statistical Methods and Model

We employed matching to reduce bias by selecting nonimpaired physicians for the control group who are similar to the impaired physicians in the background variables on which we had data in order to account for relevant differences other than impairment between impaired and nonimpaired physicians. For example, to the extent that impaired physicians are disproportionately represented in lower-risk specialties, their malpractice claims rates will be lower because of this confounding factor, making a direct comparison of impaired and nonimpaired physician malpractice risk misleading. To the extent that each impaired doctor ("case") can be matched to one or more similar nonimpaired doctors ("controls"), we improve our ability to attribute any differences in outcome measures to impairment status.

From a presentational point of view, an advantage of successful matching is its persuasiveness for nontechnical audiences. While the matching algorithms themselves can be complex, simple comparisons of the means and standard deviations of the explanatory variables of the two groups can indicate whether the outcome variables of the two groups may be compared without bias.

For a given impaired physician, we selected a "control group" of nonimpaired physicians that is similar to the impaired physician with respect to age, training, years in practice, specialty, board certification, and practice pattern. It is particularly important to include patient load in the matching criteria to avoid possible biases that could result from impaired physicians seeing fewer (or more) patients.

4A. Matching to Create the Analysis File

As discussed in Subsection 1D, we began with 141 impaired physicians for analysis, and 11,945 potential nonimpaired physicians to match. We went through three successive steps in performing matching, as depicted in Figure 6.1.

Screening. First, we eliminated 512 nonimpaired physicians for whom there were no impaired physicians to match. As Figure 6.1 shows, these were mostly physicians in administrative positions but also included physicians who practiced at Veterans Administration, rehabilitation, or neuropsychiatric hospitals, whose primary hospital was out-of-state, or whose residency was not completed.

Matching Procedure. Because we wished to match on a substantial number of factors, we combined exact matching with propensity score matching (Rosenbaum and Rubin 1983, 1984, 1985; Rosenbaum 1995). After screening, our second step was propensity score matching, which we describe in more detail below. It is a multivariate procedure for creating a "similarity index" from selected covariates. Using propensity scores, we created six approximately equal-sized groups of physicians. In our third and final step, we did exact matching within each of the six propensity score groups.

First, we divided our population of physicians into two broad groupings of specialties: "Medical" ($N = 6441$) and "Surgical/Ancillary" ($N = 5133$). To describe the propensity score matching step, we digress to define propensity scores. Let x be the vector of covariates for a particular physician, and let z be a binary variable indicating whether the physician is impaired ($z = 1$) or not impaired ($z = 0$). The propensity score $p(x)$, is the conditional probability of impairment given x. That is, $p(x) = \text{Prob}(z = 1 \mid x)$. We estimate the propensity score using logistic regression:

$$\log\left(\frac{p(x)}{[1 - p(x)]}\right) = \beta'x$$

where β is the vector of regression coefficients to be estimated.

We did propensity score matching separately within each of the two broad specialty groupings as follows. We regressed impairment (z) on the list of selected exposure and quality variables in Table 6.2 using logistic regression. The logistic regression output for the two broad specialty groups is shown in Tables 6.3a (medical specialties) and 6.3b (surgical specialties). Within each specialty group, we then used the fitted probabilities or propensity scores to group physicians into six approximately equal-sized categories. The reader may wish to think of this process as creating a single matching variable with six levels.

Table 6.2. Propensity Score Variable Definitions

Variable	Description
off_pats	Number of office patients seen each week
surg	Any surgeries performed (medical specialties only)
maj_surg	Number of major surgeries performed each week (surgical specialties only)
hrsopert	Hours per week spent in operating room
hrspspec	Hours per week spent in primary specialty
hrssspec	Hours per week spent in secondary specialty
hrsother	Hours per week spent in activities other than direct patient care
pracpat	Indicator: Responded to practice patterns survey
resflag	Indicator: Residency training obtained at flagship teaching hospital
teachprv	Indicator: Privileges at teaching hospital
flagpriv	Indicator: Privileges at flagship teaching hospital
crdstat2	Indicator: Board certified in specialty
hrsprac	Total patient care hours per week

Table 6.3a. Logistic Regression to Generate
Propensity Scores: Medical Specialties

Variable	Coefficient	Prob > |t|	Mean of Variable
off_pats	−0.00	0.28	47
surg	0.01	0.99	.01
hrspspec	0.00	0.53	24
hrssspec	−0.06	0.10	2.3
hrsother	0.01	0.58	3.4
pracpat	0.22	0.53	.27
resflag	−0.84	0.04	.19
teachprv	0.21	0.36	.54
flagpriv	−0.59	0.42	.50
crdstat2	−0.28	0.22	.58
hrsprac	−0.00	0.84	29
constant	−4.11	0.00	1.0

NOTE: $N = 6441$, p-value for overall regression = .04.

Table 6.3b. Logistic Regression to Generate
Propensity Scores: Surgical Specialties

Variable	Coefficient	Prob > |t|	Mean of Variable
off_pats	0.00	0.54	40
maj_surg	0.04	0.17	2.0
hrsopert	−0.01	0.82	3.4
hrspspec	−0.01	0.16	30
hrssspec	−0.05	0.41	.77
hrsother	−0.03	0.32	3.6
pracpat	0.05	0.94	.23
resflag	−0.20	0.30	.32
teachprv	−0.25	0.39	.57
flagpriv	0.90	0.04	.06
crdstat2	0.23	0.49	.75
hrsprac	0.01	0.27	31
constant	−4.61	0.00	1.0

NOTE: $N = 5133$, p-value for overall regression = .28.

Finally, within each of the six propensity score categories we exact-matched on age, sex, medical specialty category, part-time practice, primary hospital affiliation, and starting period of coverage with the medical insurer; these measures are described in Table 6.4. Within each broad medical specialty category, our clinical consultant (R. Kravitz, M.D.) created the smaller specialty categories (see Table 6.4). These categories were defined using the criterion that the cognitive activities for the specialties and subspecialties within a category be similar.

All variables in the table were used for matching, with one exception. Three impaired physicians had no exact matches for starting period of coverage. We therefore widened the window in order to find matching controls in these three cases.

Matching resulted in 695 controls matched to 141 impaired cases comprising 137 matched sets of impaired and nonimpaired physicians. Most (133) sets were 1-to-N case-control matches; that is, these sets consisted of one impaired and N nonimpaired physicians, with N ranging from 1 to 32 (mean = 5). Four matched sets contained two impaired physicians and N nonimpaired physicians since both impaired physicians were identical on all control variables within the set.

4B. Analytic Model

Given the matched sets, our analysis method was two-way main effects analysis of variance (ANOVA) with impairment status (two levels) and matched set (137 levels) being the two factors. We used physician years of coverage as weights. The tables reporting the results give the estimated coefficients for im-

Table 6.4. Exact-Match Variable Definitions

Variable	Description
agecat	Under 40, 40–55, over 55
sex	Male, female
specialty category	Medical specialties: –Internal medicine –Pediatrics –General/family practice –Emergency room –Radiation therapy –"Other" nonsurgical specialties
	Surgical specialties: –General surgery and major surgery specialties –Obstetrics, with or without gynecology –Office-based surgery and gynecology –Anesthesiology –Radiology –Pathology
parttime	Part-time coverage, full-time coverage
cluster	Type of hospital: No hospital practice or not at regular hospital Rural Small Large inner city (teaching + nonteaching) Other large teaching Other large nonteaching
startcov	Founder, 1st, 2nd, 3rd, 4th, 5th periods

NOTE: Startcov periods are 2/1/77, 2/2/77–6/30/78, 7/1/78–6/30/81, 7/1/81–6/30/84, 7/1/84–6/30/87, and 7/1/87–12/31/89, respectively.

pairment status only. Malpractice claims rates for impaired physicians were used for those coverage periods that fall within the identified window of impairment. We did not include claims rates either before or after the impairment period for impaired physicians due to the sparseness of the data.

5. Results

5A. Claims Rate Comparisons for Impaired and Comparable Nonimpaired Physicians

As described in Section 6.1, we used three different claims definitions to capture different aspects of malpractice. They were successively narrower definitions of claims: total claims, negligence claims, and paid claims. The claims rate is defined as the total number of claims divided by the total number of person-years. Summaries stratified by impairment severity and type of impairment are given in Tables 6.5 and 6.6 and shown graphically in Figures 6.2, 6.3, and 6.4.

Figure 6.2 gives a bar chart of claims rates by type of malpractice claim. Impaired physicians have about a 25% higher total claims rate than nonimpaired controls. Impaired physicians have about twice the negligence claims rate as the matched nonimpaired ones. Impaired physicians have a 60% higher paid claims rate than nonimpaired ones. About 30% of total claims have an indemnity payment.

Figure 6.3 shows that the smallest differences in negligence claims rates between the impaired and nonimpaired groups are associated with drug problems in contrast to alcohol and psychological impairment. Figure 6.4 shows how differences vary by the severity of the impairment. Surprisingly, the largest differences are for physicians classified as being moderately impaired; impaired physicians have about double the claims rate of those nonimpaired controls. In-

Table 6.5. Claims Rates by Severity of Impairment

| | No. of | Total Claims | | Negligence Claims | | Paid Claims | |
| | | | Non- | | Non- | | Non- |
Severity	Claims	Impaired	impaired	Impaired	impaired	Impaired	impaired
Low	1308	0.13	0.15	0.05	0.04	0.05	0.03
Medium	5392	0.29	0.22	0.14	0.06	0.11	0.05
High	2665	0.15	0.14	0.06	0.05	0.05	0.04
All	9365	0.23	0.18	0.10	0.05	0.08	0.05

NOTE: Significance probabilities are not shown. However, claims rate differences between the impaired and nonimpaired groups are statistically significant ($p < .01$) for each claim type/severity level. All differences across severity levels within claim type/impairment indicator are also statistically significant ($p < .01$).

Table 6.6. Claims Rates by Type of Impairment

| Impairment | No. of | Total Claims | | Negligence Claims | | Paid Claims | |
| | | | Non- | | Non- | | Non- |
Type	Claims	Impaired	impaired	Impaired	impaired	Impaired	impaired
Alcohol	5410	0.26	0.21	0.10	0.06	0.08	0.05
Drugs	2081	0.15	0.12	0.07	0.05	0.05	0.04
Psychol.	1874	0.24	0.17	0.13	0.05	0.12	0.04
All	9365	0.23	0.18	0.10	0.05	0.08	0.05

NOTE: Significance probabilities are not shown. However, claims rate differences between the impaired and nonimpaired groups are statistically significant ($p < .01$) for each claim type/impairment type level. All differences across impairment type within claims type/impairment indicator are also statistically significant ($p < .01$).

terestingly, physicians in the severely ("high") impaired group have only slightly higher negligence claims rates than their controls (0.06 vs. 0.05), and impaired physicians diagnosed with a low severity of impairment experience *fewer* negligence claims than similar unimpaired controls. We have no explanation to offer for this reversal.

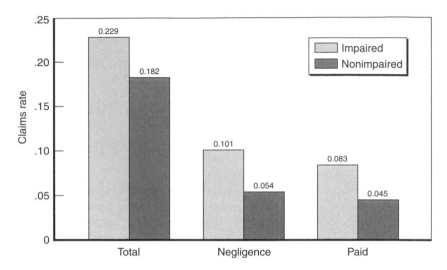

Figure 6.2. Claims Rate by Type of Claim. This bar chart graphically summarizes some of the results shown in Tables 6.5 and 6.6.

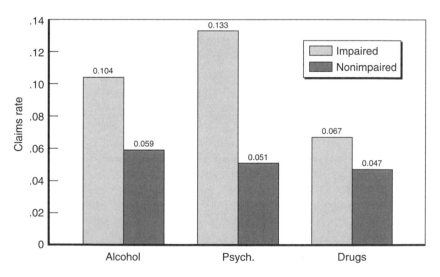

Figure 6.3. Negligence Claims Rates by Type of Impairment. This bar chart graphically summarizes some of the results shown in Table 6.6.

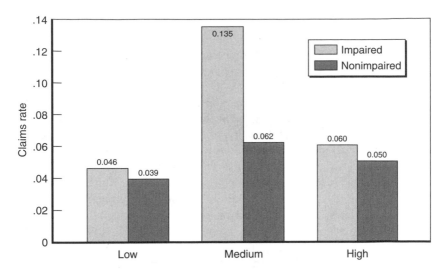

Figure 6.4. Negligence Claims Rates by Severity of Impairment. This bar chart graphically summarizes some of the results shown in Table 6.5.

In summary, compared to control physicians, nonimpaired physicians have:

- 25% more claims;
- 100% more negligence claims;
- 59% more paid claims.

These differences persist to varying degrees for different types of impairment. While severity of impairment matters, it has a mixed pattern, with only the group of physicians with a medium level of impairment having consistently higher claims rates of all types than their control group.

6. Discussion

6A. Policy Issues

This study presents evidence of a positive relationship between malpractice claims rates and impairment over most of the comparisons examined. Impaired physicians have higher total claims rates, negligence claims rates, and paid claims rates than matched nonimpaired controls. While the evidence for differing negligence claims rates is not as strong as for the other claim definitions, the difference is substantial and in the expected direction. These differences persist across all impairment types: alcohol abuse, other substance dependence, and psychological impairment. Surprisingly, estimates of the "impairment effect" do not increase with the degree of severity—it is highest for the moderately impaired category. There may be an interaction between type of impairment and severity which could explain some of this observed relationship, but our sample size limits our ability to detect such an interaction if it is present.

The reader should bear in mind some caveats about the measures we used in this study. Physician demographics, specialty, training, and practice pattern information were self-reported measures at a single point in time. In particular, practice pattern information is subject to possible reporting bias. Differential reporting bias might affect the estimates of the effects of impairment. If impaired physicians tend to overreport their practice activity—that is, if they are more likely than unimpaired physicians to overreport patient loads, perhaps to mask the effects of impairment—then we have systematically matched impaireds to controls who tend to have higher underlying claims rates. This would bias the estimate of impairment effect downward. A less intuitively plausible possibility is that the differences in reporting are reversed so that impaired physicians understate their self-reported workloads as compared to controls. This would bias the estimated effect of impairment upward.

Missclassifying nonimpaired physicians as impaired also has the potential to bias our estimates of observed differences. We carefully excluded physicians initially labeled as impaired who were found to be unimpaired or for whom we had inadequate evidence to support a diagnosis of impairment. Given the level of case review and exclusion of ambiguous cases, we are reasonably certain that our impaired group is uncontaminated, but some percentage of controls are probably unidentified impaired physicians. Since impaired physicians have higher claims rates on average, the presence of unidentified impaired physicians in the control group would raise our estimate of claims rates for the controls, thus decreasing the difference in claims rates between the impaired and unimpaired groups. Under this scenario, the observed differences would be a lower bound for the effect of impairment on malpractice claims rates.

Given these caveats, our results suggest that physician impairment may be a risk factor for malpractice claims. Claims where negligence is established by peer review or an indemnity being paid indicate quality-of-care problems at the extreme end of the spectrum. But malpractice claims are, at best, an imperfect indicator of poor-quality care. A comprehensive study in New York in the 1980s (Harvard Medical Practice Study 1990) shows that paid malpractice claims occur at a rate of fewer than 1 per 16 adverse medical events. Thus, without further research, no firm conclusions can be drawn about how strongly the incidence of adverse medical outcomes and iatrogenic injury is associated with physician impairment. Also, while we found statistically significant disparities in claims rates between impaired physicians and their matched controls, this does not translate into an especially large overall risk to patients since impaired physicians in this study comprise fewer than 2% of the practicing physicians covered by this insurer.

However, it is important to find ways to reduce the risk of unnecessary adverse outcomes to patients. State medical society sponsored Impaired Physicians Programs may be serving an important role in identifying problem behaviors and helping induce recovery for physicians with behavioral impairments.

6B. Statistical Issues

Although a randomized controlled trial is the gold standard of evaluation design, selection of controls in observational studies such as this one must necessarily be done "after the fact." Matching controls to subjects in the treatment group on important characteristics that are plausibly related to outcome measures is the observational study analog to the designed experiment. Specifically, by matching on relevant characteristics, one can reduce bias introduced by confounding factors. In this study, we measured the success of our matching by assessing the comparability of the impaired and control groups on the characteristics used to match physicians. Because we had a relatively large number of potential variables to match on compared to the number of impaired physicians, we augmented exact matching on the most important variables with propensity score matching. Propensity score matching is an efficient way to incorporate a large number of control variables in the matching criterion (Rosenbaum and Rubin 1985).

In selecting a bias-reducing method, one must consider the tradeoff between reducing bias and increasing variance. Matching is a particularly effective bias-reduction method because of its constructive nature and its avoidance of the assumptions about functional form and error structure required by regression, its main competitor. However, matching has lower precision (higher variance) in the resulting estimates as compared to regression because much of the available data are not used—those control physicians who cannot be matched to an impaired physician. In making this tradeoff for this study, we were faced with a small number of treatment observations (impaired physicians) relative to the overall sample size. Thus, the dominant contribution in the variance of differences in claims rates associated with impairment comes from the claims rate estimate for the impaired physicians. This is precisely the situation where matching dominates regression since its strong bias-reduction attributes need not be traded off against substantially higher standard errors of estimates.

7. Exercises

The dataset and accompanying documentation for the following exercises are available on our website (www.rand.org/centers/stat/casebook).

1. Using the outcomes on paid claims, use a two-way ANOVA without interactions to estimate the "effect" of impairment. Your two factors are impairment (0–1) and matched group. List the assumptions for this model and interpret your results.

2. Fit a two-way ANOVA to paid claims where impairment has four levels (not impaired, low impairment, medium impairment, and high impairment). Write an explanation of your findings in no more than one page.

3. Using paid claims as the outcome variable, use a two-way ANOVA without interactions to estimate the "effect" of impairment *only for those matched groups where the type of impairment is alcohol.* Your two factors are impairment (0–1) and matched group. List the assumptions for this model and interpret your results.

4. Discuss the pros and cons of using regression in this study rather than matching. In this study, there were 141 physicians with confirmed impairment. Now suppose you were faced with the same dataset as in this study except that the number of physicians whose impairment is confirmed is 1410. Would you prefer regression to matching in this situation? Why or why not?

Further RAND Reading

Kravitz, R., Rolph, J. E., and McGuigan, K. A. (1991), *Malpractice Claims Data as a Quality Improvement Tool. I, Epidemiology of Error in Four Specialties,* N-3448/1-RWJ, Santa Monica, CA: RAND.

Lewis, E., and Rolph, J. E. (1993), *The Bad Apples? Malpractice Claims Experience of Physicians with a Surplus Lines Insurer,* P-7812, Santa Monica, CA: RAND.

Rolph, J. E., Kravitz, R., and McGuigan, K. A. (1991), *Malpractice Claims Data as a Quality Improvement Tool. II, Is Targeting Effective?* N-3448/2-RWJ, Santa Monica, CA: RAND.

Note

[1]This research was funded by the Robert Wood Johnson Foundation and the Office of the Assistant Secretary for Policy and Evaluation in the Department of Health and Human Services. Elizabeth Lewis, M.S., carried out the initial datafile construction. David Canavan, M.D., shared his expertise and quantitative information on impaired physicians, Neal Thomas, Ph.D., advised on matching methods, and Richard Kravitz, M.D., advised on specialty groupings.

Understanding Relationships

7

Supply Delays for F-14 Jet Engine Repair Parts: Developing and Applying Effective Data Graphics

Lionel A. Galway

Executive Summary

In 1989, RAND undertook a project for the U. S. Navy to study supply problems at Naval Aviation Depots, which are responsible for repairing aircraft engines, airframes, and electronics. Many repairs were being delayed because needed repair parts were not in stock locally and were taking significant time to arrive at the repair depot. A number of potential causes were proposed, including delayed reorder of depleted stocks at the depot, inefficient distribution of parts from the Navy and Department of Defense (DoD) supply systems, and depletion of stocks across DoD, leading to lengthy delays while cumbersome procurement procedures for buying parts from manufacturers were executed.

The project on which this chapter is based studied the repair of the F-14 jet engine at the depot in Norfolk, VA. For those repairs, we assembled a dataset consisting of parts orders and issues at the depot, as well as procurement actions for engine repair parts by the Navy, U. S. Air Force, and the Defense Logistics Agency. Preliminary data analysis using aggregate statistics verified the supply problem but did not show enough detail on problem parts to support or disprove the various hypothesized causes.

Realizing that we needed to see more details of the supply delays for individual parts, we developed a graphical display, the *supply transaction profile* (STP), which displayed orders, issues, and relevant procurement actions for each repair part ordered chronologically in a compact layout which allowed easy comparison between different parts. We found that for a majority of the problem parts, delays in receiving them were due to lengthy shipping times from other sections of the Navy or DoD supply system. In particular, reparable parts that were stored at the local Naval Supply Center took several days to move to the depot. For some parts, however, delays were due to the necessity of procuring the part. This suggested that efforts to streamline procurement procedures, while useful, should be secondary to efforts to reengineer internal distribution in the Navy and the DoD as a whole.

1. Introduction

1A. Policy Problem

In its broadest sense, military logistics is the support of a nation's armed forces. This support includes procuring and repairing equipment and distributing supplies. Military logistics consumes a substantial part of the U. S. defense budget: roughly $50 billion out of a budget of $250 billion. While part of this task is done by military personnel, a large role is also played by civilian-manned organizations such as the equipment repair depots operated by the Army, Air Force, Navy, and Marines.

In 1989, the Navy asked RAND to do a study of supply problems with repair parts in the naval aviation maintenance system.[1] Repair work was often stopped because needed repair parts were out of stock and it took days or even weeks to get these parts. These delays were extremely costly to the Navy; not only were depot manpower and shop space used inefficiently, but extra items were purchased for Navy use while the broken ones waited to be repaired. Although all agreed the problem existed, agreement on the cause of it was harder to come by. The responsibility for providing repair parts for naval aviation falls not only to the Navy itself but also to other parts of the U. S. Department of Defense (DoD), including the Defense Logistics Agency (DLA) and the U. S. Air Force. Each organization has its own perspectives, concerns, and performance measures, and each organization named another as a potential source of the parts problem.

1B. Research Questions

We initially hypothesized several sources of the problem:

- The depot itself delays reordering depleted stock.
- Distribution of parts from Navy and DoD supply systems is delayed even when the part is in stock.
- When a part is not in stock anywhere in DoD, the lengthy procurement procedures delay restocking and hence delay the part's availability.

Given the widespread disagreement on the sources of the problem, we divided our task into two questions:

- Is the supply problem due to a small number of problematic parts or does it affect most of the repair parts used by the depot?
- What are the potential causes of the problem, and how can we focus improvement efforts where they can be most effective?

1C. Statistical Questions

The depots collect large amounts of detailed data, as described below, about the use of parts in repair at the depots. Our initial goal was to summarize that data and to extract any underlying patterns in how the delay to get various parts differed over types of parts, sources of supply, and other characteristics. Even though we hypothesized some plausible causes for the problem, we wanted to be able to look at the patterns in enough detail to be able to suggest other candidate causes as well. We were faced with a complex system, and we wanted to detect features of our data that we could not clearly specify in advance. Our problem was one of *discovery and exploration*, rather than confirmation of a single a priori hypothesis, which is the more usual mode of statistical inference (Meyer and Fienberg 1992). We had to be able not only to assess the plausibility of our candidate hypotheses but also to see evidence for other unanticipated hypotheses. We were aware of the danger of drawing spurious conclusions from exploratory analysis, but given the complexity of the dataset, we knew that we needed a more detailed understanding of it before we attempted to apply rigorous formal statistical methods (Cleveland 1993).

In reducing the data from thousands of numbers, we needed more detailed information than a few summary statistics (e.g., mean and standard deviation of the time it takes to receive a part) because of the many potentially different aspects of the supply process that could drive the parts delivery process. One of the primary ingredients of exploratory data analysis is to use graphical displays of the data as a guide to analysis. Theory has been developed to guide the construction of graphical tools (Velleman and Hoaglin 1981). Our statistical question for this project was: Can we develop a graphical method to "reduce" the data, exhibit its important features, and help us discover unanticipated aspects? This case study illustrates our variant on the adage: "The right picture is worth a thousand numbers."

1D. Summary of Data and Methods

Our research focused on the repair of the F-14 jet engine for reasons given below. A first step was to get transaction data on parts orders and issues for each engine repair job and for the depot stock supply. Second, we obtained information on contracting and purchasing from the supply and procurement organizations responsible for buying repair parts for the engine. To display this supply history concisely, we developed a graphical method, the supply transaction profile (STP). This tool efficiently displayed the patterns of requests and issues for individual parts and allowed us easily compare histories for large numbers of different parts. With this graphic, we identified and ruled out hypothesized problems and generated new hypotheses.

This chapter necessarily shortens some of the material in the original project. The interested reader is invited to peruse Galway (1992a, b) for more details.

2. Study Design, Data Collection, Description of Data Sources, and Description of Data Elements

2A. *Study Design*

There were two sources of data: (i) detailed depot data on the parts ordered for each repair job; and (ii) procurement contracts (purchase orders to buy an item) from the various national stock points in the Navy, Air Force, and Defense Logistics Agency that buy repair parts for the F-14 engine. To understand the data collection and ensure we could get particular needed data elements, we visited several depots and each procurement organization. We defer a detailed description of the data to give a summary of naval aviation logistics that sets the data in context and to describe the focus of this case study, the F-14 engine.

U. S. Naval Aviation Logistics. Naval aircraft are repaired either by the Navy on aircraft carriers, ashore at Naval Air Stations, or by civilian-manned repair depots. Aboard ship, Navy personnel do maintenance ranging from basic repairs to fixing integrated circuit boards, while the depots do more complex repairs such as complete overhauls of aircraft and jet engines.

To repair broken items, depot workers diagnose the failure and order the parts required. (See Figure 7.1 for a diagram of the supply organizations that support the depots.) These orders are submitted to the depot's store, which stocks repair parts. For a part that either is not stocked by the store or is temporarily out of stock, the order goes to the local Naval Supply Center. At the time of our project, the depot store stocked only *consumable* repair parts, such as gaskets or bolts, that are discarded after use. *Reparable* parts, which are themselves subject to repair (e.g., fuel pumps from jet engines) were stocked only at the supply center and were ordered by the depot when needed by a worker to complete a repair.

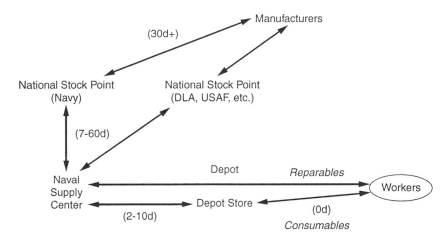

Figure 7.1. Orders and Parts Flow for Naval Aviation Depots (1990). This figure illustrates the supply organizations that support the depots (d = days).

Parts not available at the supply center are ordered from the appropriate national stock point, which is responsible for keeping sufficient stocks of the parts it manages to cover demands throughout DoD. Each DoD part is managed by only one national stock point. For most reparable parts used in naval aviation, the responsible national stock point is the Navy's Aviation Supply Office ("Navy" in Figure 7.1), but a substantial fraction of consumable parts are purchased and managed by the national stock points of the Defense Logistics Agency ("DLA" in Figure 7.1) or of the Air Force ("USAF" in Figure 7.1). The national stock points replenish their stocks by procuring them from the manufacturer. Bids, negotiation, and manufacturing delays all contribute to making the time to procure a part from a vendor quite lengthy.

The F-14 Jet Engine Case. After consultation with our Navy sponsors, we selected as the focus of our study the jet engine of the F-14, which is the current air superiority fighter of the U. S. Navy and is repaired at the depot in Norfolk, VA. Our reasons for selecting this engine were:

- Delays in getting repair parts at the depot were an important problem in repair of the engine.

- Since the F-14 was introduced into the fleet in 1972, the plane and all its equipment are mature. This eliminated the presence of transient support problems of newly fielded weapon systems.[2] Also, the aircraft and many of its components are not in production, and so depot repair was central to keeping the F-14 operational.

- Repair parts support for the engine did not differ significantly from that for other Navy jet engines, so the F-14 could serve as a "representative case."

- The F-14 engine's parts were managed by several different national stock points.

- The repair parts data for this engine's repair had undergone special validation, so it was considered to have the best-quality data of all items repaired at the depot. Maintaining accurate lists of parts for items repaired by Navy depots has been a long-standing problem (Galway 1992a).

2B. Repair Parts Data

Our primary source of data for parts requests and issues was the NIMMS (Naval Industrial Materiel Management System) data system, which logs all repair parts transactions at the depot (orders, issues, returns).

The data in each transaction record include:

- Transaction date.

- Part number ordered. This number is known as the National Item Identification Number and is assigned by the DoD.

- Transaction type code. This code indicates whether the transaction was an issue (the part was given to a worker for use in a repair job), an order (a worker request for a part not carried by the depot store), a backorder (a worker request for a part that the depot store carried but was currently not in stock) or another of the rarer types of transactions, such as a return of an unneeded part.

- Document number. Each different part request was assigned a unique document number, which was put on any further transactions pertaining to that request (e.g., issues, or increasing or decreasing the quantity) so that all transactions for that request could be linked together. The document number included the date of the initial request. Thus for any set of transactions, its document number alone told us when it was initiated, regardless of whether our data contained the first transaction.

- Job order number. Each transaction record had a unique number identifying the engine repair job for which the part was requested. This allowed us to identify all parts used on a particular engine.

The parts requests for each engine job (unique job number) therefore consisted of one or more documents (document numbers), each requesting a single part type for the repair job. Repairs that required more than one of the same type of part could place such an order on a single document or on multiple documents. Each document consisted of one or more transactions, depending on whether the item needed was in stock at the depot store or needed to be ordered. There are three basic patterns of transactions for a single document:

- A single *issue* transaction. The item requested by a worker was in stock at the depot store and was issued. Note that a request is implicit in the issue.

- A *backorder* transaction, followed by an issue. The part requested was normally carried in the depot store but was temporarily not in stock. When a part is out of stock, NIMMS keeps a record of the request as a backorder so that when the part is received it can be issued to the jobs that requested it. Since the part is normally stocked at the depot, a backorder implies that the depot store has already placed an order with the higher levels of the supply system to replenish its stock.

- An *order*, followed by an issue. The part requested is not normally carried by the depot store and so must be ordered. Again, NIMMS records which job has requested the part so that when the part arrives it can be issued to the correct job. In this case, the part is ordered only when a request has been made.

We expected only two variations from these three basic patterns. First, an order or backorder with quantity greater than one may be satisfied by several different issues if the entire quantity requested is not received at one time by the depot store. Second, the depot workers may increment or decrement the quantity ordered as the repair proceeds. As noted above, the other possible transactions were rarely seen.

NIMMS was also used to record parts orders the depot store itself made to replenish its stocks. Each order was made under a special job number to distinguish it from worker orders on repair jobs. These documents consisted exclusively of order and receipt transactions.

2C. Procurement Data

To see whether the problems observed were being caused by low levels of stock at the national level, we also acquired data from the national stock points. Most of the national stock points do not keep historical information on the stock levels of individual repair parts, but all of them do keep information on contract actions so that their procurement staffs can compare prices, lead times, performance, and other characteristics among different manufacturers. This information includes contract award dates, dates of shipments, and/or receipts from manufacturers. A purchase action, for example, indicates that national stocks are getting low; a receipt by the national stock point indicates that a part is available for issue to the supply centers and repair depots.

Our procurement data sources were:

- The Navy national stock point, the Aviation Supply Office (ASO), which maintains the ASO Contract Datafile (purchase dates and shipment receipt dates).

- The Air Force national stock point that manages many F-14 engine parts is the Oklahoma City Air Logistics Center. It maintains a procurement history file for its purchases (contract award date and a first receipt date).

- The Defense Industrial Supply Center (DISC) is the Defense Logistics Agency national stock point that manages many of the consumables used in the repair of the F-14 jet engine. Its database is extensive but organized differently from the Navy and Air Force databases, and we were only successful in acquiring paper reports for a limited set of parts. These reports provide the contract award dates for each purchase and shipping dates for each shipment, but not receipt by DLA.

In addition to national procurement, the local supply center is also authorized, under certain circumstances, to buy parts locally for use by the depot. Some parts are only bought on an emergency basis, while others are always procured locally. The Norfolk supply center's local purchase history information included purchase dates only, not receipt dates.

3. Datafile Creation, Descriptive Statistics, and Exploratory Analysis

3A. *Datafile Creation*

The most complex and time-consuming part of the study was preparing the repair parts data analysis file from the depot data. In contrast, our major effort with the procurement data was to determine whether the needed data elements existed. We give considerable detail about the data acquisition, data editing, and file creation process, both to give the reader an appreciation of how important these often tedious steps are and to provide the detail needed to understand our graphical method.

Worker Parts Requests. As is common in using secondary data, we initially could not read the tape of NIMMS data because of an error in record size. A more precise specification met with success.

It generally is much simpler to ask for a superset of raw data that includes the records of interest rather than to ask for a very precisely defined subset. The initial understanding of the data may be incorrect, or continuing research may require a broader dataset than initially expected. Thus, we requested NIMMS data from repair jobs on all engines and components repaired by the depot. After learning more about the depot repair process from the depot staff, we focused our attention strictly on those transactions from repair jobs on the entire F-14 engine plus orders from the depot store for parts it stocked that were used on the engine.

The data contained 475 F-14 engine jobs with 48,243 transactions, ranging from 1 to 280 transactions per job, and covered January 1989 through January 1991. Initial data editing included eliminating those jobs that had only a single old transaction (apparently maintained in the database in error) and orders for parts not from the three major national stock points of interest or local procurement. In particular, this eliminated orders for items that were not repair parts (e.g., lubricants and fuel for testing). This reduction left 451 engine repair jobs. We sorted the transactions by job order number, then by document number (which includes the date of the first transaction), and then by date of each individual transaction, so that our data consisted of a list of transactions grouped first by engine job, then within engine job by individual part order, and within that by the chronological order of the transaction.

Our mental picture of the data at this point was simple. Each part order would consist of one of the three basic patterns. For a simple issue (part requested is carried by the depot store and in stock), the delay to get a part is zero. For backorders (part normally carried but temporarily out of stock) and orders (part not normally carried), the difference in transaction dates between the request and issue gives us the time it took for the worker to receive the part. Roughly three quarters of the data followed this pattern: 60% were simple requests, 13% were backorders with issues, and 13% were orders followed by issues.

The remaining 14% of the data, however, contained much more complex patterns than our simple expectations.[3] These patterns required care for two reasons. First, they implied that there were aspects of the depot repair process that we did not understand but that caused modifications to the usual repair process. Second, we needed to reduce these special cases into a request/issue form for the further analysis we planned. Each special case required custom treatment in our data processing.

Our final analysis dataset consisted of one record for each parts order. It contained the part number, order date, and, if present, an issue date. Every order/backorder that was satisfied by multiple partial issues was split into a set of separate simple order/backorder-issue pairs. The rest of the requests were flagged as "unresolved."

Depot Store and Procurement Data. In contrast to parts requests for specific engine repair jobs, the vast majority of parts orders and receipts by the depot store were well behaved, consisting almost exclusively of simple order/receipt transaction pairs. Preparing procurement data was even simpler since we needed only the part number and the order and receipt dates, which were easily extracted if available from our national data.

We now had three sets of data consisting of broadly defined request (either order or backorder) and receipt (issue) pairs. These pairs correspond to parts requests, and parts receipts and issues by the worker, depot store, and national stock points.

3B. Descriptive Statistics and Exploratory Analysis

One initial concern was that the workload at the depot had been skewed by the Gulf War operations Desert Shield and Desert Storm, which began in August 1990 and lasted through the first quarter of 1991. A surge in demand for engine repair could strain the supply system and result in problems getting repair parts which either did not exist in peacetime or whose characteristics were anomalous. Further, during the crisis, special expediting procedures were used to cut delays, which would obscure the problems occurring during the normal functioning of the supply system. Table 7.1 gives the engine job starts (first NIMMS transaction) by quarter and shows little effect from the Gulf War. If anything, the num-

Table 7.1. Engine Job Starts (First NIMMS Transaction) by Quarter

Quarter	1989	1990
Jan–Mar	59	49
Apr–Jun	47	37
Jul–Sep	40	42
Oct–Dec	55	35

ber of engine repairs started at the depot seems to have dropped. See Galway (1992a) for more discussion of the adaptations used to meet wartime demands.

As we expected, the suppliers for the repair parts for this engine were varied. Table 7.2 shows the breakdown of orders for parts from the top three national stock points (the consumables and reparables from the Navy have been shown separately because there are differences in the ways these two categories of parts are handled). "Orders" is the number of separate orders for any quantity; "parts" is the number of different types of parts ordered.

Although Navy sources assured us that when all repair parts are in stock even the most extensive repairs should only take two or three weeks, the repair jobs in our data were taking much longer. Figure 7.2 plots the duration of each engine job against the number of parts required. Each point represents one engine job. Note that the median time to complete a job was 102 days, far in excess of the 15 to 20 days that it should require. It is also striking that the time to complete a repair does not vary with the number of parts required, which is a rough proxy for complexity of repair. Since manpower and facility space at the depot were adequate at this time for the number of repairs, availability of repair parts seemed to be a key contributor to delays.

Aggregate analyses of mean delay times after stratifying the requisitions by priority[4] and responsible national stock point revealed no substantial difference between stock points or different priorities. The vast majority of the requisitions in our data were the same priority, in any case. See Galway (1992b) for more details on this part of the analysis.

The aggregate statistics clearly demonstrate that problems exist, but give little insight into the causes. Examining the patterns of supply transactions for individual parts might reveal what problems were causing the delay in receiving parts. For example, if procurement delays at the national level were causing a part's delay, the data would show a series of requests indicated by immediate issues at the depot, followed by a series of backorders, with the final satisfaction of those backorders being preceded by the receipt of the part at the national level. The timing of depot store orders and national orders would show whether the ordering was being done well in advance of the date when stocks were exhausted. Conversely, if the delayed resolution of a backorder was not correlated

Table 7.2. Number of Parts and Orders by National Stock Points

National Stock Point	Orders	Parts
Navy (consumables)	8431	432
Navy (reparables)	1377	42
DLA (consumables)	8130	791
Air Force	8638	619
Other	1483	225
Total	28,059	2109

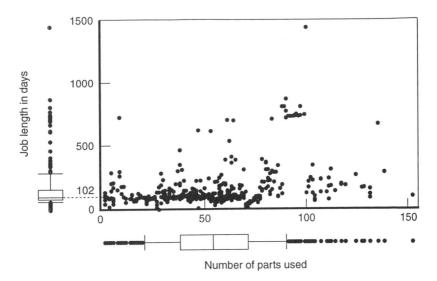

Figure 7.2. Job Duration and Number of Parts Required. Each point represents one engine job. The boxplots in the margins of the plot are percentile boxplots, with crossbars at the 10th, 25th, 50th (median), 75th, and 90th percentiles, and data values outside the 10th and 90th percentiles are individually plotted.

with a national receipt, the cause of the delay would have to be internal problems in getting the part from another organization in the Navy or DoD supply system.

Before we examined the details of supply transactions for individual parts, we computed for each part the number of days that part was not available for each engine job and summed over all jobs; we called this number *engine-days of delay*. A part contributed positive engine-days of delay equal to the time between order and issue. This allowed us to rank parts in order of their overall effect on the depot's engine repair program so that we could focus on those parts causing the most delay.

4. Statistical Methods and Model

In moving from using aggregate statistics to analyzing the detailed transaction histories of individual parts, we faced a large data visualization task. There were several hundred parts; many of the parts had hundreds of transactions. This motivated us to devise a graphical approach that would symbolically display both supply and procurement transactions in chronological order.

The use of graphical methods to display information and to assist in statistical analysis has a long history (Tufte 1983, 1990). Traditionally, even simple graphical methods were used sparingly because of the difficulty of plotting even modest amounts of data by hand. Now, of course, computer software allows the manipulation and display of complex graphics based on immense amounts of data. With ease of preparation of graphics assured, interest has now turned to the question of what qualities make for good graphical information.

The advantage of graphics, according to Cleveland (1985, 1993), is that a dataset can be displayed graphically as a whole, allowing the user to take a careful, penetrating look at the structure of the data. In Deming's words, quoted by Cleveland (1993, p. 5): "graphical methods retain the information in the data," in contrast to classic statistical methods, which seek to reduce the data in various ways. Cleveland points out that most statistical methods make a variety of assumptions, which graphical methods can help to check, and he (Cleveland 1993) cites many examples of data analyses that produced misleading analyses because the analysts missed important features in the data which were easily detectable graphically. The disadvantage of graphical methods is that the human eye has a well-known propensity to see structure where none exists. This is where statistical inference takes over by testing whether supposed structure is only due to statistical noise.

The first test of a good exploratory data graphic is whether it preserves the important structure of the data so that we can see patterns that we can interpret and which then form the focus of further study. For our analysis of the repair parts data, we developed a graphic that we called the *supply transaction profile* (STP) of the combined NIMMS-procurement data to allow us to identify and interpret patterns and relationships.

We build up an example in several steps to explain the STP. Our example is a consumable part whose pattern of transactions is particularly easy to interpret; it is managed by the Navy, stocked by the depot store, and locally procured by the depot. We will call the part NC10 for Navy-managed Consumable, 10th in order of engine-days of delay of repair.

The STP starts with a timeline covering the window of our repair parts data (see Figure 7.3). The X-axis is the months of 1989, 1990, and January 1991 with quarters marked by dotted vertical lines. The left caption gives descriptive information about the part: its identifier, the total engine-days of delay caused by lack of this part, the number of jobs in which it was required, and its unit cost.

First, we display baseline information on the requests that were satisfied immediately out of the depot store stock. Figure 7.4 displays these requests as solid black dots arranged on the baseline at the time of the issue.

The next set of transactions are those requests that were not satisfied by the depot store at the time of the request, but which were issued later when the store had received more stock. We display these times with a three-part symbol: a solid black dot on the baseline at the time of the request, a solid black dot above the baseline at the time of issue, and a line connecting the two points. Figure 7.5 shows that NC10 has alternated between being in and out of stock over the time period covered by the data.

Third are requests unresolved in our data; that is, those that did not have an issue transaction for the quantity requested. Figure 7.6 represents these requests

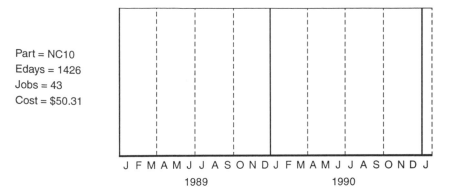

Figure 7.3. Supply Transaction Profile Framework. This timeline covers the period of our repair part data, and the left caption gives information about the part.

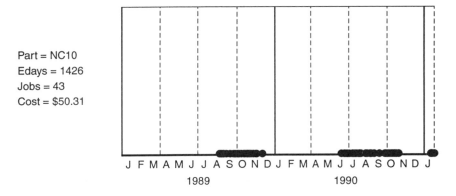

Figure 7.4. Supply Transaction Profile with Requests Satisfied from Depot Stores. Each request is represented by a solid black dot on the horizontal axis plotted at the time the request is made and when it is issued (i.e., immediately).

by open (empty) circles slightly above the baseline to allow them to be visible even when overplotted on the satisfied requests. The figure shows that these un-resolved requests are not randomly distributed, implying that they are not due to random errors in record keeping. Instead they are concentrated between a series of requests that were satisfied from stock and some that were backordered.

To this point, the STP shows only the worker requests and issues but not the depot store orders and receipts or action by local procurement and the responsi-ble national stock point. Since this part is purchased locally, the Navy national stock point made no purchases of this part.

We add that information to the STP by plotting in the upper half of Figure 7.7 three horizontal dotted lines for the orders/receipts of the depot store ("NIF"), purchases/receipts by local procurement ("LOC"), and the responsible national stock point ("ICP"). An order or purchase is an open diamond ("empty") and a

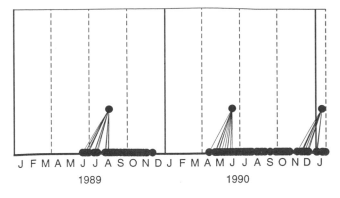

Part = NC10
Edays = 1426
Jobs = 43
Cost = $50.31

J F M A M J J A S O N D J F M A M J J A S O N D J
1989   1990

Figure 7.5. Supply Transaction Profile Plus Delayed Receipts. This figure builds on Figure 7.4. A delayed receipt is plotted as a solid black dot on the horizontal axis at the time of the request, a solid black dot above the axis at the time of the issue, and a line connecting the two points.

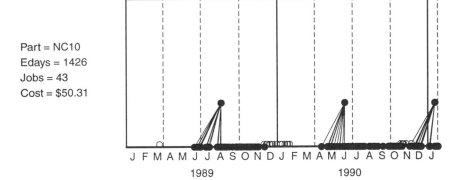

Part = NC10
Edays = 1426
Jobs = 43
Cost = $50.31

J F M A M J J A S O N D J F M A M J J A S O N D J
1989   1990

Figure 7.6. Supply Transaction Profile Plus Unresolved Requests. This figure builds on Figure 7.5. Unresolved requests are shown as empty circles at the time of the request.

receipt a closed diamond ("filled"). Thus, the store receipts tally neatly with the issue date for the resolved (explicitly satisfied) orders. Further, the store's orders for part NC10 seem very timely, with both orders in our data occurring between two and three months in advance of running out of the part. However, somewhat surprisingly, there is no local procurement activity. The part may have been acquired from another Naval Supply Center, but we would now need to go back to the depot to try to determine the origin of the parts to satisfy the demands.

The complete STP in Figure 7.7 summarizes the repair parts information on worker requests for the part, issues, unresolved requests, depot store orders and receipts, and procurement activity in a compact graph that can be compared with similar graphs for other parts and assembled in larger displays.

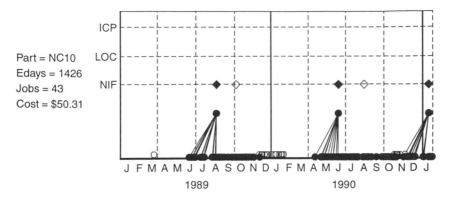

Figure 7.7. Complete Supply Transaction Profile. This figure builds on Figure 7.6. Orders and receipts by the depot store ("NIF") and purchases and receipts by local procurement ("LOC") and the national stockpoint ("ICP") are shown as empty diamonds and solid diamonds, respectively, on the horizontal lines labeled "NIF," "LOC," and "ICP."

The STP is not a standard data plot, so packages with only canned routines such as scatterplots cannot produce this graphic. We therefore used the statistical package S-PLUS (Becker, Chambers, and Wilks 1988; MathSoft Inc. 1997) to draw the STP plots because of its flexibility in data graphics. It allows users to mix data plotting with line drawing in a single coordinate system, so that the development of the plot was easy and we could alter the plot in response to suggestions. A number of graphics packages have been developed for personal computers as well as UNIX workstations that have various mixtures of drawing and plotting capabilities, so it seems unlikely that our choice of S-PLUS is the only one that will serve. What does seem clear is that the full graphical exploration of complex datasets usually cannot be achieved by attempting to force the complex structure into a set of standard plots.

Cleveland (1985) enumerates a number of technical characteristics to which graphics users should be attentive. We will defer discussing the performance of the STP in terms of these characteristics until the results have been presented.

5. Results

Our study generated STPs for ten selected parts from each of the three major national stock points (Navy, Air Force, and Defense Logistics Agency) that provided support to F-14 engine repair. For the Navy, we looked at ten reparables and ten consumables, three of which are locally procured. These parts had the maximum delays among parts used in at least ten different engine repair jobs. We present the STPs for the Navy parts; the STPs for the parts managed by the Air Force and the Defense Logistics Agency were qualitatively similar.

5A. Navy-Managed Reparables

Figure 7.8 shows the STPs for the top ten Navy-managed reparables, labeled NR1 through NR10 in order of decreasing engine days of delay. We can immediately see that for eight of the ten parts (except NR3 and NR6) virtually all of the issues are delayed uniformly by several days; that is, there are no simple issues represented by a dot on the baseline, all transaction histories consist of an order followed by an issue joined by a line, and most of the lines incline at the same angle, indicating identical delays. Recall that at this time reparable parts were not kept at the depot store but needed to be ordered from the local supply center. The time delays for the eight items were consistent with shipment times from the supply center, which were typically several days, depending on work schedules at the depot and the supply center. Furthermore, four of the eight (NR2, NR4, NR5, and NR8) were in heavy demand fairly continuously over the period covered by our data (NR5 does have a gap in demand of about six months), meaning that their use in F-14 engine repair is roughly predictable.

The remaining two parts, NR3 and NR6, differ from the others in two ways. Their delays seem to have occurred because the supply system was out of these parts, since no issues were made until a set of receipts was logged by the Navy national stock point (filled diamonds on the "ICP" row). Note that there is a long gap of at least a month between the final receipt (last filled diamond on the "ICP" line) and the final issue at the depot. One possible explanation is that these parts are rarely used in F-14 engine repair: both were demanded only in the first half of 1989 and were ordered for roughly the same set of jobs.

There are two general points about reparable parts support for engine repair that are suggested from the STPs, although we need to remember that we are only looking at ten parts, albeit admittedly the most troublesome:

- For all reparables except NR3 and NR6, the delay is mostly from the consistent several-day delay to get the part from the local supply center—the eight parts were virtually always in stock.

- Only delays for NR3 and NR6 were due to lack of stock in the supply system, requiring national purchases. All other parts, with the exception of NR9, were supplied to the depot with no receipts by the national stock point; for NR9 the national receipts did not affect the delay in getting the part to the depot.

5B. Navy-Managed Consumables

Figure 7.9 shows the STPs for the top ten problem Navy-managed consumables. The patterns differ considerably from those of the reparables, with the predominant pattern being periods when the depot store was out of the part, resulting in lengthy delays, alternating with periods when the part was in stock and an issue was made immediately. All of the Navy-managed consumables that were problems were stocked by the depot store at some time during the two years covered by the data.

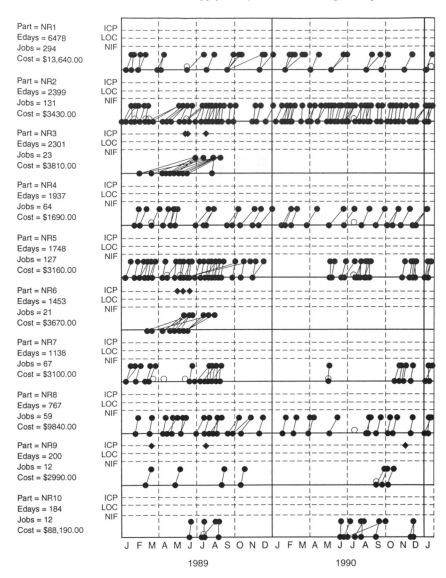

Figure 7.8. Supply Transaction Profiles for Navy-Managed Reparables. The STPs are shown for the ten reparables with the maximum delay among parts used in at least ten different repair jobs, ordered by decreasing engine-days of delay (Edays) from top to bottom.

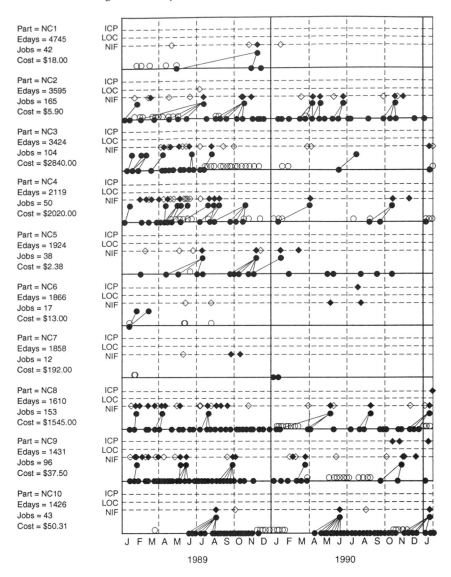

Figure 7.9. Supply Transaction Profiles for Navy-Managed Consumables. The STPs are shown for the ten consumables with the maximum delay among parts used in at least ten different repair jobs, ordered by decreasing engine days of delay (Edays) from top to bottom.

Consider part NC9: through all of 1989 and early 1990, the part was out of stock four times (late January, May, September, 1989; March 1990), indicated by delays in issues at those times separated by longer periods with immediate issues. In each instance, a depot store receipt satisfied the outstanding requisitions and provided enough parts for several months. From April through November, 1990, the part was apparently not available from the supply system since the store was ordering the part (open diamonds on the "NIF" line in May and late September), but the demands that were made were never resolved in our data. Finally, the national stock point received parts in October–November 1990 (closed diamonds on the "ICP" line), which was followed by depot receipts in November and December (closed diamonds on the "NIF" line), and satisfaction of the last few orders that had been made in September and October. A final demand in January 1991 was apparently satisfied directly from stock.

As with reparables, in only two cases does the delay seem to have been caused by procurement activities. For item NC2, a local purchase date was recorded in mid-1989 following a quarter of unfilled demands. However, there is no record of a local purchase receipt, although two depot store receipts follow the local action, and, as noted for item NC9, the Navy national stock point logged a receipt in late 1990 after almost half a year of unresolved orders and about a month before the depot store recorded a receipt and satisfaction of two outstanding backorders. For all of the other items, there is no evidence of either local purchase or purchase or receipt of the item by the national stock point. Most of the delays were therefore probably caused by locating the part elsewhere in the DoD supply system and getting it to the depot.

Figure 7.9 illustrates the data problem of unresolved orders. The mid-1990 NC9 orders were undoubtedly somehow satisfied in late 1990, but no issue transaction was recorded in NIMMS. Further, the unresolved orders for several parts (e.g., NC2, NC3, NC8, NC9, and NC10) are clustered at times when local supplies of parts had run out: a period of issues from the depot store was followed by a cluster of unresolved orders, sometimes mixed with orders eventually satisfied by an issue. We speculated that this pattern of unresolved orders was caused by cannibalization of other engines in repair by depot workers; that is, an order was made, was taking a long time to be satisfied so the needed part was taken from another engine in repair, and an order made for the part against that engine.[5]

As for reparables, the STP analysis for consumables suggests that:

- For most parts, the problem is a long delay in getting the part from within the system.

- A minority of problems result from a lack of stock in the entire DoD system.

In addition, we notice that

- The depot store usually orders well in advance of running out of stock but still repeatedly runs out.

6. Discussion

6A. *Extensions of the Study*

This STP analysis of the "top ten" parts illustrates graphical integration of information from several sources to reveal patterns of problems with parts supply. To learn more, we could examine individual patterns in more detail and analyze all parts that delay F-14 engine repair. Our graphical technique could be used to inform the interaction of the study team with the depot and the supply system in order to identify potential problems. Analysts could also check with depot staff to make sure that data abstraction and graphical reduction do not mask important issues that may not be detectable from the repair parts data.[6]

Our study treated parts independently, much in the flavor of classical inventory theory (e.g., Hadley and Whitin 1963). Alternatively, we could focus on the pacing parts, those that delay engine repair for the longest time. Our top 40 parts were the pacing parts for 131 (almost 30%) of the 451 engine jobs we studied. But for another 151 jobs there were 125 different pacing parts. Brauner, Hodges, and Relles (1993, 1994) quantify the impact of pacing parts in a more sophisticated analysis. Sherbrooke (1992) takes another approach to stocking spare parts for repair.

6B. *The STP as a Graphic*

The STP graphical display in this study is a compelling example of exploratory data analysis to attain insight. It enabled us to examine quickly the mass of transaction types and dates and allowed us to compare and contrast the patterns of supply transactions for different repair parts. Also, the ability to relate national procurement activity to depot orders for parts and receipt of parts in a single display was both vital to the study and gave useful information to managers.

Overall, the STP meets the basic requisite for an exploratory graphic: it retains the entire structure of the data on a single graph, so that we can look at the performance of the depot stockroom and the various procurement agencies in anticipating shortages and ordering replenishment stocks. It is a very dense graphic as well. Each of the two graphs displayed in Subsections 5A and 5B of this chapter display about 2500 different data points. While the graph seems overwhelming at first glance, its primary purpose is analysis, not communication, so that it is not required that a viewer be able to grasp every pertinent characteristic of the data from a single brief look at an STP.

Key concepts that Cleveland emphasizes are to "make the data stand out" and "use visually prominent graphical elements to show the data" (Cleveland 1985, p. 100). The STP certainly meets these criteria in that the points that represent the fundamental data, the times of transactions, dominate the graph. Other elements of the graph that support our first analysis goal, which was to look at the time relationships between repair parts usage and the actions of the organizations responsible for stock procurement, are the faint vertical lines at each calendar quarter, which facilitate the horizontal comparison between dates across the four parallel lines of data for each part.

The STP has some drawbacks as well. Cleveland advised that "overlapping plotting symbols must be visually distinguishable" (Cleveland 1985, p. 100), and that is not the case for the STP: part requests that are satisfied from the depot stockroom on a given date are overplotted and cannot be distinguished. In fact, requests on closely spaced days are difficult to distinguish. Since unresolved requests (orders and backorders) are open circles, they are a bit more easily discriminated even when closely spaced. Another drawback is that it is difficult with an STP to get a quantitative estimate of the distribution of times to get a part. The times are represented both by a series of separated intervals on the X-axis and by the slope of the line from the time of the request to the time of the issue. Cleveland notes that both of those tasks are difficult to do accurately and recommends that other graphic constructions (such as box-and-whisker plots) be used for visualizing distributions (Cleveland 1985, p. 235). However, in the case of Navy-managed reparables, the slopes as indicators of time to issue are enough alike to alert us that the times are very similar. In our original study, this insight led us to do a box-and-whisker plot look at this distribution, thereby executing another of Cleveland's suggested general strategies for graphical analysis: "Graph data two or more times when it is needed" (Cleveland 1985, p. 94).

The STP can no doubt be improved further, both to show more detail and to display certain features of the data more accurately. It certainly went though several iterations during our research as we saw new features in the data and focused on different questions. To quote Cleveland one last time: "Graphing data should be an iterative, experimental process" (Cleveland 1985, p. 93).

6C. Conclusions and Recommendations

We concluded, pending a comprehensive analysis of all repair parts for the F-14 jet engine, that the majority of the delays for some of the most troublesome parts did not result from a lack of stock at the depot store or at the national level (i.e., a part being unavailable throughout the supply system). Instead, the delays arose when a part had to be delivered from another part of the supply system where delivery usually took between 12 and 40 days. Unfortunately, the data from NIMMS do not pinpoint where the delay was occurring in the DoD supply system except for Navy-managed reparables, for which it came mainly from the local supply center. The NIMMS data has a field in the transaction for receipt of an ordered or backordered part (where the depot acknowledges receipt, usually on the same day as the part is issued for use), which indicates the source of supply. We had hoped that this field might indicate which supply entity (e.g., another supply center) had provided the part. Unfortunately, most of the entries were for the Norfolk supply center, since all shipments to the depot were routed through that point.

We made three recommendations to the Navy:

- Fix the repair parts availability problem by speeding up delivery for parts already in the supply system, particularly from the local supply center but also from the other DoD supply centers. Stock reparable parts at the depot that are in heavy demand at the depot.

- Delays arising from lack of stock in the entire supply system are not as important, so efforts in streamlining procurement, though worthwhile, should be secondary.

- Fix relevant data problems to make analysis easier. The preliminary validation of repair parts for the F-14 engine is a start, but we also need to edit data for consistent quantity increments and decrements and for multiple orders for the same part on the same order number.

Our hope was that the Navy would use the STP to analyze many repair parts over many different items to see if our conclusions about the relative importance of distribution and procurement held. Because of the requirement for getting regular access to data from outside the Navy, this would have required strong direction from the leadership of organizations such as the Aviation Supply Office (ASO). Unfortunately, as we finished our project, the admiral commanding ASO, who had been very supportive, retired, as did the admiral in charge of Naval aviation depots. These changes were followed by significant legislative restrictions on the ability of RAND, which is contractually related to the Army, Air Force, and Office of the Secretary of Defense, to do work for the Navy, so many of the results and insights generated by the project were not implemented by the Navy.

In the foreseeable future, changes in national security threats coupled with domestic budget constraints will force even more cuts in Navy forces and equipment. Spare part stocks will be adequate in the short term, since demand will lessen and parts will be available from scrapped systems. Attention to management rather than procurement should lead to efficient use of these parts. As the overstock is reduced, the balance should shift back toward more equal roles of management and procurement in maintaining adequate supplies of repair parts.

7. Exercises

The dataset and accompanying documentation for the following exercise are available on our website (www.rand.org/centers/stat/casebook).

A warehouse manager comes to you for some help with an inventory problem. His story:

> I have three parts whose management I've just recently consolidated in one place as of 1 January. Each has the same demand rate, about three per day. I computed this over a year, since I know that I need a fair amount of data to get

a stable estimate. Before consolidating, I made sure that there were no outstanding orders, and I started off with 50 of each part. I told the manager to reorder when the on-hand plus due-in (on order) stock gets down to 25, and the reorder quantity is 30. The shipment time for an order (from time of order to time of receipt) is a fixed 7 days. I thought that with those policies I would have very few problems.

However, at the end of the year I found vastly different performances. Part A had backorders (a demand arriving when it is out of stock) 5% of the days. But Party B had backorders for 23% of the days and Part C had backorders for 38% of the days! I need to know why. This dataset contains the order and sale information on the three parts. The first column is the part ID (A, B, or C), the second column is the Julian date of the demand, and the third is the Julian date of the sale. The fourth column has the price (which you won't need). I want to know why parts B and C have such problems. Are the clerks following my policy? Is my policy wrong?

Oh, by the way, I don't have the reorder information. The clerk accidentally erased that during the holiday party. But I did start off with 50 of each and no backorders, and the ship time is definitely 7 days, so maybe that will be enough.

Use the data to diagnose the problem. Can you develop a graphic display to show the problem easily? Be careful with the data; if the clerk erased the reorder information, there might be other errors too.

Further RAND Reading

Brauner, M. K., Hodges, J. S., and Relles, D. A. (1993), *Using Value to Manage Repair Parts: A Documented Briefing,* MR-311-A/USN, Santa Monica, CA: RAND.

Brauner, M. K., Hodges, J. S., and Relles, D. A. (1994), *An Approach to Understanding the Value of Parts,* MR-313-A/USN, Santa Monica, CA: RAND.

Galway, L. A. (1992), *Management Adaptations in Jet Engine Repair at the Naval Aviation Depot in Support of Operation Desert Shield/Storm,* N-3436-A/USN, Santa Monica, CA: RAND.

Galway, L. A. (1992), *Materiel Problems at a Naval Aviation Depot: A Case Study of the TF-30 Engine,* N-3473-A/USN, Santa Monica, CA: RAND.

Notes

[1]The project was to address selected aviation maintenance issues at all levels of the Navy and was designed to draw on previous RAND experience with U.S. Air Force

logistics. The RAND Navy project was initiated by the Undersecretary of the Navy for Shipbuilding and Logistics and was jointly sponsored by the Navy Secretariat, Naval Air Systems Command, and Naval Supply Systems Command.

[2]However, the F-14 engine's repair was not in "steady state." After our study had been underway for about a year, a chance conversation with one of the Norfolk depot staff revealed that the engine had gone through a comprehensive rework program about three years before, which meant that the repairs at the time of our study might not have been representative.

[3]Some were orders followed by multiple issues with quantities adding up to the original order, indicating that the parts order had been satisfied in several shipments. Others had multiple *order* transactions (when there should have been only one order) or a sequence of modification transactions (incrementing or decrementing the quantity of the original) with the same quantity as the initial order, or sets of transactions without any recorded issue, even though a later order for the same part was satisfied immediately from the depot store.

Our questioning of depot personnel revealed that many of the anomalous patterns resulted from ad hoc actions stimulated by problems in getting repair parts. For example, the multiple orders were often entered by frustrated workers who had not received an ordered part and were trying to "jog" the system. This was also the cause of the series of increment transactions that had the same quantity as the initial order. Another common anomalous pattern was one or more issues for a part of the quantity ordered, followed by a decrement transaction reducing the outstanding number of items to zero and thus "terminating" the order. Here, depot workers had acquired the undelivered parts from another order and were "canceling" this order by reducing the outstanding quantity to zero.

[4]DoD shipments are assigned transportation priorities of 1, 2, or 3 (highest to lowest) depending both on how urgent the need is for the item and the military importance of the requester (in Naval aviation aircraft carriers get top rating in the latter category). The majority of the depot orders were assigned priority 2.

[5]Navy policy strongly discourages cannibalization on grounds of safety and efficient use of manpower: an installation requires only the installation work, while a cannibalization requires an additional removal and an additional installation. The NIMMS data have a transaction code for cannibalization, but there were only three uses of the code in our entire dataset for the F-14 engine.

[6]During one conversation with a materiel manager at the depot, we mentioned that a cursory analysis of orders for inexpensive bench stock (such as common bolts and gaskets) showed no backorders, indicating that they had no problems with this class of parts. He just laughed and said that when they had problems with these cheap parts they didn't bother with backorders but simply started expediting shipments and doing local procurement.

8

Hospital Mortality Rates: Comparing with Adjustments for Case Mix and Sample Size

Neal Thomas and John E. Rolph

Executive Summary

There has been growing interest in publishing "report cards" in the form of mortality rates for hospitals and other health care providers. We present alternative methods to those used by the Health Care Finance Administration for estimating medical patient mortality rates. We used an empirical Bayes model to capture the variations in observed hospital-specific mortality rates. Our model-based formulation yielded much more accurate estimates and resolves the severe multiple-comparison problem that arises when extreme rates are used to identify exceptional hospitals. We estimated models for each of four conditions using the national Medicare mortality database. We found substantial between-hospital variation in underlying death rates using our Bayesian approach. However, because the empirical Bayes procedure is more conservative than standard methods, we will tend to understate or miss the problem of an exceptionally bad hospital.

1. Introduction

1A. Policy Problem

Release of hospital-level mortality data by the Health Care Finance Administration (HCFA), state organizations, and private groups has focused attention on how hospital-level mortality rate data can be used to evaluate the quality of hospital care. Since we concluded our original study, there has been a growing interest in publishing "report cards" describing the performance of doctors, hospitals, and large HMO networks. The hospitals in the Cleveland metropolitan area, for example, have agreed on a common system for collecting and reporting patient severity and outcome data, which is available to insurance companies, large corporate purchasers of health care, and individual consumers.

For consumers and managers within large health care organizations, information about individual hospitals, and even specific doctors (Rolph, Kravitz, and McGuigan 1991; Bumiller 1995), is required to make informed choices and to monitor potential problems. We focus on statistical methods that improve the reporting of hospital-specific mortality rates, although many of the statistical issues involved in reporting mortality rates are common to reports of other measures of quality when applied to other organizations.

1B. Research Questions

There are several research questions that must be addressed in any successful effort to provide consumers with information that can inform their choice of health care providers. These include:

- develop understandable and relevant measures of quality of care, such as death rates and immunization rates, that can actually be implemented in practice;

- develop methods of presenting data on these quality-of-care measures that consumers can easily access and understand;

- ensure that any quality-of-care measures presented to the public adequately account for differences in case mix across providers; and

- ensure that the quality requirements presented adjust for differences in the number of cases when making comparisons across providers.

In this study, we addressed only the latter two questions. Our quality-of-care measure was mortality rate and our providers of care were hospitals. In our original study, we used a refined case-mix measure and made adjustments in estimated mortality rates based on it. For expositional purposes, we do not describe the case-mix adjustments in this chapter. However, the interested reader will have no difficulty in seeing how our logistic-regression-based adjustment method fits into the notation of the methods described in this chapter. We concentrate here on the last question, accounting for sample-size difference. We addressed this issue using empirical Bayes methods.

1C. Statistical Questions

Our goal is to produce a method that:

- provides more accurate, stable estimates of hospital-specific mortality rates;

- creates confidence or high-probability coverage intervals that account for the severe *multiple comparisons* problem that arises when identifying exceptional hospitals from among (potentially) thousands, because identifying *exceptional* hospitals is perhaps the most important use of hospital-specific estimates of mortality rates; and

- explicitly quantifies the variation in hospital-specific mortality rates not attributable to small sample fluctuations; previous studies, such as that of Park et al. (1990), have focused on establishing the existence of such variation.

There is some controversy about the value of hospital mortality data for measuring the quality of care (Dubois, Brook, and Rogers 1987; Kahn et al. 1988). The principal objection is that mortality rates obtained from administrative data sources are difficult to interpret because there has been little adjustment for the clinical condition of patients on admission (Green, Wintfeld, Sharkey, and Passman 1990). This concern can be addressed by collecting better but much more expensive information about the condition of patients when they enter the hospital by using the patients' medical records. In addition, patients can be compared within smaller, more homogenous medical condition subgroups, thereby avoiding situations such as the comparison of a specialty hospital treating only heart disease patients with a general care hospital. The collection of expensive data within more homogenous subpopulations, however, tends to result in small sample sizes at each hospital, thus decreasing possible bias at the price of increased variance.

The primary statistical question we address is: how can we use empirical Bayes methods to "pool" data from all hospitals to improve estimates for each individual hospital? These methods use a weighted combination of the average for all hospitals and that of an individual hospital. Shrinking the individual hospital estimate toward an overall average reduces variance at the expense of introducing a bias. The "bias" created by the empirical Bayes methods is different from the bias that results from comparing patients with differing medical conditions. Overall, these methods can result in more accurate estimation through a variance/bias tradeoff when variance can be reduced significantly at the cost of little bias.

1D. Summary of Data and Methods

For this chapter, we used National Medicare Mortality data from approximately 5500 hospitals during 1986. We focus on the common statistical issues involved in the analysis of hospital-specific mortality rates using empirical Bayes methods.

The application of these methods to improve reports on health-care quality is a rapidly expanding area of research. Recent work since the completion of our project includes that of Daniels and Gastonis (1997), Kahn and Raftery (1996), and Normand, Glickman, and Gatsonis (1997). The advent of the Gibbs sampler, in particular, has increased the contribution that Bayes methods can make in this area.

2. Study Design, Data Collection, Description of Data Sources, and Description of Data Elements

We used hospital-specific mortality data for the entire U.S. population of Medicare patients for fiscal year 1986 for each of four medical conditions: stroke, pneumonia, heart attack, and congestive heart failure. In the datafile associated with each medical condition, there was one line of data for every hospital. The number of hospitals varied somewhat across medical conditions. There were two numbers on each line; first is the number of qualifying patients at a hospital, followed by the number of these patients who died within 30 days of hospital admission.

3. Datafile Creation, Descriptive Statistics, and Exploratory Analysis

3A. Summary of the 1986 Medicare National Data

Table 8.1 gives a summary of the death rates for Medicare patients at U.S. hospitals in the four medical conditions. Hospitals with fewer than five patients with the condition were excluded from our analyses because they are certainly too small to yield useful hospital-specific estimates. The five number summaries in Table 8.1 (minimum, 25th percentile, 50th percentile (median), 75th percentile, maximum) display substantial differences in observed death rates across hospitals and the very long upper tail of the death-rate distribution.

Table 8.2 contains five number summaries of the number of patients treated for each medical condition. Some hospitals treat many patients, but most treat less than 75 patients with each medical condition during a year.

Table 8.1. Distribution of Hospital Death Rates for Four Medical Conditions

	Death Rate at Hospital			
	Stroke	Pneumonia	Heart Attack	Congestive Heart Failure
Minimum	0.00	0.00	0.00	0.00
25th percentile	0.15	0.13	0.20	0.12
Median	0.21	0.18	0.26	0.15
75th percentile	0.27	0.23	0.32	0.19
Maximum	0.90	1.00	0.83	0.67

NOTE: Hospitals with fewer than five patients treated for the condition in 1986 are excluded.

Table 8.2. *Distribution Across Hospitals of Number of Patients Treated for Four Medical Conditions*

	Number of Patients Treated at Hospital			
	Stroke	Pneumonia	Heart Attack	Congestive Heart Failure
Minimum	5	5	5	5
25th percentile	18	31	17	27
Median	38	58	35	58
75th percentile	78	101	72	117
Maximum	571	529	471	719

NOTE: Hospitals with fewer than five patients treated for the condition in 1986 are excluded.

3B. Information on Variation Among Hospitals

We represent the 30-day mortality outcomes for a particular hospital's qualifying patients during a year by $Y_1, \ldots, Y_n$, where Y_j is a 0/1 survival variable equal to one if the jth patient dies. The observed death rate among the patients admitted to a hospital is the average of their survival variables

$$\overline{Y} = \frac{1}{n}\sum_{j=1}^{n} Y_j \ .$$

The mortality data obtained from a large population of N hospitals are distinguished by subscripting the death rate and the number of patients, $\overline{Y}_h$ and n_h, for $h = 1, \ldots, N$, and the patient survival variable with the condition at hospital h by $Y_{hj}, j = 1, \ldots, n_h$. A very simple model for the death rates assumes that each patient at hospital h has the same independent probability of death, which we denote by P_h. Note that the probability of death can be different for different hospitals. These assumptions imply binomial distributions for the number of deaths at each hospital conditional on P_h and n_h so that

$$n_h\overline{Y}_h \sim \text{Bin}(n_h, P_h) \ . \tag{8.1}$$

Because of small sample fluctuations, $\overline{Y}_h \neq P_h$, and the model in (8.1) determines how much the $\overline{Y}_h$ vary about the P_h. The actual variation in the observed death rates is a combination of the variation of the $\overline{Y}_h$ about the P_h and the variation between the P_h at different hospitals.

A very simple and strong hypothesis is that the P_h are the same for each hospital. Using data from the Medicare database for pneumonia, we can check this hypothesis using plots similar to those presented by Jencks et al. (1988). The upper left (a) plot in Figure 8.1 is a histogram of the observed death rates for

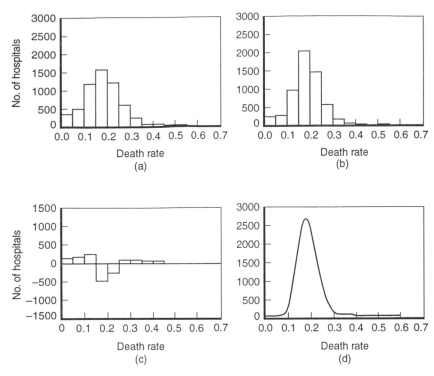

Figure 8.1. Death Rates for Pneumonia Patients. The upper left plot (a) is a histogram of the death rates for pneumonia patients at each hospital based on the Medicare datafile. The upper right plot (b) is a histogram of death rates at each hospital simulated under the assumption that the underlying death rates are the same at all hospitals in the nation. The lower left plot (c) is the difference in the two upper histograms. The lower right plot (d) is the variation in underlying death rates needed to explain the extra variation present in the observed rates.

pneumonia patients at U.S. hospitals. The upper right plot (b) in Figure 8.1 is a histogram of death rates simulated under the assumption that all of the P_h are equal.

The lower left plot (c) in Figure 8.1 is a barplot formed by subtracting the counts in the bins in the observed-rate histogram (a) from the simulated-rate histogram (b). It shows that there is more spread in the histograms of the actual death rates than we expect if all the P_h were equal. To explain this extra variation—called extrabinomial variation in the statistics literature—we allow the P_h to be different. But rather than allowing them to be arbitrarily different, we will assume they differ in a way described by a common statistical model. The methods described in Section 4 in this chapter will be used to derive the distribution of P_h displayed in the lower right corner (d) of Figure 8.1. It shows the spread in the P_h necessary to explain the extra variability in the histograms of the observed death rates.

4. Statistical Methods and Model

4A. Statistical Formulation

In this section, we present a statistical framework for quantifying the variation in the 30-day mortality rates across hospitals. The proportion of patients who die among all patients in the nation with a given medical condition is denoted by P. The (hypothetical) death rate for all patients in the nation if each patient could be observed receiving treatment at a *particular hospital* is denoted by P_h (where h is for hospital). To estimate P_h directly, imagine an experiment in which we take a random sample of all patients in the country and assign them to hospital h. This is not a feasible experiment, though an attempt at such an experiment involving a small number of nearby hospitals within an HMO is not unthinkable.

Comparing hospitals based on data from nonexperimental conditions in which patients are self-selected into hospitals by a poorly understood mechanism is an example of an "observational" study. For our comparisons of hospitals, we will assume that the patients treated at each hospital are like a random sample of all patients in the nation. This assumption can be substantially wrong, and thus our comparisons based on mortality data must be interpreted skeptically. For example, hospitals serving poor inner city and rural areas, as well as large research hospitals, may attract more difficult-to-treat patients. We discuss the case-mix issue later in this chapter.

We also assume that the survival of a patient in a hospital does not depend on which other patients are treated. This is a defensible assumption provided there is no competition for limited hospital resources and because our medical conditions are not contagious.

With the assumption that patients are assigned to a hospital independent of their survival outcomes, the observed death rate at a hospital, $\bar{Y}_h$, is an unbiased estimate of P_h. In Subsection 4B, we describe how the $\bar{Y}_h$ vary among hospitals and what this implies about the variation of the hypothetical death rates P_h.

4B. Model

Recall that $\bar{Y}_h, n_h$, for $h = 1, ..., N$, are the death rates and sample sizes at a collection of hospitals, and P_h is the underlying death rate at hospital h. We will denote the overall observed death rate in the nation by $\bar{Y}$. Since P_h and $\bar{Y}_h$ are probabilities and proportions, respectively, they take values between 0 and 1. We transform P_h and $\bar{Y}_h$ to take values between $-\infty$ and $+\infty$ using the logit transformation. We use a normal distribution to describe how the logit-transformed values of P_h vary across hospitals,

$$\text{logit}(P_h) = \log\left(\frac{P_h}{(1 - P_h)}\right) \equiv \delta_h \sim N(\mu_\delta, \sigma_\delta^2) . \tag{8.2}$$

The model in (8.2) assumes that logit-transformed values of the P_h are normally distributed.

The logit-transformation assures that the estimates of the P_h, which are obtained by back-transforming estimates of δ_h, are in (0, 1). The formula for back-transforming logit values to proportions is

$$P_h = \frac{e^{\delta_h}}{\left(1 - e^{\delta_h}\right)}. \tag{8.3}$$

This is a common device used in the study of rates and binary variables.

We estimated μ_δ and σ_δ in (8.2) using the method of moments. More efficient estimators are usually used in practice. One minor complication is that the logit function equals $-\infty$ or $+\infty$ when $\overline{Y}_h = 0$ or $\overline{Y}_h = 1$, respectively, so we used a common device for rate data and add 1/2 to the observed number of deaths and 1 to the number of patients at each hospital,

$$\overline{Y}_h = \frac{\sum\limits_{j=1}^{n_h} Y_{hj} + \frac{1}{2}}{n_h + 1},$$

and $\tilde{\delta}_h = \text{logit}(\overline{Y}_h)$. We estimated μ_δ by

$$\tilde{\mu}_\delta = \frac{1}{N} \sum\limits_{h=1}^{N} \tilde{\delta}_h.$$

Each $\tilde{\delta}_h$ is an approximately unbiased estimate of δ_h so that $\tilde{\mu}_\delta$ is an approximately unbiased estimate of μ_δ.

The estimated variance of the observed logits is

$$V = \frac{1}{N-1} \sum\limits_{h=1}^{N} \left(\tilde{\delta}_h - \tilde{\mu}_\delta\right)^2 \tag{8.4}$$

and is composed of the variance σ_δ^2 plus the small sample "chance" fluctuations of the $\tilde{\delta}_h$. The $\tilde{\delta}_h$ vary about δ_h because most of the n_h are relatively small. We denote the estimated variance of $\tilde{\delta}_h$ given δ_h by

$$V_h \approx \left\{\overline{Y}_h\left(1 - \overline{Y}_h\right)n_h\right\}^{-1}$$

[see Morris and Rolph (1981)].

The observed variance V is approximately equal to the average of the V_h plus the variance σ_δ^2. When $\sigma_\delta^2 = 0$, there is no extra variance and V is equal to the average V_h. We estimated the extra variance by the difference between V and the average V_h,

$$\tilde{\sigma}_\delta^2 = V - \frac{1}{N}\sum_{h=1}^{N} V_h \ . \tag{8.5}$$

Estimates of μ_δ and σ_δ are given in Subsection 5A.

4C. Bayes Shrinkage Estimators

We apply Bayesian ideas using the models in Subsection 4B to calculate estimates of the *individual* hospital mortality rates based on the posterior distribution of δ_h. The Bayesian approach "shrinks" $\tilde{\delta}_h$ toward the national average and produces a more stable, improved estimator (Morris 1983a). As just discussed, the $\tilde{\delta}_h$ have a larger variance and are more spread out than the δ_h. Shrinking the empirical logits compensates for this fact. See Carlin and Louis (1996) for a comprehensive treatment of shrinkage estimates.

An oversimplified version of our problem may offer some intuition. Using (8.2) and (8.4), assume that the observed logit death rates have a normal distribution,

$$\tilde{\delta}_h \sim N(\mu_\delta, V) \ .$$

Then the posterior distribution of δ_h given $\tilde{\delta}_h$ is

$$\delta_h | \tilde{\delta}_h \sim N\left(w\tilde{\delta}_h + (1-w)\mu_\delta, w\left(V - \sigma_\delta^2\right)\right) , \tag{8.6}$$

where $w = \sigma_\delta^2 / V$ and we ignore for simplicity that the sample size n_h vary across hospitals. The Bayes estimate of δ_h from (8.6) is thus

$$w\tilde{\delta}_h + (1-w)\mu_\delta \ . \tag{8.7}$$

The values of σ_δ^2 and μ_δ (and thus w) can be estimated as described in Subsection 4B to produce the "empirical Bayes" estimator corresponding to (8.7). Note that (8.7) shrinks the hospital h value of δ_h toward the central value for all hospitals μ_δ. Loosely speaking, this shrinkage yields an estimator with a small variance at the expense of introducing a bias. Overall, the result is an improvement.

Results from our analyses of the national data in Subsection 5A produce very precise estimates of μ_δ and σ_δ that we can substitute into the distribution of δ

in (8.2). Methods that account for the fact that we are using estimates of μ_δ and σ_δ instead of the actual values of μ_δ and σ_δ have been developed (Kass and Steffey 1989), but they make very little difference in our examples because our estimates are based on a large number of hospitals.

Once we compute the posterior distribution of δ for a particular hospital, we must still back-transform the results to obtain estimates and confidence intervals for the difference between the hospital and national death rates, $P_h - P$. This is easily done using (8.3).

5. Results

5A. Estimates of σ_δ

The estimates of μ_δ and σ_δ for the logit-normal model in (8.2) and the overall national death rate $\overline{Y}$ based on the national database are given in Table 8.3. Standard errors for the estimates of μ_δ and σ_δ were less than 0.01 because the sample sizes are very large since they came from a database of all the hospitals in the nation. Consequently, the p-value for the hypothesis that $\sigma_\delta = 0$ is less than 0.0001 for each medical condition. As another example of a hypothesis test, the difference between σ_δ for stroke and congestive heart failure is $0.22 - 0.16 = 0.06$ compared with a standard error for the difference in the σ_δ estimates of

$$\sqrt{2(.01)^2} = 0.014 \ .$$

Hypothesis tests for the assumption that μ_δ is the same in each medical condition are also highly statistically significant.

5B. Comparing Empirical Bayes and Conventional Estimators

We simulated the statistical properties of the empirical Bayes and conventional estimators of hospital-specific mortality rates to determine if there are practically important differences between them. We compared two estimators: the empirical Bayes posterior mean *shrinkage* estimator and its standard error,

Table 8.3. *Estimates for Model (8.1) Without Severity Conditioning Based on the National Database for 1986*

Medical Condition	$\overline{Y}$	$\tilde{\mu}_\delta$	$\tilde{\sigma}_\delta$
Stroke	0.20	−1.303	0.22
Pneumonia	0.19	−1.530	0.25
Myocardial infarction	0.26	−1.026	0.17
Congestive heart failure	0.15	−1.699	0.16

which are described in Subsection 4C; and the standard estimator $\overline{Y}_h - \overline{Y}$ along with its standard error $\left(\overline{Y}\left(1 - \overline{Y}\right) / n_h\right)^{1/2}$. This standard-error formula does not include a term for the variance of $\overline{Y}$ because it is based on the national data. The variance of $\overline{Y}$ is negligible compared to the variability at each individual hospital.

We generated a large population of 2000 hypothetical hospitals to simulate the current hospital-level mortality distribution and its sources. We summarize the performance of our two estimators when they are applied to a large collection of hospitals, as is typically the case in practice.

The size of the sample at each hospital was randomly selected from the values (25, 50, 100, 200) with probabilities (0.35, 0.35, 0.25, 0.05), respectively, yielding an average hospital size of 61, in rough agreement with the national data. Because the performance of the estimators did not appear to vary with the different medical conditions, we only simulated one condition, heart attack data.

A death rate P_h was simulated for each hospital by selecting a random number from the distribution in (8.2) using the parameter values from the heart attack data in Table 8.3 and then back-transforming. The number of deaths at each hypothetical hospital was then generated using the binomial model in (8.1).

Finding the Worst Hospitals. The empirical Bayes shrinkage estimators and conventional estimators produce similar rankings of the extreme hospitals, and both have difficulty identifying extreme hospitals. However, the empirical Bayes intervals have the correct coverage properties when applied to samples of hospitals identified as extreme by their estimated death rates. This is because the Bayes intervals explicitly account for the large number of individual hospital estimates with the prior distribution. The conventional estimator and its commonly used standard error, in contrast, produced misleading significance levels and confidence intervals for these hospitals because the procedure failed to account for the large number of hospitals ranked.

To demonstrate these assertions, the conventional estimator $\overline{Y}_h - \overline{Y}$ was used to select the 50 worst hospitals out of the 2000 hospitals. Figure 8.2 displays histograms of actual $P_h - P$ selected using $\overline{Y}_h - \overline{Y}$, and the 50 most extreme values of $P_h - P$ among the 2000 simulated hospitals (recall that P is the overall death rate in the population).

The usual 95% confidence intervals for the 50 hospitals selected using $\overline{Y}_h - \overline{Y}$ cover only 24/50=48% of the generating population values while the Bayes 95% interval covers 48/50=96% of these hospitals.

6. Discussion

The analysis of the national data in Section 5A together with the results of Park et al. (1990) and Jencks et al. (1988) provide very strong evidence that hospitals vary in their underlying death rates after accounting for sampling variation.

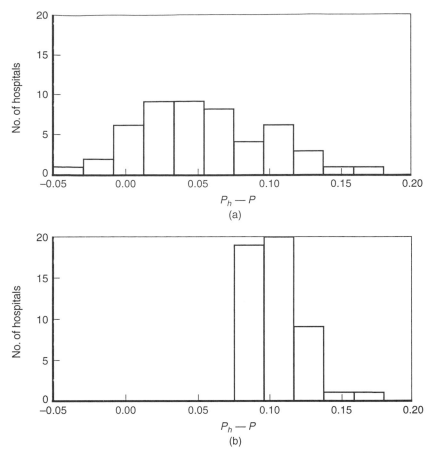

Figure 8.2. Extreme Death Rate Deviations Across Hospitals. The upper plot (a) is a histogram of the 50 values of $P_h - P$ selected using $\overline{Y}_h - \overline{Y}$. The lower plot (b) is the histogram of the 50 most extreme values of $P_h - P$ from the simulation sample of 2000 hospitals.

6A. Implications for Individual Hospital Reporting

For all but the largest hospitals and most prevalent medical conditions, the information contained in the hospital-specific mortality data is relatively uninformative compared to national data sources that inform us about the likely range of hospital mortality differences. We anticipate that sparse information about the quality of hospitals and doctors will be typical of other databases.

The simulation comparisons, while for hypothetical hospital populations, reveal some interesting conclusions. The most common use of the estimators of mortality rates is for identifying exceptional hospitals. The Bayes procedure is more conservative than the conventional estimator $\overline{Y}_h - \overline{Y}$ in judging that a hospital is extreme. Overall, the two procedures perform similarly and rather poorly in identifying the best and worst hospitals. The procedures based on the conventional estimator $\overline{Y}_h - \overline{Y}$ give incorrect and misleading significance levels and confidence intervals for hospitals selected on the basis of their estimated mortality rates and exaggerate the evidence about the extreme nature of these hospitals. The Bayes-based procedure, in contrast, gives correct significance levels and confidence intervals for the hospitals identified by their extreme estimates.

In practice, most attention is focused on apparently extreme hospitals and medical conditions, so coverage properties of the statistical procedures are most important in this situation. The failure of the standard procedure when applied to extreme hospital rates, and the success of the empirical Bayes procedure, are examples of a much broader property of empirical Bayes and Bayes procedures.

6B. Policy Consequences of the Empirical Bayes Methods

The empirical Bayes procedure is much more conservative than the standard procedure because it tends to report a common value for all hospitals unless there is much stronger evidence of a difference. As a consequence, it will tend to understate or miss the poor performance of an exceptionally bad hospital. The tradeoff between empirical Bayes and the standard estimators is determined by the relative importance of potentially overlooking a bad hospital versus misrepresenting the performance of some good ones. The more conventional procedure will identify some hospitals as bad regardless of the actual variation in hospital quality, even when the procedures work as they are designed. This property can lead to resistance to report mortality data among hospital leaders as well as a tendency to discount all mortality reporting.

Since public reporting of hospital-specific mortality rates began, some of the strongest objections have come from administrators at certain types of hospitals, most notably from hospitals serving poor inner-city populations, who complain that their patients are more difficult to treat. In the original study, we addressed the case-mix problem by doing a logistic-regression-based adjustment. This is a straightforward extension of the method presented here.

Another way to address this concern that can be used with both the standard statistical procedure and the empirical Bayes procedure is to divide the hospitals into more homogenous groups (e.g., public hospitals serving inner city populations) and compare hospitals only with other more similar hospitals. This amounts to doing a separate analysis for each type of hospital considered. This approach is appealing because it is likely to reduce unmeasured differences in the patients across hospitals, which could result in misleading differences in mortality. Such an approach would result, however, in the establishment of different standards of good performance for hospitals serving different portions of the U.S. population. In particular, a hospital serving concentrated populations of low-income patients would be allowed a higher death rate before it would be identified as having potential quality problems because its death rate would be compared to a higher standard death rate. Statistical procedures establishing different standards would be politically and ethically acceptable only if there exists very strong evidence that current observed differences in the survival rates across different types of hospitals are fully attributable to differences in the patients they treat.

Because addressing the question of why there are differing mortality rates at different types of hospitals is very difficult, how to report rates for different types of hospitals is likely to remain controversial.

7. Exercises

The dataset and accompanying documentation for the following exercises are available on our website (www.rand.org/centers/stat/casebook). Select one of the four medical conditions to work with for each of the following exercises.

1.   Form $\bar{Y}_h$ and the logit of the death rate $\tilde{\delta}$ for each hospital. Remember to add 1/2 to the number of deaths and 1 to the number of patients. Plot a histogram of the observed death rates.

2.   Recompute $\tilde{\mu}$, $\tilde{\sigma}$, and $\bar{Y}$ in Table 8.3 using the estimators in Subsection 4.B (for $\bar{Y}$, use (number of deaths)/(number of patients)).

3.   Compute the empirical Bayes estimate for the hospitals with the lowest and highest values of $\tilde{\delta}$. Back-transform these estimates to the death-rate scale and compare them to $\bar{Y}_h$ and $\bar{Y}$.

4.   Divide the hospitals into two groups: those with 25 or more patients in the medical condition and ones with more than 100 patients. Plot histograms of the logit for each group. Do you notice any differences in the two histograms?

Further RAND Reading

Dubois, R., Brook, R. H., and Rogers, W. H. (1996), *Adjusted Hospital Death Rates: A Potential Screen for Quality of Medical Care,* RP-132, Santa Monica, CA: RAND.

Dubois, R., Rogers, W. H., Moxley, J. H., Draper, D., and Brook, R. H. (1991), *Hospital Inpatient Mortality: Is It a Predictor of Quality?* N-3372-HHS, Santa Monica, CA: RAND.

Park, R. E., Brook, R. H., Kosecoff, J. B., Keesey, J., Rubenstein, L. V., Keeler, E. B., Kahn, K. L., Rogers, W. H., and Chassin, M. R. (1991), *Explaining Variations in Hospital Death Rates: Randomness, Severity of Illness, Quality of Care,* R-3887-HCFA, Santa Monica, CA: RAND.

Thomas, N., Longford, N. T., and Rolph, J. E. (1992), *A Statistical Framework for Severity Adjustment of Hospital Mortality Rates,* N-3501-HCFA, Santa Monica, CA: RAND.

9

Eye-Care Supply and Need: Confronting Uncertainty

Daniel A. Relles, Catherine A. Jackson, and Paul P. Lee

Executive Summary

This chapter describes a RAND project initiated by the American Academy of Ophthalmology. The project attempted to answer several questions related to the eye-care need of the U. S. population, including whether there were enough eye-care providers, what combinations of optometrists and ophthalmologists might be sufficient, and whether there were enough subspecialists to meet need within areas of specialization.

The project performed three basic tasks. First, it acquired a substantial amount of utilization information from national surveys and published literature. Second, it computed estimates of total supply and need using a series of deterministic computations. Third, it compared aggregate estimates of supply and need to see what combinations of eye-care providers could fulfill the need. Figure 9.1 provides a schematic diagram of these steps and their interrelationships.

The statistical steps entailed preparing a number of datasets, gathering sample survey data to supplement information on provider workloads, and developing models to calculate total supply and need. The main statistical challenge was to assess uncertainty in the estimated totals. We did this by randomly varying all of the input datasets and writing a series of UNIX computer programs that enabled us to rerun all of our data preparation and analysis steps hundreds of times. We think this is a useful technique in general for producing interval estimates where standard statistical models are hard or impossible to apply.

1. Introduction

1A. Policy Problem

Due to a concern about growing health-care costs, policy-makers have focused recently on the distribution of physicians across specialties (Greenfield et al. 1992). In this health-policy context, the American Academy of Ophthalmol-

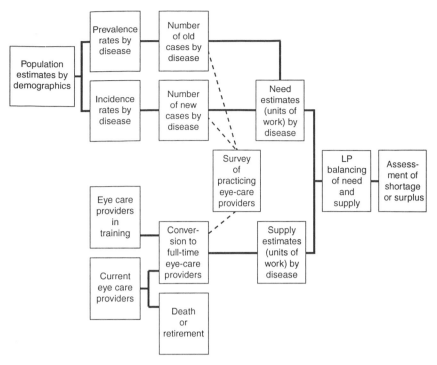

Figure 9.1. Process for Modeling Need and Supply. Boxes denote the steps in the modeling process. The top set of boxes describes public-health need: disease rates are applied to national population estimates to determine the number of persons requiring care, and these numbers are converted to required hours of work through data obtained in our sample survey of eye-care providers. In the bottom panel, the supply model determines the current number of ophthalmologists and optometrists in practice, as well as the estimated inflow (new trainees) and outflow (retirement or death) of these providers. The survey data are again used, this time to convert numbers of providers to available hours of work. A direct comparison of need and supply is now possible. The need and supply work estimates are run through a linear programming (LP) algorithm that attempts to allocate work loads by types of training and need. Finally, the imbalances between allocated need and supply are assessed.

ogy (AAO) commissioned RAND to study the composition of the eye-care-professional workforce and appointed an advisory panel to help us. The study was aimed at determining whether too many or too few eye-care providers of various types were being trained.

1B. Research Questions

The goal of the study was to compare the supply of eye-care providers with the need for such providers. To do this, we focused on four questions:

- What was the number of providers (supply)?
- What was the public-health need for eye-care services and professionals (need)?
- How do the estimates of supply and need compare?
- What is the uncertainty in these comparisons?

1C. Statistical Questions

We faced the following methodological questions:

- What method to use to estimate supply and need.
- How to reconcile the supply and need estimates to determine where workforce shortages or overages might be.
- How to gauge the uncertainty in the estimates.
- How to carry out the computations.

As we describe in detail below, our biggest challenge was designing methods to assess systematically the uncertainty in our estimates and efficiently vary the inputs to redo the computations.

Estimation. Our data came from several sources:

- descriptions of the population of ophthalmologists and optometrists;
- population-based estimates of disease incidence and prevalence;
- nationally representative health-care utilization surveys; and
- an ophthalmologist work-time survey that we conducted to elicit clinical judgments by ophthalmologists.

We estimated the supply for 12 categories of eye-care providers (e.g., general ophthalmologist) and we estimated the need for 197 categories of disease or eye condition (e.g., cataracts).

Comparing Estimates of Supply and Need. To assess the balance between supply and need, we matched estimates of subspecialty providers to the work they could perform. This process required determining which providers were eligible to perform which procedures, matching specific types of providers with specific procedures based on subspecialty training, and using a linear programming optimization algorithm to assign providers to procedures to satisfy eligibility constraints and to minimize a cost-based desirability measure.

Uncertainty. We assessed the stability of our results using standard errors of important quantities such as excess providers by subspecialty. Because the computations were so complex, it was infeasible to derive analytic expressions for the standard errors of many quantities. Instead, for some types of data we statistically varied the input data, produced estimates for each variation, and summarized the distribution of the resulting estimates. Sample surveys provided the bulk of our data; for these, we used the bootstrap to sample the datasets

(Efron and Tibshirani 1993). Other data came from the medical literature or from the clinical judgment of the study team and advisory board members. Since nothing comparable to a standard error was available for these data sources, we rescaled these data by a random multiplier to simulate our uncertainty.

Computing. Estimates of the quantities of interest came from producing supply and need estimates and then applying a linear program to assess imbalances between supply and need. We developed a computing environment that allowed us to vary the inputs and collect hundreds of analyses, each involving more than two dozen separate computer programs, to explore the uncertainty in the linear program. A UNIX computing environment (Kernighan and Pike 1989) enabled us to schedule and manage the runs by "watching" us do the analysis the first time and recording this in a script (computer program). We edited the script so that the steps were completely automated, enabling us to easily rerun the analysis multiple times.

1D. Summary of Data and Methods

In this chapter, we estimate supply and need by combining data from numerous sources. Assessing the uncertainty of computed values from different types of information on the uncertainty of the input data was a unique feature of the study.

Typical problems we addressed in building these datasets were:

- combining data from numerous sources;
- assessing the stability of inferences; and
- fielding our own surveys since readily available data were not sufficient.

To assess the variation in the input data, we use bootstrap methods; we also vary input parameters to assess the sensitivity of inferences to assumptions.

2. Design, Data Collection, Description of Data Sources, and Description of Data

2A. Study Design

We built two arrays of provider counts: the supply by specialty class and the public-health need for eye-care services by type of condition or disease. Both supply and need are expressed in units of full-time equivalent (FTE) providers. We compared these counts, assigned providers to service the need, and thereby calculated any deficit or excess. Note that this comparison is on a public-health need basis. It assumes need is given and does not factor in any economic considerations.

Supply. We defined the different types of providers, estimated the current number of each, and developed a model to forecast their number in the future. We also estimated provider characteristics, including training, demographics, and productivity. We defined categories of eye care by subspecialty in Table 9.1. The datasets used to estimate and forecast the number of providers in the 12 categories are given in Table 9.2.

Need. We developed a disease/eye-condition taxonomy representing all categories of eye care, which distinguished different types of treatment and different categories of providers and has been collapsed into four identifiable types of eye care in Table 9.3.

Table 9.1. Categories of Provider Supply Defined by Subspecialty

1.	Cataract
2.	Cornea
3.	Glaucoma
4.	Low vision
5.	Neuro-ophthalmology
6.	Pediatrics and strabismus
7.	Oculo-plastics
8.	Retina
9.	Uveitis
10.	General ophthalmology
11.	Optometrists without therapeutic privileges
12.	Optometrists with therapeutic privileges

Table 9.2. Datafiles Used in Developing Supply Estimates

American Academy of Ophthalmology (AAO) Member Master File	Reports member and nonmember, demographics (age and gender), geographic location (address), training (year graduated, board certification status), clinical preference (self-designated specialty), and medical practice type (solo, health maintenance organization). File identifies over 98% of all ophthalmologists.
Ophthalmology Match Program	Association of University Professors of Ophthalmology (AUPO). Number of positions and applications to residency and fellowship positions for U. S.
American Medical Association (AMA) Data	Annual sample survey of member practice characteristics reported in part by specialty geographic region.
Public Use Micro Sample (PUMS) Census Files	Five percent sample of 1990 census households receiving long-form questionnaire. Used to estimate number of optometrists by age, sex, and state.

Table 9.3. General Types of Eye Care

Problem-oriented medical care	Diagnosis and treatment of physical maladies or problems; typically covered by insurance plans as "medical–surgical" care
Rehabilitative services	For patients in which preventive and medical care have not been successful or for patients who need assistance in adjusting to a chronic condition or in lessening or reversing its effects.
Preventive care	Periodic well-eye visits or visits to detect early disease.
Elective services	Includes the fitting of cosmetic contact lenses, refractive surgery, and cosmetic eyelid surgery, which are valued by patients and performed by many eye-care providers.

We focused most of our efforts on problem-oriented and rehabilitative medical care, which encompass the largest share of eye-care services. We broke down disease groups according to clinically relevant available information, resulting in 15 major disease categories and 97 specific disease groupings within them.

There were numerous sources of information on incidence and prevalence of disease (need). Table 9.4 shows the disease categories we attempted to cover and the data sources associated with each. The sources included certain national health-survey datasets as well as surveys of some local populations.

Table 9.4. Data Sources of Need Information by Provider Supply Category

Disease Category:	NAMCS	FR	BD	BA	NHIS	NHDS
Cataract		X	X	X		
Conjunctivitis	X					
Cornea	X					
External disease	X					
Glaucoma		X		X		
Rehabilitation				X		
Neuro-ophthalmology	X				X	
Orbital	X					
Plastics	X					
Refractive		X			X	
Retina	X	X	X		X	
Strabismus	X				X	
Trauma	X				X	X
Uveitis	X					
Other	X					

NOTE: NAMCS: National Ambulatory Medical Care Survey, 1989–1991; NHIS: National Health Interview Survey, 1994; FR: Framingham Eye Study, 1980; BA: Baltimore Eye Study, 1991; BD: Beaver Dam Eye Study, 1994; and NHDS: National Hospital Discharge Survey, 1986–1990.

2B. Population Estimates

The Bureau of the Census forecasts population totals by age, sex, and race. We estimated the patient population through the year 2010 by rescaling Census population projections by current prevalence and incidence rates.

2C. Supplemental Survey

We surveyed practicing ophthalmologists to produce resource requirements (e.g., the time it takes to care for a patient with a given disease, the number of disease-specific follow-up visits required, etc.). The survey requested disease-specific estimates of initial visit length, the number and length of follow-up visits, the proportion of patients who required surgical treatment, preoperative assessment time, intraoperative time, other same-day surgical time, and the number and length of postoperative (within 90-day) visits. The survey was sent to a stratified random sample of 2007 ophthalmologists and had a 40% response rate.

3. Datafile Creation, Descriptive Statistics, and Exploratory Analysis

3A. Datafile Creation

Our analysis required four datasets:

- population estimates by age, race, and sex;
- provider supply estimates by subspecialty, age, sex, and training status (if applicable);
- prevalence and incidence rates by 97 disease groupings and utilization per year for persons with these diseases, including the number of visits per year, the lengths of such visits, the amount of follow-up for a given condition, and the division of work between medical and surgical procedures; and
- parameter values describing the physicians' capability to provide services, including the number of work hours per year, the percentage of visits with multiple eye problems, and the relative efficiencies in treating persons with multiple versus single conditions.

We were assembling information from numerous sources, including an ongoing sample survey, but we needed to do all of the model computations before the survey data were in to check the model and provide a preliminary assessment of the results. We required the different datasets to be independent. Thus, we could update a file without regard to the relationship between the data being entered and the data in other files. We also used automated scripts to update the files so that we could maintain a precise history of our activities. We did the scripting using the UNIX history mechanism to record the series of commands required to update files, which we modified to produce UNIX shell scripts for repeated processing.

3B. Details of Dataset Construction

Dataset construction consisted of deterministic computations, which had varying degrees of uncertainty at different points. See Lee, Jackson, and Relles (1995) for additional details.

Estimating Provider Supply. We estimated the supply of ophthalmologists and optometrists as follows:

- Determine the number of practicing eye-care providers and trainees by subspecialty.

- Add a cohort of first-year trainees to maintain a targeted number of trainees.

- Adjust to obtain current-year full-time equivalents (FTEs): add a fractional equivalent of trainees (depending on where they are in their training cycle) and subtract deaths and retirements using age- and sex-specific rates (Greenberg 1992).

- Adjust for next year by graduating trainees (depending on where they are in their training cycle) into their subspecialty areas.

- Iterate this procedure to the year 2010.

We projected the number of FTE ophthalmologists to 2010, and Table 9.5 shows the results through 2000.

Estimating Need for Disease and Rehabilitation Services. We defined incidence and prevalence rates to be as consistent as possible with our model and current medical practice. Where we had demographic-specific (e.g., race and sex) rates, we used them to increase precision. We imputed prevalence and incidence rates for ages outside the ranges established by the large eye studies. For younger ages, when the rate was known to be zero for some specified age interval, we smoothly interpolated from that age to the earliest age for which rates were available. For older ages, we set the rate equal to the value for the oldest age available. As a check, we compared our need estimates with estimates of national prevalence and incidence (National Ambulatory Medical Care Survey 1991).

Using disease- and condition-specific incidence and prevalence rates and population estimates, we estimated the population of individuals affected by each disease or condition. Since not all individuals with a condition actually require regular clinical care, we adjusted these numbers downward to produce a "clinical population" by applying a disease-specific fractional multiplier.

Table 9.5. Estimation of Current and Future Supply of Providers

Year	Current-Year Status and Adjustments				Next -Year Status	
	Full	In-Training	FTE	Full	In-Training and Graduates	Full
	Ophthalmologists					
1994	14,225	1961	14,091	13,882	485	14,367
1995	14,367	1958	14,215	13,907	484	14,391
1996	14,390	1957	14,225	14,070	482	14,552
1997	14,553	1957	14,370	14,238	482	14,720
1998	14,721	1957	14,523	14,412	482	14,894
1999	14,894	1957	14,677	14,580	482	15,062
2000	15,063	1957	14,828	14,749	482	15,231
	Optometrists					
1994	27,510	2000	27,646	26,910	997	27,907
1995	27,907	1997	27,974	27,294	993	28,287
1996	28,287	1997	28,287	27,662	993	28,655
1997	28,655	1997	28,589	28,032	993	29,025
1998	29,025	1997	28,892	28,412	993	29,405
1999	29,405	1997	29,206	28,802	993	29,795
2000	29,796	1997	29,531	29,209	993	30,202

Estimating Need for Preventive and Elective Services. We used the AAO Preferred Practice Pattern for well-eye exams for adults to estimate preventive services need. For children and infants, we used the AAO-sponsored March 1994 National Eye Care Forum Consensus Conference recommendations (AAO 1994) and assumed that persons getting clinical care receive full eye care and thus are not included in the preventive service estimate.

Estimating Resource Requirements. The resource requirements (work-time) for each of the 97 disease groupings were estimated from the supplemental survey in the following manner:

- For each of the 97 disease groupings, assemble all related survey work-time responses regardless of the subspecialty category of the respondent and regardless of whether the particular item is a procedure that relates to other diseases as well.

- Average the numbers of visits and visit lengths for each disease grouping using unweighted averages and medians, respectively. For percentages (e.g., proportion proceeding to surgery), compute unweighted means. Means rather than medians were used because these data had asymmetric distributions. There were many zeroes in the percentages of patients proceeding to surgery, and the median rates of surgery were often lower than our advisory panel thought was appropriate.

- Disease groupings not covered by the questionnaire items use estimates from a similar disease grouping (17 out of 97 disease groupings for office activity, 24 for incisional procedure times, and 19 for laser procedure times). These accounted for less than 15% of all patients.

We multiplied provider work-times and the estimated population affected by each disease or condition, or in need of each preventive or elective service, to produce the number of FTEs required in 197 different categories of type of service provided: two (medical and surgical) for each of the 97 disease and rehabilitative groupings, and one each for cosmetic contact lens, refractive surgery, and preventive care.

3C. Data Limitations

Our results are affected by the following data limitations:

- Variation in the clinical definitions of disease used among the different data sources we used may affect the precision of the model.

- How optometrists practice, how much time they take to provide these medical services, and how much time optometrists spend on services not covered in this study are not captured in our estimates.

- We estimated the clinical population by applying a disease-specific fractional multiplier to the population with a particular condition (using incidence and prevalence information) to get the number of persons needing disease-specific care.

- The accuracy of estimated hours per FTE is affected by ongoing changes in the U. S. health-care system. While our 2016 estimate was a value that the advisory panel favored, there were arguments both for increasing and decreasing the number.

4. Statistical Methods and Model

4A. Linear Programming

Given estimated supply by 12 different categories of providers and need by 197 different categories of type of service required, we had to match providers to need in an efficient and cost-effective way. Because eye-care needs are best served if the provider has appropriate training and expertise for a specific disease/condition, detailed matching is appropriate. Furthermore, some areas of care are not covered by the training of certain providers (e.g., optometrists do not perform cataract surgery).

Linear programming (LP) introduces these constraints in an efficient way. Using a linear objective function and given constraints, the LP algorithm finds parameter values that minimize the objective function (Wagner 1969). The most difficult part of the procedure is coming up with an appropriate objective function.

4B. Problem Setup

We allocate providers into a two-way matrix (Table 9.6). The rows in the table index all eye-care-specific work categories (need), and the columns identify the subspecialty categories of eye-care providers, optometrists, and ophthalmologists (supply). The leftmost column, "Need Grouping," lists the 197 different classes of work: two (medical and surgical) for each of the 97 disease and rehabilitative groupings, and one each for cosmetic contact lenses, refractive surgery, and preventive care. The rightmost column, "Need FTE," gives the FTEs calculated to be needed, as discussed in Subsection 3B of this chapter. A total of 30,757 FTEs is required to meet the estimated need. The bottom row, "Total Supply," shows the number of eye-care providers by subspecialty area available. There are 41,737 FTE providers to perform 30,757 FTEs worth of work.

Let x_{sp} be the "cost" associated with the (s,p)th cell (row s indexing service, column p indexing provider); that is, the cost associated with a given type of provider performing a specific service.

The linear program provides N_{sp}, the number of eye-care providers of type p allocated to perform service s. The algorithm attempts to minimize $\Sigma\ x_{sp}N_{sp}$, subject to the constraints.

Table 9.6. Format of Provider Allocation Table

Need Grouping (197 Categories)	Provider Subspecialty Category							Need FTE
	Cataract	Cornea	General	...	Uveitis	DPA	TPA	
Medical								
Cataract								1567
Aphakia								1812
Congen	the number of eye-care providers in each cell is filled in by the linear programming algorithm							9
...								...
Surgical								
Cataract								2788
Aphakia								1229
Congen								6
..								...
								30,757
Total supply	2266	840	8347	...	77	14,440	13,206	41,737

NOTE: $\Sigma\,N_{sp}$ = row total (i.e., meet all the need) < column total.

If x_{sp} truly reflects costs, this is the most cost-effective assignment. The lower x_{sp}, the higher the value N_{sp}, that the linear program assigns to the cell. Conversely, if x_{sp} is extremely large, the linear program will set $N_{sp} = 0$, because the product $x_{sp}N_{sp}$ contributes to the quantity being minimized.

In assigning the values x_{sp}, we faced two major problems: we did not know the costs; and we did not know the relative quality of care. Since optometrists and ophthalmologists do not agree on such matters, assigning values is contentious. We chose to focus discussion on priorities accorded to type of supplier rather than costs and efficiencies, and varied x_{sp} as a sensitivity analysis. To see the effect of allocating optometrists to all categories of work they could do before allocating ophthalmologists, we assigned optometrists as a group lower values of x_{sp} as input to the linear programming algorithm. Similarly, if ophthalmologists were assigned lower costs, we could see how many excess optometrists would result. We used the following considerations in determining x_{sp}:

- Diseases that optometrists cannot treat, by law, were assigned to receive a "6" in their cells.

- Optometrists without therapeutic privileges (DPA optometrists) got the highest priority (lowest x_{sp}) in the initial model in order to establish a lower-bound estimate of DPA excess. Since optometrists with therapeutic privileges (TPA optometrists) and ophthalmologists are substitutable for DPA optometrists, any excess in the number of other providers can replace DPA optometry assignments, increasing the DPA excess. Therefore, we can get both upper and lower bounds on the need for DPA optometrists by using this initial allocation strategy. We put "1" in the cells in which, by law, DPA optometrists are able to function. This initial model is the most flexible and illustrative; it is not an allocation based on quality, cost, or other judgments.

- For similar reasons, the TPA optometrists get the next highest priority, and we put a "2" in the cells in which, by law, they are able to function. Again, this provides a lower bound on any excess.

- The next priority is to allocate ophthalmologist subspecialists to their surgical area of expertise in recognition of subspecialty training and experience. By maximizing the use of subspecialists in areas where they are particularly well trained, we satisfy public-health goals. We put "3" only in those cells of subspecialists and subspecialty conditions.

- Allocate general ophthalmologists next because if subspecialists are restricted to their specialty area of training, we want to know how many subspecialists will be used. We gave general ophthalmologists a "4" in all entries and gave ophthalmologist subspecialists a "5" outside their area of surgical expertise.

Note that the linear programming assignment depends only on the ordinal ranking of "1" through "6." Table 9.7 gives these inputs used in the linear program to produce N_{sp}.

4C. Accounting for Uncertainty

Our judgments and data extrapolations, combined with inherent variation and uncertainty in the data elements themselves, may affect the stability of our results. To create a range of estimates within which we would have a higher degree of confidence, we used bootstrap techniques and other randomization schemes to vary the survey data elements and data based upon judgment.

The bootstrap replaces analytic calculations with computer simulations in the following way. To calculate a statistic that is based on a sample x_1 through x_n, estimate the statistic's variation by randomly sampling n cases with replacement from $(x_1, \ldots, x_n)$, compute the statistic, sample again with replacement and compute the statistic, iterate many times, and summarize variation in the statistic from the resulting distribution of the statistic across these bootstrap samples (Efron and Tibshirani 1993). The bootstrap technique worked well for our survey data.

Some parameters, such as the percentage of the population requiring clinical care, were not obtained through surveys but were simply reviewed and accepted by our advisory board. We wanted to see how sensitive our final inferences would be to such parameter choices, so we randomly varied each parameter by a random gamma (4)/4 multiplier to give it a standard deviation of half its value. We did this separately for each of the bootstrap runs.

Table 9.7. Assignment of Multipliers (x_{sp}) for the Linear Programming Algorithm

Need Grouping	Provider Subspecialty Category							
	Cataract	Cornea	General	.....	Uveitis	DPA	TPA	Need
Medical								
Cataract	5	5	4		5	1	2	1567
Aphakia	5	5	4		5	6	2	1812
Congen	5	5	4		5	1	2	9
..	..	..	..	..	..	..	..	..
Surgical								
Cataract	3	5	4		5	6	6	2788
Aphakia	3	5	4		5	6	6	1229
Congen	3	5	4		5	6	6	6
..	..	..	..	..	..	..	..	..
								30,757
Total supply	2266	840	8347	..	77	14,440	13,206	41,737

We did not do sensitivity analysis based on a more formal model for practical considerations relating to the large number of sources of variation and parameters. Our philosophy was to vary everything by a large amount to see if "things broke."

4D. Computing Environment

The complexity of our calculations necessitated a "smart" computing environment. We needed to vary inputs at the earliest stage of data management: estimates of prevalence and incidence from the national surveys and our own survey results were fed into estimating need, which later fed into the linear programming package. Our problem was much more complex than the usual bootstrap situation where there is a given database and bootstrapping is done on the statistical design matrix. We needed to propagate variations in parameter inputs through several programs.

Our solution was to encode the entire set of computations—data management, estimation of inputs, production of linear program results—into a single computer system that could be run with a push of a button. An analysis project of this complexity typically requires running programs, manually leafing through output, and pulling out parameters for the next stages of analysis. We needed to automate this process so we could run it hundreds of times. UNIX provides a congenial environment for doing this by:

- letting you "watch" what you are doing, via its "history" mechanism, which records and allows playback of commands; and

- letting you produce scripts that contain the commands that would otherwise be executed at the keyboard.

In order to program the analysis sequence, we had UNIX watch what we did the first time through, including the commands to track successful completion of programs and to save values from program outputs for subsequent runs. We coded these commands into a series of UNIX shell scripts. These scripts used mostly the standard UNIX utilities ("grep," "awk," "sed"), making it easy to execute an entire analysis, including specifying random number seeds. For a good reference on UNIX, see Kernighan and Pike (1984).

5. Results

5A. Linear Programming Results

Recall that the purpose of comparing eye-care provider supply and need is to answer the following:

- Are there enough eye-care providers to serve the needs of the U. S. population?

- What kinds of combinations of optometrists and ophthalmologists can meet the eye-care needs of the U. S. population?

- Are there enough subspecialists to meet surgical need for care and treatment of eye diseases within their specialization?

Differences Between Supply and Need. The linear programming algorithm allocates eye-care providers to each cell of Table 9.6. These allocations add across rows to get need and add down columns to less than or equal to the total supply. Thus, eye-care needs are met with an excess of providers.

Table 9.8 gives the results of our model runs by calendar year and three priority-driven models (optometry first, ophthalmology first, and generalist provider first). The three models allocate priorities differently; Table 9.7 shows the allocation for the optometry-first model. In the first two runs, either optometrists or ophthalmologists are allocated all the care they can provide; any unmet need that this provider type cannot fill is then given to the other type of provider. In the last model, optometrists and general ophthalmologists are allocated all care first, with residual care (if any) then going to subspecialist ophthalmologists. Within this model, care is allocated to optometrists first to provide maximum flexibility; again, no quality or cost of care judgments are implied.

Table 9.8. Summary Description of Supply, Need, and Excess FTEs

Year	Provider Type	Supply	Optometry-First Model		Ophthalmology-First Model		Primary-Care Provider Model	
			Need	Excess	Need	Excess	Need	Excess
1994	Gen	8347	3261	5086	8347	0	7800	547
	Spec	5744	4539	1205	5744	0	0	5744
	Tot-Oph	14,091	7800	6291	14,091	0	7800	6291
	Optom	27,646	22,957	4689	16,666	10,980	22,957	4689
	Total	41,737	30,757	10,980	30,757	10,980	30,757	10,980
2000	Gen	8220	3896	4324	8220	0	8220	0
	Spec	6608	5010	1598	6608	0	686	6608
	Tot-Oph	14,828	8906	5922	14,828	0	8,906	5922
	Optom	29,531	25,335	4196	19,413	10,118	25,335	4196
	Total	44,359	34,241	10,118	34,241	10,118	34,241	10,118
2010	Gen	8371	4717	3654	8371	0	8371	0
	Spec	7603	5332	2271	7603	0	1678	7603
	Tot-Oph	15,974	10,049	5925	15,974	0	10,049	5925
	Optom	33,492	27,480	6012	21,555	11,937	27,480	6012
	Total	49,466	37,529	11,937	37,529	11,937	37,529	11,937

The total number of FTE eye-care providers currently required, according to our estimate of need, is 30,757. In contrast, we have 14,091 FTE ophthalmologists and 27,646 FTE optometrists available for a total surplus of 10,980 FTEs.

Alternative Model Scenario 1: Optometry-first model. In this setting, surgical-care priorities go to the subspecialty ophthalmologists. There are 4689 surplus FTE optometrists and over 6291 surplus FTE ophthalmologists (Table 9.8); the surplus is relative to the number of FTEs sufficient to satisfy the public-health need for eye-care services.

Alternative Model Scenario 2: Ophthalmologist-first model. In this case, ophthalmologists provide routine primary eye care. No ophthalmologists are surplus in any specialty area. The effect on optometry under this structure would be severe because optometrists would be displaced in a one-to-one relationship. When need is considered, 16,666 optometrists would be required, resulting in a remaining total surplus of 10,980 optometrist FTEs (Table 9.8).

Alternative Model Scenario 3: Primary-care provider model. In this setting, generalist ophthalmologists can perform any of a subspecialist's functions. In this model, need can be satisfied without using any sub-specialist ophthalmologists. Excess general ophthalmologists are 547 FTEs (Table 9.8) for current need under a system of full utilization of optometric capabilities. The results reported here assign optometrists first, but the model is indifferent to optometrists being displaced by ophthalmologists. To the extent that general ophthalmologists perform preventive services, this displacement would decrease their surplus while increasing that of optometrists.

5B. Bootstrap and Simulation Results

In 100 bootstrap runs of the model, the extremes fell between 28,500 and 33,500 FTEs required for need, with a bootstrap standard deviation of about 1500. Likewise, the surplus ranged from about 8500 to 13,500 FTEs, with a standard error of 1500. Surplus FTE ophthalmologists under the optometry-first model have a mean of about 6000 and a standard error of 1200; surplus FTE optometrists have a mean of about 4500 and a standard error of 900.

Given that the overall numbers were fairly consistent with previous workforce studies and that the intervals generated by the bootstrap and other randomizations were fairly tight, we felt comfortable with the model's projections of the number of FTEs required as well as the supply of FTEs. All the inferences drawn are stable across parameter variations.

6. Discussion

Our analysis of eye-care workforce supply and need requirements shows that there currently is an excess supply of eye-care providers of between 8000 and 14,000 FTEs relative to the public-health need. How the excess supply is divided between ophthalmologists and optometrists depends on the structure of the eye-care delivery system. Defining the socially, medically optimal, or economically optimal allocation would require normative judgments and was beyond the scope of this project.

When we examined the supply of ophthalmologists, we exploited the generalist/specialist distinction reflecting the current interest in general (or comprehensive) ophthalmology (i.e., a primary-care provider model). The requirements for subspecialist ophthalmologists can vary from zero to 100% of those available according to how ophthalmic surgical care is assigned. When we consider the workforce requirements for the public-health need under an ophthalmologist-first scenario, there is no subspecialty surplus; all 5744 subspecialty FTEs are required. However, under the comprehensive primary-care provider model, virtually no subspecialist ophthalmologists are required. Under the primary optometric care model, while subspecialists provided all the surgical care and were restricted to providing only surgical care, there is still an excess of subspecialists in most ophthalmic subspecialty areas. Only when a significant portion of the medical office care is included as a component of surgical treatment are all subspecialists allocated. Clearly, a policy designed to enhance the skills of comprehensive ophthalmologists to approximate those of subspecialists would reduce the need for subspecialists.

6A. Policy Implications

The results of this study raise two important policy implications:

- There are more eye-care providers than required to meet the current level of need for eye-disease care, vision rehabilitation, and preventive care.

- More data are needed so that the skills and capabilities of the different types of eye-care providers, including the optometrist/ophthalmologist and generalist/subspecialist comparisons, can be better optimized.

We are able to construct three different eye-care system scenarios, each an extreme. However, the practical reality falls somewhere within the bounds of these estimates. More data are needed so that allocations among providers can be made on the basis of measured quality of care or costs. Such data would inform a mechanism to determine workforce requirements with an explicit goal, such as determining the number of eye-care providers (optometrists, ophthalmologists, and ophthalmic sub-specialists) that would maximize quality of care, minimize costs, or maximize quality per unit cost.

6B. Statistical Issues

From a methodological perspective, this chapter provides one approach to an apparently difficult deterministic computation. The computation consisted of a significant amount of processing of survey and other datasets plus running a linear programming algorithm with hundreds of constraints. Through a series of

UNIX scripts, we did more than the standard "do the computations once and report the results." We first recorded how to run the myriad of programs that carried out the data management and fitting tasks. Then, we modified the input data using the bootstrap or random multipliers, and we replicated the data management and analysis sequence hundreds of times to get a sense of how much variability there might be in the final results. While this method does not produce formal standard errors, it does give information about uncertainty. The inferences about excess providers were robust to this level of uncertainty, which gives us some comfort that we are correct. In a situation where the inference might have tilted in another direction, we would have looked at the values of the parameters that affected this shift and asked whether the inputs were plausible.

The methods described here will work under general conditions. It is always possible to script an analysis in UNIX because of the richness of the UNIX utilities. Even text editor activities, such as extracting parameter values out of one program's output and inputting them to another program, can easily be carried out by standard routines such as "grep," "sed," or "awk." Indeed, in the scripts written for the present application, these were the routines most frequently called.

The advantages of such scripting go beyond assessing the effects of input uncertainties. It often becomes necessary to rerun an entire analysis as new data arrive, errors are discovered, you get a new idea, or because a referee requires you to do it. If the process is scripted, it is relatively easy to rerun everything. If it is not, one has to rely on memory or documentation: run this program before that, delete this dataset before you run that program, etc. The redo can become extremely difficult and time-consuming. Analysts should recognize that replication is inevitable. Scripting is the key to facilitating replication.

7. Exercises

The datasets and accompanying documentation for the following exercises are available on our website (www.rand.org/centers/stat).

There are five data matrices:

work = Minutes of work provided for each disease group, from a sample survey

prev = prevalence of disease, recorded as the number of visits to an ophthalmologist in a year

xwk = crosswalk relating disease to provider type

prov = count of providers

hours = hours per year reported by a sample of providers

Small parts of each matrix are displayed below.

7A. Need Computations

Assuming the number of visits represents true need, estimate the total amount of time required to serve the population.

1. Do a base-case computation using matrices "work" and "prev."

2. Do a computation that captures uncertainty in the "work" sample survey via the bootstrap.

3. Do a computation that captures uncertainty in the number of visits per year using a chi-squared multiplier with 8 degrees of freedom.

work			prev			xwk			prov			hours
dse	mins		dse	visits		dse	ptyp		ptyp	nprov		ptime
1	15		1	10000		1	cat		cat	1000		1800
1	18		2	20000		2	cat		gen	6000		2400
1	20		.	.		.	.		.	.		2200
1	15		.	.		.	.		.	.		2000
2	15		.	.		.	.		.	.		1900
2	18		97	15000		97	gen					
2	20											
2	15											
.	.											
97	45											
97	40											
97	25											

4. Summarize total need variation in terms of a mean and variance.

5. Matrix "xwk" maps disease into major disease groups. Summarize need by these groups.

7B. Supply Computations

1. Estimate the amount of supplier work-time available in a year.

2. Incorporate uncertainty in the supply estimates using the bootstrap.

7C. Need versus Supply

1. Match supply with need by provider-type/major-disease group and compute excess providers.

    a. Are there enough providers?

    b. What is the uncertainty in these estimates?

2.   What information would you need to perform a cost-minimizing allocation of supplier to need? Do you think this is feasible? Why or why not?

Further RAND Reading

Lee, P. P., Jackson, C., and Relles, D. A. (1998), *Demand-Based Assessment of Workforce Requirements for Orthopaedic Services,* RP-719, Santa Monica, CA: RAND.

Lee, P. P., Jackson, C., and Relles, D. A. (1995), *Estimating Eye Care Provider Supply and Workforce Requirements,* MR-516-AAO, Santa Monica, CA: RAND.

10

Modeling Block Grant Formulas for Substance Abuse Treatment

Daniel F. McCaffrey and John L. Adams

Executive Summary

The growing use of block grants to allocate federal dollars among states raises a number of important and politically sensitive issues. Block grants are unrestricted Federal grants given to states to pay for services supported by the Federal government but performed by state and local agencies. Such grants currently fund many Federal programs, and their increasing use invites close scrutiny of the relative size of allotments given to the states. Ideally, allocation of funds should be equitable and should reflect a program's goals.

In this chapter, we will use a case study of the allotment of block grants for substance abuse services, both treatment and prevention, to demonstrate the role of statistical analysis in ensuring equitable distribution of such funds. The existing block grant formula determines allotments by estimating what each state needs for substance abuse services; estimating the costs of these services; and calculating each state's taxable resources. Our study explores alternative ways of estimating needs and costs and demonstrates that well-informed estimates of the formula's components can greatly improve the equity of block grant allocations.

This chapter describes fitting logistic regression models to estimate needs, including a discussion of variable selection and sensitivity analysis. Additionally, it summarizes a simulation study on the equity of alternative specifications in the allotment formula. Our main finding was that estimates of need for treatment have the greatest effect on the allotment formula, and that alternative estimates would shift about 18% of the block grant dollars, reallocating funds away from large-population states toward smaller-population states.

Our study demonstrates that if the federal government plans to rely more heavily on block grants, accurate estimates of need for the services funded by such grants are required. We conclude that robust statistical methods are essential for equitable block grant allocation and good policy.

1. Introduction

Block grants are unrestricted Federal grants given to states to pay for services supported by the Federal government but performed by state and local agencies. Such grants are currently used by many Federal programs, including substance abuse services, and have been proposed for future welfare and Medicaid expenditures. An important and politically sensitive issue is the relative size of the grant allotments among the states. Of special concern is that allocation of funds be equitable and reflect a program's goals.

In this chapter, we use a case study of the allotment of block grants for substance abuse services, both treatment and prevention, to demonstrate the role of statistical analysis in ensuring funding equitability. Formulas for block grants involve estimating the size of the population in need of substance abuse services by state. Our approach is to introduce a new means of making these state estimates and then to consider the effect on current allotments.

1A. Policy Problem

In 1992, Congress passed the Alcohol, Drug Abuse, and Mental Health Administration Reorganization Act. One outcome was a revision of the Federal Substance Abuse and Mental Health Services Block Grant Allotment Formula, the formula used for allocating federal block grant dollars for substance abuse and mental health treatment. Because of the contentious nature of the debate, and the fact that proposed changes to the formula threatened to reduce the funding in some states while increasing it in others, Congress mandated a study of the formula. The study (Burnam et al. 1997) described in this case study fulfilled that mandate. In this chapter, we focus only on the substance abuse services analyses.

History of the Block Grant Formula. Our goal was to assess the equity of the current substance abuse block grant allocations and to identify possible improvements. The issue of equity in the allotment process was complicated because of the way block grants had developed. The initial grant authorization and early reauthorizations allocated the block grants according to the historical funding patterns of the categorical grants that block grants replaced as part of the 1981 Omnibus Budget Reconciliation Act (OBRA). These early allocations resulted in wide variations in per capita funding across the states, and the allotments were perceived to be inequitable. As a result, in 1988 Congress revised the allocation formula using a combination of a state's total taxable resources and its population, weighted by age and urbanicity, to determine that state's grant. Urbanized populations received a larger weight than populations of high-risk age cohorts, reflecting belief that the prevalence of drug abuse was higher in urban areas. In the 1992 reauthorization, Congress continued to attempt to ensure greater equity. The resulting allocation changes did not adequately demonstrate that Congress had achieved equity.

Equity. To measure equity, we must have a clear concept of it. In general, equity means creating an "equal" allocation of block grants across states. An equal allocation, however, does not necessarily imply equal dollars or equal per capita allotments to all states. Congress has chosen to forgo per capita equity in favor of taxpayer equity. Taxpayer equity means that the burden of providing a standard service level for all persons in need should be equal for taxpayers in every state. The aggregate expenditure required within a state to provide a standard service level for all persons in need is known as "expenditure need." Taxpayer equity means that Federal funding should fill the gap between expenditure need and the funding that could be provided by state and local governments, assuming these governments taxed their fiscal capacities at the same rate.

The difference between taxpayer equity and other measures of equity, such as per capita or beneficiary equity (equal share of expenditure need across states), is that taxpayer equity is sensitive not only to services provided but also to state wealth. A consequence of using taxpayer equity is that achieving equitable allotments requires accurate estimates of two factors: the expenditure need and the fiscal capacity of each state. This requirement creates interesting empirical challenges.

The Current Formula. The current formula for determining substance abuse allocations demonstrates Congress' commitment to taxpayer equity:

$$g_i \propto \left(P_i \times C_i\right) - T_i, \tag{10.1}$$

where g_i denotes the grant for state i, P_i denotes a measure of the state's population needing substance abuse treatment services, C_i denotes the cost of providing a standard package of services to an individual in state i, and T_i denotes the state's total taxable resources. The first term on the right-hand side of (10.1) is a measure of expenditure need, calculated as population in need times per capita cost. The second term measures the state's fiscal capacity. Grants are proportional to expenditure need less fiscal capacity in order to maintain taxpayer equity.

To provide truly equitable allotments, Congress must accurately estimate need P_i, costs C_i, and taxable resources T_i. For substance abuse services, Congress currently estimates P_i using a weighted sum of shares of the population over 18, where people under 24 are overweighted and the urbanized population aged 18–24 is doubly overweighted (see Burnam et al. 1997 for details).

1B. Research Questions

Given that Congress had chosen taxpayer equity for allocating block grants for substance abuse services, our charge was to determine whether the current measures of the population in need, the cost of services, and the state's resources accurately reflect variations across states. Our first goal was to determine whether the current formula led to an equal burden for each state's taxpayers. If we found inequalities, we would try to minimize them by introducing alternative factors into the formula.

Our review of the block grant allotment formula for substance abuse services raised three questions that roughly corresponded to the authorizing legislation:

- What correlates of need for treatment identified in the substance abuse literature are not included in the current formula?

- What are the most accurate estimates of treatment need and service costs for all states, and are these estimates robust against model assumptions?

- In terms of equity, how do the allotments based on the current formula compare to those generated by using alternative estimates of need and costs?

We did not seek to design an estimation procedure that would be a prototype for future allotments. Instead, we attempted to provide best estimates and to suggest improvements in the existing formula. We proceeded by estimating the population in need and then presenting the results of a simulation study to answer the third question. In the simulation study, we combined our need and cost estimates with taxpayer equity to produce alternative allotments using (10.1). Although this chapter contains only a subset of our analyses, it highlights the modeling and exploration of the most interesting statistical concerns in the analysis.

1C. Statistical Questions

The statistical questions we faced were:

- Using available data, what is an appropriate method for estimating need for treatment in all 50 states and the District of Columbia?

- How sensitive are our estimates to the method's assumptions?

In answer to our first question, we turned to synthetic estimation (Ghosh and Rao 1994) and used indirect regression (Office of Management and Budget 1993) to estimate need for treatment at the state level. Our synthetic estimates followed three steps:

- using a nationally representative sample, we estimated β, the vector of coefficients for the logistic regression model

$$\log\left(\frac{p(x)}{(1 - p(x))}\right) = \beta'x \ , \tag{10.2}$$

where $p(x)$ denotes the probability of needing treatment for a person with a vector of characteristics x, which includes demographic, socioeconomic, and geographic (e.g., region and metropolitan status) predictors;

- using this model, we estimated the probability of needing treatment for each respondent in a sample of each state's population; that is, we calculated

$$\hat{p}_{ij} = \frac{e^{\hat{\beta}x_{ij}}}{1 + e^{\hat{\beta}x_{ij}}}, \text{ for each } x_{ij}, j = 1, \ldots, n_i \text{ and } i = 1, \ldots, 51$$

  with n_i respondents from the ith state's sample, and we created estimates for all 50 states and the District of Columbia;

- for each particular state, we estimated P_i, the prevalence of need for treatment, as the weighted average of the individual estimates made for the state's resident sample; that is,

$$\hat{p}_i = \sum_{j=1}^{n_i} w_{ij}\hat{p}_{ij} \bigg/ \sum_{j=1}^{n_i} w_{ij} ,$$

where w_{ij} is the sampling weight for the ijth person in the sample. The estimated number of residents in need of treatment ($NEED_i$) is calculated as $NEED_i = POP_i \times \hat{p}_i$, where POP_i denotes the population of state i.

To carry out such an estimation scheme, we needed two information sources: a dataset to estimate the parameters of the logistic regression model; and a dataset to project this model onto each state's population.

Our synthetic estimates had to provide an accurate description of state-to-state variations in treatment need. They could do so only if our logistic regression model (10.2) was well specified and if it held for residents of all 50 states and the District of Columbia.

Our primary statistical challenge was to develop a model that met these requirements and to determine if it had any shortcomings. In addition, with respect to our second statistical question, we needed to assess the effect of the assumptions made in our approach on our final estimates and study conclusions.

1D. Summary of Data and Methods

Data. The 1991 National Household Survey on Drug Abuse (NHSDA) was our primary source of data for fitting the logistic regression model. The NHSDA surveyed over 32,000 respondents and collected information on the recency and frequency of drug and alcohol use as well as associated problems. We used these data to measure need for treatment. The NHSDA also contains many demographic and socioeconomic variables, which we used as predictors of need.

To predict probabilities of needing treatment and to estimate each state's prevalence of need, we used the 1990 Census Public Use Micro Sample (PUMS) to provide each state's sample of residents. We used the 1% PUMS sample with over 2000 respondents from each state and a total of over 1 million records. The PUMS contains data from the Census long form and provides many, though not all, of the demographic and socioeconomic status (SES) variables found in the NHSDA.

Estimation Process. We adopted an eight-step process to produce state-level estimates of need for substance abuse treatment:

- identify candidate predictors by reviewing the literature;
- create proxies for these predictors from our NHSDA variables and use exploratory data analysis to find their correct form for the logistic regression model;
- use backward deletion to choose the final set of predictors;
- use diagnostics to identify model failure and search for interactions, revising the model as necessary;
- fit the final logistic model;
- use the final model to predict the probability of need for treatment for each respondent in the PUMS;
- calculate the weighted average of the estimated probabilities by state and estimate need by state; and
- conduct sensitivity analysis by altering the formulation of the logistic regression model, repeating steps 3–6, and determining the effect of the model changes.

Assessing the Effect of Our Estimates. We assessed the effect of the final estimates of state treatment needs on block grant allotments. Our procedure was to simulate allocating block grants. First, we used the current formula and the current measures of need. Second, we used the current formula and our estimates of need. To compare the allotments from these two approaches, we used three measures: the percentage of current dollars shifted from one state to another; the distribution of percentage change in funds by state; and the distribution of percentage change in funds by state, weighted by population. These three measures demonstrated the overall effect, the number of states affected, and the number of people affected.

2. Study Design, Data Collection, Description of Data Sources, and Description of Data Elements

The data used for our estimates of treatment need were the richest available. Because the NHSDA contained extensive individual-level data on drug use and associated covariates, we could fit a model for predicting individual need for treatment (10.2). The PUMS data allowed us to translate the individual predictions into state-level estimates. Without the details available in these data, our aggregate analysis would have been less precise.

However, as discussed below, the NHSDA used a complex sample design, which had important consequences for our analyses. Furthermore, although the PUMS contained extensive data from a large sample of individuals, it did not contain all the NHSDA predictors. This fact influenced our analyses and our final estimates.

2A. The National Household Survey on Drug Abuse (NHSDA)

NHSDA surveys the illicit use of drugs and alcohol of a probability sample of U. S. residents. The survey asks respondents about the recency and frequency of use of illicit substances, including heroin, other opiates, cocaine, stimulants, sedatives, tranquilizers, hallucinogenics, and marijuana. It also asks about the use of alcohol and tobacco. Demographic (age, sex, ethnicity), socioeconomic (educational attainment, income), health data, and data on problems associated with substance use are collected (National Institute on Drug Abuse 1992; Office of Applied Studies 1993). From the NHSDA data on drug or alcohol use and its related problems, we created an indicator of need for substance abuse treatment and used this variable as the outcome in our need models.

The 1991 NHSDA target population was residents in all 50 states and the District of Columbia. The sampling frame included household residents as well as college students living in dormitories and homeless people residing in shelters. The frame excludes those in prison, homeless not in shelters, and people housed on military bases. These exclusions are important because prison and homeless populations have been shown to include a large percentage of drug users (National Institute of Justice 1995). Excluding such individuals from our sample might bias our need estimates downward.

We needed to consider the complexity of the NHSDA design to avoid biasing our parameter estimates. The NHSDA employs a complex multi-stage design that oversampled six large Metropolitan Statistical Areas (MSAs) as well as young people, Hispanics, and African-Americans. Respondents from the six oversampled MSAs account for nearly half of the final sample, and people under 35 account for about 75% of respondents. Hispanics and African-Americans constitute equally disproportionate shares of the sample.

2B. The Primary Use Micro Sample (PUMS)

The PUMS is a random sample of 1990 census respondents. We used the 1% PUMS sample, which contained over 2000 respondents from each state, with more persons included from larger states. Because the PUMS oversampled rural populations within each state, we needed to use the sampling weights to generate our treatment need estimates for each state.

The PUMS data contain information on demographic characteristics (age, sex, ethnicity, and marital status); social characteristics (education enrollment and attainment, place of birth, citizenship, ancestry, language spoken at home, disability, fertility, and veteran status); and economic characteristics (labor force participation, occupation, place of work, journey to work, income, and last year worked). Many of these variables are analogous to NHSDA variables, a fact that allowed us to project the NHSDA models onto state populations via the PUMS data.

3. Datafile Creation, Descriptive Statistics, and Exploratory Analysis

Although we used public-release datafiles, we needed to create derived variables from the NHSDA database. Specifically, we constructed a measure of need for treatment as well as predictors.

3A. Datafile Creation

While creating the actual analysis files, we had to determine how to both measure treatment need and deal with missing data.

Measuring Need for Substance Abuse Treatment. Although the NHSDA is a rich source of data about drug and alcohol use, it does not identify persons in need of treatment. Such need must be inferred from responses to questions about use and related problems. We defined need for treatment as equivalent to drug or alcohol dependence.[1] Thus, any person meeting the criteria for drug or alcohol dependence was defined as in need of substance abuse treatment. This definition meant that we were using the NHSDA to model the probability of substance dependence.

Substance dependence is identified as a clinical disorder according to criteria established in the standard manual for mental health disorder diagnoses, the DSM-III-R.[2] These criteria are listed in the Appendix of this chapter. If the NHSDA had contained questions about the DSM-III-R criteria, we could have identified respondents with substance dependence simply by checking these criteria. While the NHSDA does not contain such items, it does contain a series of questions about problems relating to substance use, and we used these questions to create a proxy for the DSM-III-R criteria (Table 10.1). We chose this proxy based on face validity and did not conduct empirical tests to determine whether this measure accurately identifies substance dependence.

Missing Data. Missing data, or item nonresponse, is a common survey problem, and most public-use datafiles such as the NHSDA provide missing data codes or imputed values for missing items. The long NHSDA face-to-face survey on sensitive issues such as the use of illicit drugs produced item nonresponse, and the public-use datafile contains missing data codes and imputed values for a small percentage of respondents on most items (Table 10.2). The

*Table 10.1. Operational Definition of Persons Needing Substance
Abuse Treatment*

Definition of Dependence (Proxy for DSM-III-R Criteria)

Experienced three or more of the following problems with a specific type of drug or alcohol in the past year:

- tried to cut down on use or unable to cut down
- needed greater quantities to achieve the same effect
- used a substance daily for two or more consecutive weeks
- felt dependent on substance
- felt sick due to substance use
- psychological problems due to substance use (i.e., depression, loneliness, nervousness, feeling upset, suspiciousness, or concentration difficulties)
- social problems due to substance use (arguments, problems at work or school, problems harder to handle due to substance use)
- substance use contributed to physical health problems (i.e., substance use precipitated medical emergencies or contributed to physical health problems)

*Table 10.2. Missing Data Statistics for the 1991 National Household
Survey on Drug Abuse*

Variable	Percentage of Responses Missing Item	Percentage of Responses with Imputed Value
Sex	0.01	0.01
Marital status[a]	1.34	0.00
Age	0.02	0.02
Number in household	0.51	0.00
Education (years)	0.74	0.00
Work status	1.56	1.00
Student	0.51	0.00
Veteran status	0.69	0.00
Health insurance	1.84	1.84
Race	0.06	0.06
Population density	0.00	0.00
Region	0.00	0.00
Welfare	0.00	0.00
Income	28.12	28.12

[a]For example, the table entries for this variable means that 1.34% of respondents did not report marital status, and no imputation (0%) was performed.

NHSDA uses hot-deck imputation (Ford 1983) to impute some missing items.[3] Hot-deck imputation incorporates responses from similar respondents to fill in the missing data.

Because logistic regression requires complete data from each respondent, we decided to use imputed data and treat them as observed data. Properly imputed data do not cause bias in estimates, and using the imputed values provided by the NHSDA allowed us to proceed. Sensitivity analyses performed later showed that this decision had little effect on our final parameter estimates.

Although the NHSDA used imputation for items in the *Main Findings* and *Population Estimates* publications (NIDA 1992; Office of Applied Studies 1993), other items are left missing. We found that about 10% of the records in the datafile lacked the data necessary to create a measure of treatment need. Because we were using self-reported need, we imputed missing values as not indicating need for treatment. Although this conservative approach may have led us to underestimate need, it ensured that we counted only those who were clearly in need of treatment.

Cases that had missing data for predictor variables were excluded from our study. Such exclusion affected less than 2% of cases in our final model and, given our large sample size, did not have a significant effect on the final estimates.

3B. Descriptive Statistics and Exploratory Data Analysis

Table 10.3 gives unweighted descriptive statistics from the 1991 NHSDA. Of the 32,594 respondents, a total of 2421 (7.4%) met our criteria (Table 10.1) for needing substance abuse treatment. Table 10.3 also shows the effect of the oversampling. About 25% of the respondents are Hispanic, and another 25% are African-American. Nearly 75% of respondents are under 35 years of age, and 68% of respondents reside in large (population over 1 million) MSAs. This oversampling is also apparent in other characteristics. For example, a large number of respondents have never married or are students, characteristics typical of younger people.

As mentioned previously, we needed to ensure that our logistic regression model (10.2) was correctly specified. If our model was missing important predictors, or if the relationship between need and a predictor was nonlinear, then our final need estimates would be biased. We used exploratory analyses to identify predictors and to determine their functional forms for the model. Our modeling procedure is summarized in Figure 10.1 (boxes L1 to L3):

- we reviewed the literature to create a candidate list of predictors;

- we used items from the NHSDA to derive predictors that corresponded to those identified by our literature review; and

- we used exploratory data analysis (EDA) techniques to determine an appropriate functional form for each predictor.

Table 10.3. Unweighted Descriptive Statistics from 1991 NHSDA

	N	Percentage of Total
Total sample	32,594	100
In need of substance abuse treatment	2421	7
Predictor variables		
Male	14,422	42
Marital status		
Married	11,860	36
Widowed/divorced/separated	3220	10
Never married	17,079	52
Age		
12–17	8005	25
18–24	6831	21
25–34	9232	28
35–44	3239	10
45–54	1875	6
55–64	1477	5
65+	1935	6
Education (years)		
0–8	6785	21
9–11	6465	20
12 (HS diploma/GED)	9418	29
13–15	5491	17
16+	4195	13
Work status		
Full-time	12,679	39
Part-time	3969	12
Not working	15,772	48
Race		
Hispanic	7916	24
White (not Hispanic)	15,648	48
African-American (not Hispanic)	8050	25
Other (not Hispanic)	980	3
Population density		
MSA of over 1,000,000	22,087	68
MSA 250,000–999,999	5169	16
MSA less than 250,000	1406	4
Not in MSA, not rural	1513	5
Rural	2419	7
Region		
Northeast	5480	17
North central	5722	18
South	13,117	40
West	8275	25
Full-time students	10,444	32
Veterans	2288	7
Insured (have health insurance)	25,585	79
Living alone	3312	10
Welfare recipient	2989	9
Income (natural log)	mean=9.7	SD[a]=1.8

[a]SD = standard deviation.

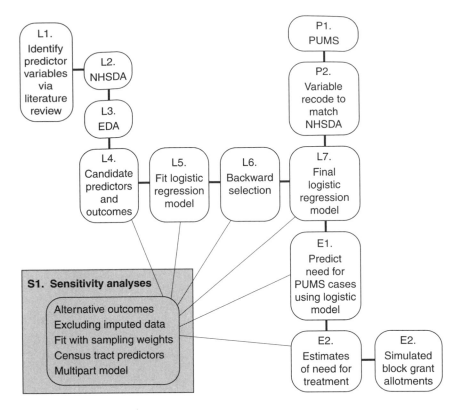

Figures 10.1. Process for Modeling Need for Treatment. Boxes denote the sequential steps in our modeling process. Boxes with labels that begin with "L" denote steps in fitting our logistic regression model. Boxes with labels that begin with "P" denote steps in preparing the PUMS data. Boxes with labels that begin with "E" denote steps that combined the regression model and the PUMS data to estimate the population in need and the simulated block grant allotment by state.

These three steps yielded a complete set of candidate analysis predictor variables (box L4 in Figure 10.1). From this list, we selected the final set of variables used in our model (boxes L5 to L7):

- we fit a preliminary logistic regression model using the entire set of candidate predictor variables; and

- we used backward deletion to choose our final main-effects model.

Candidate Predictors. The project contract specified that important demographic and socioeconomic predictors of treatment needed to be selected via a literature review. The contract further required that we identify those variables that could affect the allocation.

The demographic and socioeconomic predictors identified are listed along with descriptive statistics in Table 10.3. These predictors include age, ethnicity, sex, marital status, education, work status, veteran status, insurance coverage, welfare status, living arrangements, and geographic region and population density of city of residency. Our model exploration also included indicators for the six oversampled MSAs.

Functional Forms for Predictor Variables. After identifying candidate predictors, we needed to create the variables appropriate for our study by using items from the NHSDA. Most of the variables were categorical, such as educational attainment, sex, and ethnicity. Other predictors, such as age or income, were available on a continuous scale. However, because the literature and previous NHSDA analyses demonstrated that the relationships between some of these continuous predictors and substance abuse were nonlinear, we decided to categorize many of these variables. For example, we grouped age into seven categories: 12–17, 18–24, 25–34, 35–44, 45–54, 55–64, and older than 65 years old.

Although nonlinear transformations might have improved statistical efficiency, using categorical variables yielded more interpretable models. The relationship between age and the prevalence of treatment need, for example, is clearly nonmonotonic, as shown in Figure 10.2. The prevalence increases rapidly from young adolescence through early adulthood (early 20s) and then falls off sharply in the late 20s before a more gradual decline after age 30. Simple transformations are inappropriate for this type of relationship, and a complex polynomial approximation would be hard to interpret. But the prevalence for six age groups is both interpretable and gives the necessary flexibility to yield an accurate model fit.

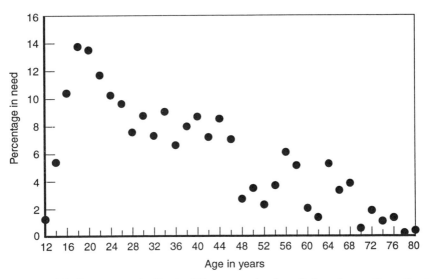

Figure 10.2. Percentage in Need of Treatment by Age. Points denote the estimated percentage of the population in need of treatment by age in years.

We used several empirical techniques to determine the cut points for our categorical variables. First, we used generalized additive models (Hastie and Tibshirani 1990) to identify the nonlinear relationships between treatment need and predictors. We adopted this approach for both continuous and ordinal variables. Using these smoothed fits, we determined the appropriate categories for capturing the nonlinear structure in the data. Second, in an alternative approach, we used classification trees (Breiman, Friedman, Olshen, and Stone 1984) to identify important splits in the data that explained the outcome variance. We combined the results of these two approaches to choose the final categories of our variables and to identify residual structure and interactions.

Final Variable Selection. After determining the appropriate forms for each predictor, we fit logistic regression models using backward deletion. Beginning with all candidate predictor variables, we dropped the least significant variable and refit the model. To determine when to stop dropping variables, we used Akaike's AIC criterion.

Individual dummy variables for each value of a categorical variable were treated as separate predictors. As an alternative approach, we could have treated each categorical variable as a single grouped variable and tested for inclusion of the entire group. That is, we might have used a six degree of freedom χ^2 test to decide whether to include age as a predictor, rather than exploring the six age dummies (indicator variables) separately. We did not use this procedure because the global χ^2 might exclude an important predictor for which not all levels differ significantly. For example, if people over 35 have similar probabilities of needing treatment, then a six degree of freedom test might not be significant, even though younger people differ significantly from older people. We could not afford to miss important sources of variability, so we treated dummies separately, risking greater Type I errors while avoiding more troublesome Type II errors.

We chose backward deletion, rather than forward or stepwise selection algorithms, in part because backward deletion is not sensitive to the order in which variables are included in the models. Also, backward deletion is more likely to identify all important predictors. Inclusion of all relevant predictors was important because one of our goals was to identify variables excluded from the current allocation formula. There are other variable selection approaches, such as best subsets, that have some of the favorable characteristics of backward deletion. However, these approaches were not as easy to implement in a timely manner. Our prior experience also showed that backward deletion yielded accurate and parsimonious predictive models.

The use of the AIC criterion was somewhat arbitrary, though we wanted to use a criterion that accounted for model complexity as well as fit. Other measures of model fit, such as Mallows C_p, are not available for logistic regression, and again our previous experience with AIC had been favorable. See Neter, Wasserman, and Kutner (1990, Sec. 12.4) for a discussion of selection techniques.

Creation of Corresponding PUMS Variables. After fitting a final logistic regression model (box L7 in Figure 10.1), we took two additional steps:

- using the NHSDA data, we recoded PUMS items to derive predictor variables that matched our logistic regression ones; and

- we used our final logistic regression model to predict the probability of need for substance abuse treatment for each PUMS respondent (boxes P2 and P3 in Figure 10.1).

4. Statistical Methods and Model

Our primary statistical objective was to provide the best estimate of the number of people in need of substance abuse treatment by state. Our first task was to choose among three general approaches to estimation:

- design-based (direct) estimation, where we survey each state and then estimate prevalence for each state using only respondents from that state;

- model-based (synthetic) estimation, where we use a national sample of people to create a model that predicts need and then use this model to make predictions for each state; or

- a combination of direct and synthetic methods.

As mentioned previously, we chose model-based or synthetic estimation, and our reasons are explained below.

Design-Based (Direct) Estimation. Typically, if we were interested in measuring characteristics of a population, we would survey a probability sample and infer from this sample the characteristics of the entire population. We would design the sample and construct an unbiased, or as unbiased as possible, estimator with the greatest precision that our budget allowed.

Because this study required a measure of treatment need for each state, a direct estimation approach would require samples from all 50 states and the District of Columbia. Furthermore, because need for substance abuse treatment is rare, the study would need a large sample from each state to produce acceptably precise estimates (Cochran 1977). Given these requirements, a direct estimation approach was unsuitable for this project because we had neither the time nor the funds to undertake such a large survey.

A Model-Based Estimator of Need for Treatment. As an alternative to gathering a large sample of data, we elected to use an estimator based on a statistical model that explains treatment need across the entire population. Our model (10.2) assumed that we could accurately predict the probability that a person needs treatment based on that person's characteristics. We further assumed that the same model held for residents from all states.

If this model was correct, we could produce unbiased estimates of need for each state by using a synthetic estimation approach described in Subsection 1C.

The advantages of synthetic estimation (Ghosh and Rao 1994) for our project were:

- it was unbiased, provided that the model was correct;

- it did not require separate samples from each state; and

- we could explore the effects of many predictors without greatly inflating the variance of the final estimate.

We wanted an unbiased estimator to accurately reflect state-to-state variation. We could not afford primary data collection, and the available data on drug use did not include state indicators for the respondents. Thus, we needed an estimator that did not require separate state samples. Finally, part of the project mandate was to explore correlates identified in the literature and determine which ones predicted need well so our model had to be flexible in the number of predictors included.

A Combination of Direct and Model-Based Estimation. Much of the recent statistical work in making estimates at the state level, or for smaller geographical areas such as counties or school districts, has focused on methods that combine direct and model-based estimation. See Ghosh and Rao (1994) for a thorough review of this topic. This approach is appealing because it captures the strengths of direct estimation without requiring an enormous sample. At the same time, a combined method avoids some of the limitations of model-based estimates. Ideally, we would have explored such an approach for estimating treatment need. However, the NHSDA did not provide state identifiers, and we could not make any direct estimates, even as part of a combination estimator. We therefore used a model-based estimator of need, although that approach did not directly account for the unique characteristics of each state. The limitations of this model are discussed below.

Model Misspecification. To ensure that our final estimates of treatment need were adequate, we had to fit a correctly specified logistic regression model. That is, assuming that model (10.2) holds for some set of predictors, we needed to choose the correct set of predictors and the correct functional form of those predictors. Not doing so would mean that our model would be misspecified, resulting in inaccurate and biased estimates.

Model misspecification creates bias in two ways:

- If our model is missing a predictor that varies by state, then we underestimate the variability of treatment need between states. For example, suppose that even after we controlled for a wide range of predictors but did not control for criminal record, people with a criminal record are more likely to need substance abuse treatment than other people. Assume further that the number of people with criminal records varies between states. In that case, on average, we will underestimate need in those states that have a large criminal population and overestimate need in other states.

- Bias results from misspecifying the form of a predictor. For example, we grouped together 18–25-year-olds in our model. However, if 18–20-year-olds have a distinctly different risk for need than do 21–24-year-olds, then our state estimates will be biased. Our estimates will overestimate need in states with relatively fewer 18–20-year-olds, and underestimate need in states with relatively more 18–20-year-olds.

To avoid model misspecification, we explored many predictor variables and conducted exploratory data analyses as discussed in Subsection 3C of this chapter. We also explored interactions and used standard diagnostics (Hosmer and Lemeshow 1989) as further protection against misspecification.

As a last check, we refit our final model using a weighted logistic regression, where our weights were the sampling weights provided by the NHSDA. It has been shown that using sampling weights may eliminate the bias associated with missing predictors, provided that the missing predictors correlate with the sampling strata (Holt, Smith, and Winter 1980; Nathan and Holt 1980; DuMouchel and Duncan 1983; Kott 1991).[4] Furthermore, if the weighted estimates are similar to the unweighted estimates, then no misspecification has occurred.

By refitting the model using sampling weights, we could check for misspecification and guard against possible bias. Fortunately, we found little difference in the weighted and unweighted estimates, and we concluded that our logistic regression model was well specified for predicting need for substance abuse treatment among the NHSDA sample respondents.

Explorations of Exchangeability. Having fit our logistic regression model and explored misspecification, we could conclude that we had an adequate model for predicting treatment need in the general U. S. population. However, to create accurate estimates of need by state, we required a model that was adequate not only for the general U. S. population, but for each state. By using a model-based estimate, we implicitly assumed that one model was adequate for all states. However, we needed to explore the validity of this assumption of exchangeability.

Exchangeability refers to the notion that we can "exchange" NHSDA respondents with other members of the U. S. population who have similar characteristics. For example, we assume that a young White male high-school dropout from the NHSDA sample can be exchanged for all other young White male high-school dropouts in the U. S., regardless of the state where they reside. If people are exchangeable, then we can use the sample of data with respondents from most states in exchange for a direct sample from every state, and projections based on our logistic regression model yield unbiased estimates of need for every state. However, if people are not exchangeable—that is, if similar people from different states have different probabilities of needing treatment—then our model is wrong and our estimates are biased. In states where people have a propensity for needing treatment higher than the national average, we will underestimate need. The opposite is true in states with below-average propensity for treatment.

We did not expect the exchangeability assumption to hold exactly. Social norms and moral convictions range widely among the various state populations. This range is evident in the different marijuana laws, as well as the tremendous variability of alcohol consumption that exists among the states. We did not account for norms or moral convictions in our model. Variations of this type are not readily explained by the covariates we included in model (10.2). We therefore expected that our model would provide inaccurate estimates for those states where social norms differ from the rest of the nation. However, on the whole, we expect that our model provides accurate estimates for many states and is appropriate for exploring variation among states and deviations from the current block grant formula.

5. Results

This section describes the results of our logistic regression analysis for determining predictors of need for drug or alcohol treatment. It also provides our estimates of need for treatment by state. Finally, it discusses the effects of using these estimates in the allocation formula and the effects of changing other components of the formula.

5A. Predictive Models of Need for Drug Treatment

Table 10.4 shows the final model for predicting an individual's need for substance abuse treatment. For comparison, we also included the final model for predicting an individual's need for drug treatment alone, excluding alcohol. The reference group for each predictor is identified by an odds ratio of 1. For both measures of need, five demographic variables were highly predictive: males, those who were separated or unmarried, those aged 18–44, those with low educational attainment (high-school dropouts or high-school graduates who did not finish college), and those living in western states all had a higher probability of needing treatment for dependence than did other people. Also, White non-Hispanics had higher probability of being either drug- or alcohol-dependent than did people from other ethnic groups. For predicting drug dependence alone, we found an interaction between race and age: White non-Hispanics aged 12–44 were more likely to need treatment, while older Whites had no increased risk of drug dependence.

Additionally, we found that people from families that receive welfare are more likely to be drug-dependent, but they do not have a significantly greater likelihood of being either drug- or alcohol-dependent. Those living in metropolitan areas are also less likely to need drug or alcohol treatment. However, metropolitan status is not a significant predictor of need for drug treatment.

5B. State-Level Estimates of Need for Substance Abuse Treatment

Table 10.5 presents descriptive statistics and correlation coefficients for the estimated state-level rates (per 100 persons) of treatment need. Rates of persons needing treatment services vary widely from state to state. Two features of the

Table 10.4. Final Model: Factors Predicting Drug or Alcohol Dependence or Drug Dependence Alone

Predictors	Odds Ratios (and 95% C.I.s)	
	Drug or Alcohol Dependence	Drug Dependence
Sex		
Female	1.0	1.0
Male	1.8 (1.7–2.0)	1.5 (1.3–1.8)
Race		
White, non-Hispanic	1.4 (1.3–1.5)	0.7 (0.3–1.5)
Other	1.0	1.0
Marital Status		
Currently married	1.0	1.0
Separated or not married	1.7 (1.6–1.9)	1.9 (1.5–2.4)
Age		
12–17	1.0	3.5 (2.0–6.1)
18–44	2.2 (1.9–2.5)	1.0[a]
45–64	1.5 (1.2–1.8)	
65 or older	0.7 (0.5–1.0)	
Education		
0–8 years and a student	1.0[b]	0.2 (0.1–0.3)
0–8 years, not a student		2.8 (2.2–3.5)
9–11 years	2.5 (2.1–2.9)	1.0[c]
High school and a student	1.9 (1.6–2.2)[d]	
High school, not a student		1.9 (1.6–2.3)
College graduate	1.2 (1.0–1.5)	1.0
Welfare status		
Welfare recipient		1.8 (1.4–2.3)
Not welfare recipient		1.0
Population density		
In MSA	0.7 (0.6–0.8)	
Not in MSA	1.0	
Geographic region		
Mid-Atlantic/East central[e]	1.0	0.7 (0.6–0.9)
West[f]	1.6 (1.4–1.7)	1.4 (1.2–1.7)
Other[g]	1.0	1.0
Age by race interactions		
12–44 years and white		2.8 (1.2–6.6)
Other		1.0
Number of children in household		0.7 (0.7–0.8)

[a]For the drug-dependence model, age 18 and older is the single reference category.

[b]For the drug- or alcohol-dependence model, education 0–8 years is the single reference category.

[c]For the drug-dependence model, education 9–11 years or high school and a student is the reference category.

[d]For the drug- and alcohol-dependence model, education high school and a student and high school and not a student are collapsed into a single category.

[e]Includes AL, IL, IN, KY, MI, MS, NJ, NY, OH, PA, TN, and WI.

[f]Includes AK, AZ, CA, CO, HI, ID, MT, NM, NV, OR, UT, WA, and WY.

[g]In the drug- or alcohol-dependence model, "other" geographic region is collapsed with "Mid-Atlantic/East central."

*Table 10.5. Predicted Prevalence of Substance Dependence
for States (per 100 persons): Summary Statistics and
Correlation Coefficients*

	Treatment Need Indicators	
	Drug or Alcohol Dependence	Drug Dependence Only
Summary statistics		
Mean	7.72	1.73
Standard deviation	1.70	0.43
Minimum	5.61	1.10
Maximum	11.94	2.71
Correlation		
Drug dependence only	0.84	

model and dataset affect variability in state-level rate estimates. First, the variable must make a significant contribution to the final model. Second, the variable must have a significantly different distribution from state to state. For example, sex may be a significant predictor at the individual level but may have little effect at the state level because the proportion of women in the total population varies little from state to state.

As shown in Table 10.5, drug dependence alone is much less prevalent than drug or alcohol dependence (i.e., most people identified by our measure as needing treatment require alcohol treatment rather than treatment for illicit drug use). On average, across states, less than 2 in 100 people are drug-dependent, while over four times that number (7.72) are dependent on either drugs or alcohol. However, state-level estimates of need are highly correlated across the two definitions because many of the predictors of drug or alcohol dependence are also predictors of drug dependence.

We examined the relationship of state-level estimates of population rates (per 100 residents) to three key characteristics: state population size, state urbanicity (proportion of population in MSAs), and state poverty level. State-level rates of need tended to be smaller for more urbanized states (correlation coefficient, $r = -0.44$), smaller for larger states ($r = -0.30$), and smaller for states with a larger fraction of their population in poverty ($r = -0.29$).

Figure 10.3 contains a map of the estimated rates (per 100 residents) of need for drug and alcohol treatment, and Figure 10.4 contains the analogous map for drug treatment alone. The large western region effect is clearly noticeable in both maps. Also noticeable is the fact that states such as New York, New Jersey, Pennsylvania, and Illinois have small estimates partly because these states have large metropolitan populations.

The two maps also demonstrate some limitations of our estimation technique. Although the relatively high alcohol-consumption levels for western states correspond to our predicted high levels of drug or alcohol treatment need for the

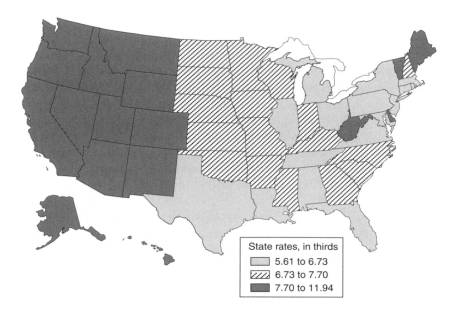

Figure 10.3. Percentage of Population Meeting RAND Criteria for Drug or Alcohol Dependence by State. The grey scale divides the estimated state rates into thirds.

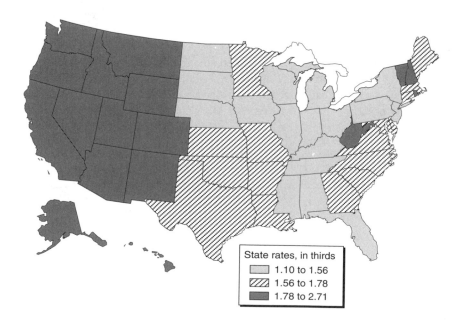

Figure 10.4. Percentage of Population Meeting RAND Criteria for Drug Dependence by State. The grey scale divides the estimated state rates into thirds.

western region, Utah is an exception. The consumption rate for Utah is much lower than for the remainder of the western states, but our estimated need for treatment does not reflect this difference. Because Utah has a youthful population consisting largely of White non-Hispanics, the state is estimated to have a high rate of dependence similar to that of other western states. This type of possibly biased estimation results from a failure in the exchangeability assumption implicit in our synthetic estimation procedure. Given the characteristics included in our model, the proportion of people from Utah who are drug- or alcohol-dependent differs from people in other states. Ideally, we would expand our model to include other predictors (e.g., religious affiliation) to capture these differences. Unfortunately, those other predictors are not readily available in either the NHSDA or the PUMS.

We could quantify the discrepancies shown on the maps by investigating model bias for the six MSAs that were oversampled as part of the 1991 NHSDA sampling plan. The public-use data included identifiers for respondents from these six regions. Using the data from each region, we created direct estimates of treatment need for each region. We also created synthetic estimates of need using our logistic regression models and the PUMS data. The results are given in Table 10.6.

Also included in the table are direct and indirect estimates for the state of California. Ebener, McCaffrey, and Saner (1994) used our definition of dependence to create estimates of treatment need in California using the California subsample of the 1991 NHSDA.

The table shows close agreement between our synthetic estimates and the direct estimates. For four of the oversampled MSAs and the entire US population, our synthetic estimates are within one percentage point of the direct estimates. For the New York MSA, our synthetic estimate is just over a percentage point greater than the direct estimate. On the other hand, our synthetic estimates underestimate need in both the Los Angeles MSA and California. Direct estimates of need in California are extremely large relative to those of other states, and this

Table 10.6. Comparison of Direct and Synthetic Estimates

Region (MSA or State)	Estimate of Need (Percentage of Population)	
	Direct	Synthetic
Chicago	5.8	5.7
Denver	8.6	9.0
Los Angeles	11.5	8.4
Miami	4.8	5.3
New York	4.2	5.4
Washington, DC	5.8	5.7
California	10.5	8.7
United States	6.8	7.7

could indicate that California residents differ from the remainder of the country, a fact that violates our exchangeability assumption.

5C. Impact of Need Estimates on Block Grant Allotments

Table 10.7 summarizes the changes in state block grant shares that result from replacing the current measure of need for substance abuse services with our alternative. Since substance abuse services include both treatment and prevention, we generated synthetic estimates of the population in need of prevention services using a procedure analogous to the one described above for estimating treatment needs. In the following discussion, we assume that 20% of the block grant allocation will be targeted for prevention and 80% for treatment. See Burnam et al. (1997) for details about this assumption and about our estimates of prevention.

As shown in Table 10.7, our alternative measure of need produces a roughly 18% change in allocations for substance abuse block grants. That is, changing only the method for estimating need for treatment leads to reallocation of about 18% of the funds currently distributed to the states. Furthermore, the shares received by nearly three-quarters of the states (37/51) would change by more than 10%, and the affected states contain over 65% of the country's population.

Table 10.7 also shows the correlation between several state characteristics and the ratio of the share given by our alternative formulation of need to that given by the current formulation. There is sizable negative correlation between

Table 10.7. Effect on Substance Abuse Allocations of Changing Estimates of Population Needs

Percentage Change in Allocation	Number of States with Allocation Changed	Percentage of U. S. Population in States with Allocation Changed
> 20% lower	6	15
10–20% lower	5	20
0–10% lower	8	22
0–10% higher	6	12
10–20% higher	4	14
>20% higher	22	16
Share of total allocation changed	17.8%	
Correlation of changes in allocations with:		
State population size	–0.42	
Percentage of state population in urban areas	–0.75	
Percentage of state population in poverty	0.08	

the ratios and both state population size and proportion of population in metropolitan areas. The negative correlation indicates that our alternative measure of need would increase shares to smaller, more rural states. This shift in allocations is not surprising given our estimates of a high prevalence of substance dependence in rural areas. These estimates do not support the heavy weight that the current formula places on urban populations. Figure 10.5 graphs these ratios, ranking them from rural to highly metropolitan states. It shows clearly that large increases in shares tend to go to rural states and large decreases tend to go to the mostly metropolitan states.

In short, the current formula appears to overemphasize the urban population and in turn may not yield equitable allocation of block grant dollars. Alternative measures of need should be considered, and the effect will most likely be a reallocation of funds from larger urban to smaller rural states.

6. Discussion

6A. Summary

Our review of the block grant allotment formula had a major statistical component and served as a good example of the role of statistics in policy analysis. Our work on the project is summarized by the following:

- We formulated the project tasks in terms of statistical analyses by identifying an approach to produce state-level estimates of need for treatment.

- We reviewed available methods and models in the context of the available data and project resources. We chose model-based estimation procedures, used the NHSDA and PUMS data to fit our model, and made our estimates, all within the constraints of the project resources.

- We used all available tools to produce the most accurate models by exploring many predictors, using diagnostics to provide a well-specified logistic regression model for predicting need for treatment and using the PUMS data to flexibly project this model onto the state populations.

- We critically evaluated the model and the results by running many analyses to test the sensitivity of both our parameter estimates and our estimates of need to model specifications.

This process is typical of the statistician's role in applied policy research. However, the highly political atmosphere of this project created some interesting twists. For example, there was considerable concern over our model selection and our parameter estimates. In fact, the project sponsor conducted an independent analysis of the NHSDA and constructed an alternative model of need for drug treatment. Their model did not find a significant effect of population density, and this conclusion led the agency to question the validity of our model.

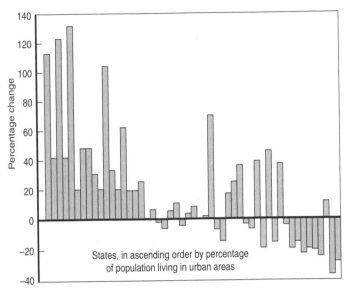

Figure 10.5. Percentage Change in Substance Abuse Allocation That Would Result from Using RAND's Estimate of Population Need Rather than the Current Estimates, by State. Let A_{io} denote the allocation for the ith state under the current allotment formula. Let A_{ir} denote the allocation for the same state using RAND's estimate of population need. The height of the bar for the ith state equals $100 \times (A_{io} - A_{ir})/A_{io}$. States are ordered by percentage of population living in urban areas, with the most rural states on the left and the most urban states on the right.

This criticism, and our own concerns over the unexpectedly large effect for Utah, led us to closely scrutinize our model and the exchangeability assumptions implicit in it. For example, we conducted numerous sensitivity analyses to test the model specification and to find means to reduce our reliance on exchangeability.

Specifically, we refit our model using sampling weights. We also fit a model that included census-tract-level predictors, data which had become newly available to us after the first draft of our report.[5] That is, for every respondent in the NHSDA, we included predictors in our model that explained the characteristics of the respondent's census tract. These included average education level, median income, number of youths, and other socioeconomic descriptors. Our hypothesis was that people were exchangeable at the local neighborhood (tract) level, and if we controlled for such characteristics in our model, our assumption of exchangeability across states would be less suspect.

In one further attempt to explore the possible biases associated with our model, we fit a three-part model. In this model, we fit a separate logistic regression model for residents of large MSAs (over 1 million people), other metropolitan areas, and nonmetropolitan areas. Such a model is appealing because there is evidence that drug use differs by metropolitan status (Office of Applied Statistics 1993), and metropolitan status indicators were available in both the NHSDA and the PUMS. However, our prime motivation for fitting this model was the oversampling of MSAs in the 1991 NHSDA. This model more fully accommodated MSA effects and better avoided bias that would have appeared if we had mistakenly excluded important MSA level predictors in our original model.

Was Our Model Robust? Through these extensive sensitivity analyses (Table 10.8), we found that for the most part our need estimates, especially the rank ordering of states, were robust to most model specifications. Including missing data or adding tract-level predictors had little impact on our parameter estimates. The use of sampling weights had almost no impact and consequently no effect on our state-level estimates of need. Similarly, the definition of need had little effect on our estimates of need. The correlation between these alternative estimates and our final estimates was over 0.93.

On the other hand, the correlation between our final estimates and estimates from the multipart model was only 0.09. The difference between the two estimates has no clear pattern, and one set is not obviously preferable to the other. Both models, for example, predict high use rates for Utah, a state with low alcohol consumption.

We took this discrepancy between the multipart model and our chosen model as a reminder that viable alternatives to our final estimates exist, a limitation inherent in any estimation procedure. However, we feel that our estimates, even if imperfect, proved very useful for identifying limitations in the current allocation formula and were valuable in framing the debate on methods for improving that formula.

Table 10.8. Approaches Used to Limit Bias in Estimates of Need

Source of Bias	Approach
Preventive Procedure	
Missing regressors	Many predictors/backward selection
Misspecified form	Exploratory analysis, diagnostics
Missing interactions	CART, backward selection
Lack of exchangeability	Included regional and geographic predictors
Sensitivity Analyses	
Missing regressors	Fit models using sampling weights
Missing data imputations	Fit model excluding records with imputed data
Lack of exchangeability	Fit multipart model
	Fit model with census tract data

6B. Contributions of Our Analysis

Our review of the block grant formula made several important contributions. First, it showed that improvements can be made in the measurement of population needs. It also demonstrated that making such improvements would greatly affect the allocation of substance abuse service funding. In particular, the changes would tend to shift more dollars to the smaller rural states.

The project also demonstrated that the process of equitable distribution of block grant funds can be broken into two distinct parts:

- Choose criteria for allotment and define the basic allotment formula that corresponds to these criteria. This is a policy decision and does not involve empirical analyses.

- Derive accurate estimates of the components of the allotment formula. This is an empirical task that requires data analysis and solid statistical methodology. For example, the current substance abuse formula is based on taxpayer equity, but bias in the component estimates could lead to inequitable allocation.

Our study also demonstrates that if the government plans to rely more heavily on block grants, it will need to work on estimates of the population in need of the services provided by these grants. For substance abuse services, variations in need for such services had a greater impact on the allotment than did variations in cost. Furthermore, as our project demonstrated, annual production of state-level estimates is not trivial and requires extensive data that may not be readily available in intercensal years. While many methodological questions remain unanswered, the contributions of good statistical research are essential for Congress to succeed in the equitable allocation of block grants.

7. Exercises

The dataset and accompanying documentation for the following exercises are available on our website (www.rand.org/centers/stat/casebook).

1. One approach to modeling clustered data is to fit a separate model for each primary sampling unit (PSU) (i.e., fit a hierarchical or random coefficients model). Discuss the limitations of this type of modeling for our synthetic estimation procedure.

2. Review the 1994 *Statistical Science* article by Ghosh and Rao. Discuss the implications of this article for synthetic estimation, and extensions of their small-area models to logistic regression.

3. Using the NHSDA data, and treating the PSUs (identified by ENCPSU) as "states," select a random sample of respondents and then create direct, indirect, and composite estimates of need for treatment and use of marijuana

(MJRYR). How do these estimates differ? How do these estimates differ from the true rate among all survey respondents? Are the differences consistent for the two outcomes?

Further RAND Reading

Adams, J. L., and Burnam, M. A. (1995), "Federal Block Grants: What Do Statisticians Have to Contribute?" *Chance*, 8, 40–42.

Burnam, M. A., and Reuter, P. (1998), *Improving Block Grant Allocation Formulas,* RB-6006, Santa Monica, CA: RAND.

Burnam, M. A., Reuter, P., Adams, J. L., Palmer, A. R., Model, K. E., Rolph, J. E., Heilbrunn, J. Z., Marshall, G. N., McCaffrey, D., Wenzel, S. L., and Kessler, R. C. (1997), *Review and Evaluation of the Substance Abuse and Mental Health Services Block Grant Allotment Formula,* MR-533-HHS/DPRC, Santa Monica, CA: RAND.

Appendix

DSM-III-R requires that three of the following nine criteria be met:

- substance often taken in larger amounts or over a longer period than the person intended;
- persistent desire or one or more unsuccessful efforts to cut down or control substance use;
- a great deal of time spent in activities necessary to get the substance, in taking the substance, or in recovering from its effects;
- frequent intoxication or withdrawal symptoms when expected to fulfill major role obligations at work, school, or home, or when substance use is physically hazardous;
- important social, occupational, or recreational activities given up or reduced because of substance use;
- continued substance use despite knowledge of having a persistent or recurrent social, psychological, or physical problem that is caused or exacerbated by the use of the substance;
- marked tolerance: need for markedly increased amounts of the substance to achieve intoxication or desired effect, or markedly diminished effect with continued use of the same amount;
- characteristic withdrawal symptoms;
- substance often taken to relieve or avoid withdrawal symptoms.

The NHSDA included items that fully or partially assessed eight of these nine criteria, with information collected specifically for alcohol and each type of drug. DSM-III-R also requires that some symptoms of the disturbance persist for at least one month or occur repeatedly over a longer period of time. We were unable to operationalize this duration requirement with the NHSDA data.

Notes

[1] We explored several other definitions. The choice of definition had little effect on the rank order of state needs.

[2] At the time of our study, the DSM-III-R was the standard diagnostic manual. The DSM-IV has since replaced that edition of the manual.

[3] The NHSDA also uses logical imputation to replace missing values (Office of Applied Statistics 1993). We do not distinguish between hot-deck and logical imputation in this case study.

[4] These results have been shown for ordinary least squares linear regression. However, they should apply directly to logistic regression for large samples.

[5] After completing the first draft of our report, we received from the project funder a new NHSDA dataset with census-tract-level predictors attached to each respondent record. We utilized these geographical data in sensitivity analyses only.

References

Allen, M. R., Read, P. L., and Smith, L. A. (1992a), "Temperature Oscillations," *Nature,* 359, 679.

_____ (1992b), "Temperature Time-Series?" *Nature,* 355, 686.

American Academy of Ophthalmology (AAO) (1994), *National Eye Care Forum Preventive Eye Care Services Schedule,* San Francisco, CA: American Academy of Ophthalmology.

Anderson, S., Auguier, A., Hauck, W. W., Oakes, D., Vandaele, W., and Weisberg, H. I. (1980), *Statistical Methods for Comparative Studies,* New York: John Wiley and Sons.

Baldus, D. (1991), *Death Penalty Proportionality Review Project Final Report to the New Jersey Supreme Court,* September 24, 1991.

Baldus, D., Pulaski, C., and Woodworth, G. (1983), "Comparative Review of Death Sentences: An Empirical Study of the Georgia Experience," *The Journal of Criminal Law & Criminology,* 74, 661–753.

Baldus, D., and Woodworth, G. (1993), "Proportionality: The View of the Special Master," *Chance,* 6, 9–17.

Baldus, D., Woodworth, G., and Pulaski, C. (1990), *Equal Justice and the Death Penalty,* Boston, MA: Northeastern University Press.

Baldus, D., Woodworth, G., Zuckerman, D., Weiner N. A., and Broffit, B. (1998), "Racial Discrimination and the Death Penalty in the Post-Furnam Era: An Empirical and Legal Overview, with Recent Findings from Philadelphia," *Cornell Law Review,* 83, 1638–1770.

Barnea, Z., Rahav, G., and Teichman, M. (1987), "The Reliability and Consistency of Self-Reports on Substance Use in a Longitudinal Study," *British Journal of Addictions,* 82, 891–898.

Barnett, A. (1985), "Some Distribution Patterns for the Georgia Death Sentence," *University of California at Davis Law Review,* 18, 1327–1374.

Baum, A. S., and Burnes, D. W. (1993), *A Nation in Denial: The Truth About Homelessness,* Boulder, CO: Westview Press.

Bauman, K., and Dent, C. (1982), "Influence of an Objective Measure on Self-Reports of Behavior," *Journal of Applied Psychology,* 67, 623–628.

Becker, R. A., Chambers, J. M., and Wilks, A. R. (1988), *The New S Language,* Pacific Grove, CA: Wadsworth and Brooks/Cole.

Bell, R., Ellickson, P., and Harrison, E. (1993), "Do Drug Prevention Effects Persist into High School? How Project ALERT Did with Ninth Graders," *Preventive Medicine,* 22, 463–483.

Berman, P., and McLaughlin, M. W. (1978), *Federal Programs Supporting Educational Change. Implementing and Sustaining Innovations,* R-1589/8-HEW, Santa Monica, CA: RAND.

Biglan, A., and Ary, D. (1985), "Methodological Issues in Research on Smoking Prevention," in *Prevention Research. Deterring Drug Abuse Among Children and Adolescents,* eds. C. Bell and R. Battjes, Rockville, MD: National Institute on Drug Abuse (NIDA).

Bloomfield, P. (1976), *Fourier Analysis of Time Series: An Introduction,* New York: John Wiley and Sons.

Bottomley, M., Folland, C. K., Hsiung, J., Newell, R. E., and Parker, D. E. (1989), *Global Ocean Surface Temperature Atlas,* Bracknell, UK: Meteorological Office.

Box, G., and Tiao, G. (1973), *Bayesian Inference in Statistical Analysis,* New York: Addison–Wesley.

Brauner, M. K., Hodges, J., and Relles, D. A. (1993), *Using Value to Manage Repair Parts,* MR-311-A/USN, Santa Monica, CA: RAND.

_____ (1994), *An Approach to Understanding the Value of Parts,* MR-313-A/USN, Santa Monica, CA: RAND.

Breiman, L., Friedman, J. H., Olshen, R., and Stone, C. J. (1984), *Classification and Regression Trees,* Belmont, CA: Wadsworth International Group.

Brewster, J. M. (1986), "Prevalence of Alcohol and Other Drug Problems Among Physicians," *Journal of the American Medical Association,* 255, 1913–1920.

Briffa, K. R., Bartholin, T. S., Eckstein, D., Jones, P. D., Karlen, W., Schweingruber, F. H., and Zetterberg, P. (1990), "A 1,400-Year Tree-Ring Record of Summer Temperatures in Fennoscandia," *Nature,* 346, 434–439.

Bumiller, E. (1995), "Death-Rate Rankings Shake New York Cardiac Surgeons," *New York Times,* September 6, 1995, p. A1.

Burnam, M. A., Reuter, P., Adams, J. L., Palmer, A., Model, K., Rolph, J. E., Heilbrunn, J., Marshall, G., McCaffrey, D. F., Wenzel, S., and Kessler, R. (1997), *Review and Evaluation of the Substance Abuse and Mental Health Services Block Grant Allotment Formula,* MR-533-HHS/DPRC, Santa Monica, CA: RAND.

Campbell, D. T., and Stanley, J. C. (1966), *Experimental and Quasi-Experimental Designs for Research,* Chicago, IL: Rand McNally.

Carlin, B., and Louis, T. (1996), *Bayes and Empirical Bayes Methods for Data Analysis,* London: Chapman and Hall.

Carter, G., and Rolph, J. E. (1973), *New York City Fire Alarm Prediction Models: I. Box-Reported Serious Fires*, R-1214-NYC, Santa Monica, CA: RAND.

———— (1974), "Empirical Bayes Methods Applied to Estimating Fire Alarm Probabilities," *Journal of the American Statistical Association*, 69, 880–885.

Chambers, J. M., and Hastie, T. J. (eds.) (1992), *Statistical Models in S*, Pacific Grove, CA: Wadsworth & Brooks/Cole Advanced Books & Software.

Clark, L. A., and Pregibon, D. (1992), "Tree-Based Models," in *Statistical Models in S*, eds. J. M. Chambers, and T. J. Hastie, Pacific Grove, CA: Wadsworth & Brooks/Cole Advanced Books & Software.

Cleveland, W. S. (1985), *The Elements of Graphing Data*, Monterey, CA: Wadsworth, Inc.

———— (1981), "LOWESS: A Program for Smoothing Scatterplots by Robust Locally Weighted Regression," *Journal of the American Statistical Association*, 35, 54.

———— (1993), *Visualizing Data*, Summit, NJ: Hobart Press.

Cochran, W. G. (1957), "Analysis of Covariance: Its Nature and Uses," *Biometrics*, 13, 261–281.

———— (1977), *Sampling Techniques* (3rd ed.), New York: John Wiley and Sons.

Cochran, W. G., and Cox, G. M. (1957), *Experimental Designs* (2nd ed.), New York: John Wiley and Sons.

Collins, L. M., Graham, J. W., Hansen, W. B., and Johnson, C. A. (1985), "Agreement Between Retrospective Accounts of Substance Use and Earlier Reported Substance Use," *Applied Psychological Measurement*, 9, 301–309.

Conlisk, J., and Watts, H. (1979), "A Model for Optimizing Experimental Designs for Estimating Response Surfaces," *Journal of Econometrics*, 11, 27–42.

Cook, T. D., and Campbell, D. T. (1979), *Quasi-Experimentation: Design and Analysis Issues for Field Settings*, Boston: Houghton Mifflin Company.

Daniels, M. J., and Gatsonis, C. (1997), "Hierarchical Polytomous Regression Models with Applications to Health Services Research," *Statistics in Medicine*, 16, 2311–2325.

Dillman, D. A. (1978), *Mail and Telephone Surveys: The Total Design Method*, New York: John Wiley and Sons.

Dubois, R., Brook, R., and Rogers, W. (1987), "Adjusted Hospital Death Rates: A Potential Screen for Quality of Medical Care," *American Journal of Public Health*, 77, 1162–1166.

DuMouchel, W. H., and Duncan, G. J. (1983), "Using Sample Survey Weights in Multiple Regression Analyses of Stratified Samples," *Journal of the American Statistical Association*, 78, 535–543.

Ebener, P., McCaffrey, D., and Saner, H. (1994). *Prevalence of Alcohol and Drug Use in California's Household Population, 1988–1991: Analysis of the California Subsample from the National Household Survey on Drug Abuse*, DRU-713-DPRC, Santa Monica, CA: RAND.

Efron, B., and Gong, G. (1983), "A Leisurely Look at the Bootstrap, the Jack-knife, and Cross-Validation, *The American Statistician*, 37, 36–48.

Efron, B., and Tibshirani, R. J. (1993), *An Introduction to the Bootstrap*, New York: Chapman and Hall.

Ellickson, P., and Bell, R. (1990a), *Drug Prevention in Junior High: A Multisite Longitudinal Test*, R-3919-CHF, Santa Monica, CA: RAND.

_____ (1990b), "Drug Prevention in Junior High: A Multi-Site Longitudinal Test," *Science*, 247, 1299–1305.

_____ (1992), "Challenges to Social Experiments: A Drug Prevention Example," *Journal of Research in Crime and Delinquency*, 29, 79–101.

_____ (1993), "Preventing Adolescent Drug Use: Long-Term Results of a Junior High Program," *American Journal of Public Health*, 83, 856–861.

Ellickson, P., and Petersilia, J. (1983), *Implementing New Ideas in Criminal Justice*, R-2929-NIJ, Santa Monica, CA: RAND.

Elsner, J. B., and Tsonis, A. A. (1991), "Do Bidecadal Oscillations Exist in the Global Temperature Record?" *Nature*, 353, 551–553.

_____ (1994), "Low-Frequency Oscillation," *Nature*, 372, 507–508.

Fisher, Sir R. A. (1953), *The Design of Experiments*, New York: Hofner Publishing Co.

Flay, B. (1985), "What We Know about the Social Influences Approach to Smoking Prevention. Review and Recommendations," in *Prevention Research, Deterring Drug Abuse Among Children and Adolescents*, eds. C. Bell and R. Battjes, Rockville, MD: NIDA.

Ford, B. L. (1983), "An Overview of Hot-Deck Procedures," in *Incomplete Data in Sample Surveys. Volume 2, Theory and Bibliographies*, eds. W. G. Madow, I. Olkin, and D. B. Rubin, New York: Academic Press, pp. 185–207.

Freedman, D., Pisani, R., Purves, R., and Adhikari, A. (1991), *Statistics* (2nd ed.), New York: W. W. Norton & Company, p. 361.

Friis-Christensen, E., and Lassen, K. (1991), "Length of the Solar Cycle: An Indicator of Solar Activity Closely Associated with Climate," *Science*, 254, 698–700.

Galway, L. A. (1992a), *Management Adaptations in Jet Engine Repair at a Naval Aviation Depot in Support of Operation Desert Shield/Storm*, N-3436-A/USN, Santa Monica, CA: RAND.

_____ (1992b), *Materiel Problems at a Naval Aviation Depot: A Case Study of the TF30 Engine*, N-3473-A/USN, Santa Monica, CA: RAND.

General Accounting Office (1990), *Death Penalty Sentencing: Research Indicates Pattern of Racial Disparities*, B-236876, Washington, DC: GAO.

Ghil, M., and Vautard, R. (1991), "Interdecadal Oscillations and the Warming Trend in Global Temperature Series," *Nature*, 350, 324–327.

Ghosh, M., and Rao, J. N. K. (1994), "Small Area Estimation: An Appraisal," *Statistical Science*, 9, 55–75.

Gibbons, R. D., Hedeker, D., Charles, S. C., and Frisch, P. (1994), "A Random-Effects Probit Model for Predicting Medical Malpractice Claims," *Journal of the American Statistical Association*, 89, 760–767.

Green, J., Wintfeld, N., Sharkey, P., and Passman, L. (1990), "The Importance of Severity of Illness in Assessing Hospital Mortality," *Journal of the American Medical Association*, 263, 241–246.

Greenberg, L. (1992), *Forecasting the Future Supply of Physicians: Logic and Operation of the BHP Physician Supply Model*, OHPAR 3-93, Washington, DC: Department of Health and Human Services.

Greenfield, S., Nelson, E. C., Zubkoff, M., Manning, W., Rogers, W., Kravitz, R. L., Keller, A., Tarlov, A. R., and Ware, J. E. (1992), "Variations in Resource Utilization Among Medical Specialties and Systems of Care," *Journal of the American Medical Association*, 267, 1624–1630.

Hadley, G., and Whitin, T. N. (1963), *Analysis of Inventory Systems*, Englewood Cliffs, NJ: Prentice–Hall.

Haggstrom, G. (1976), "The Pitfalls of Manpower Experimentation," in *Perspectives on Attitude Assessment: Surveys and Their Alternatives,* eds. H. W. Sinaiko and L. A. Broedling, Champaign, IL: Pendleton Publications.

Hansen, J. E., and Lebedeff, S. (1986), "Global Trends of Measured Surface Air Temperature," *Journal of Geophysical Research*, 92, 13345–13372.

_____ (1988), "Global Surface Air Temperatures: Update Through 1987," *Geophysical Research Letters,* 15, 323–326.

Harvard Medical Practice Study (1990), *Patients, Doctors and Lawyers: Medical Injury, Malpractice Litigation and Patient Compensation in New York: The Report of the Harvard Medical Practice Study to the State of New York*, Cambridge, MA: Harvard Medical Practice Study.

Hastie, T. J., and Tibshirani, R. J. (1990), *Generalized Additive Models,* London: Chapman and Hall.

Hogg, R. B., and Craig, A. T. (1995), *Introduction to Mathematical Statistics* (5th ed.), Engelwood Cliffs, NJ: Prentice–Hall.

Holt, D., Smith, T. M. F., and Winter, P. D. (1980), "Regression Analysis of Data from Complex Surveys," *Journal of the Royal Statistical Society*, A143, 474–487.

Hosmer, D., and Lemeshow, S. (1989), *Applied Logistic Regression*, New York: John Wiley and Sons.

Hughes, P. H., Brandenburg, N., Baldwin, D. C., Storr, C. L., Williams, K. M., Anthony, J. C., and Sheehan, D. V. (1992), "Prevalence of Substance Use Among US Physicians," *Journal of the American Medical Association*, 267, 2333–2339.

James, W., and Stein, C. (1961), "Estimation with Quadratic Loss," in *Proceedings of the Fourth Berkeley Symposium (Vol.1)*, Berkeley, CA: University of California Press, pp. 361–379.

Jencks, S., Daley, J., Draper, D., Thomas, N., Lenhart, G., and Walker, J. (1988), "Interpreting Hospital Mortality Data: The Role of Clinical Risk Adjustment," *Journal of the American Medical Association*, 260, 3611–3616.

Jones, P. D. (1988), "The Influence of ENSO on Global Temperatures," *Climate Monitor*, 17(3), 80–89.

Jones, P. D., Wigley, T. M. L., and Briffa, K. R. (1993), *Trends '93*, eds. T. A. Boden, T. A., D. P. Kaiser, R. J. Sepanski, and F. W. Stoss, ORNL/CDIAC-65, Oak Ridge, TN: Oak Ridge National Laboratory, pp. 603–608.

Jones, P. D., Wigley, T. M. L., and Wright, P. B. (1986), "Global Temperature Variations Between 1861 and 1984," *Nature*, 322, 430–434.

Kahn, K., Brook, R., Draper, D., Keeler, E., Rubenstein, L., Rogers, W., and Kosecoff, J. (1988), "Interpreting Hospital Mortality Data: How Can We Proceed?" *Journal of the American Medical Association*, 260, 3625–3628.

Kahn, M. J., and Raftery, A. E. (1996), "Discharge Rates of Medicare Stroke Patients to Skilled Nursing Facilities: Bayesian Logistic Regression with Unobserved Heterogeneity," *Journal of the American Statistical Association*, 91, 29–41.

Kass, R. E., and Steffey, D. (1989), "Approximate Bayesian Inference in Conditional Independence Models," *Journal of the American Statistical Association*, 85, 717–726.

Kattenberg, A., Girogi, F., Grassl, H., Meehl, G. A., Mitchell, J. F. B., Stouffer, R. J., Tokioka, T., Weaver, A. J., and Wigley, T. M. L. (1996), "Climate Models—Projections of Future Climate," in *Climate Change 1995: The Science of Climate Change*, eds. J. T. Houghton, L. G. Meira Filho, B. A. Callander, N. Harris, A. Kattenberg, and K. Maskell, Cambridge, UK: Cambridge University Press, pp. 285–357.

Kernighan, B. W., and Pike, R. (1984), *The UNIX Programming Environment*, Englewood Cliffs, NJ: Prentice–Hall.

Kiefer, J. (1959), "Optimum Experimental Designs," *Journal of the Royal Statistical Society, Series B*, 21, 272–319.

Kish, L. (1965), *Survey Sampling*, New York: John Wiley and Sons.

Klein, S. P., Petersilia, J., and Turner, S. (1990), "Race and Imprisonment Decisions in California," *Science*, 247, 812–816.

Klein, S. P., and Rolph, J. E. (1991), "Relationship of Offender and Victim Race to Death Penalty Sentences in California," *Jurimetrics Journal*, 32, 33–48.

Kott, P. S. (1991), "A Model-Based Look at Linear Regression with Survey Data," *The American Statistician*, 45, 107–112.

Kravitz, R. L., Rolph, J. E., and McGuigan, K. A. (1991), "Malpractice Claims Data as a Quality Improvement Tool: I. Epidemiology of Error in Four Specialties," *Journal of the American Medical Association*, 266, 2087–2092.

Lavori, P. W., Louis, T. A., Bailar J. C., III, and Polansky, M. (1983), "Design for Experiments—Parallel Comparisons of Treatment," *New England Journal of Medicine*, 309, 1291–1298.

Lee, P. P., Jackson, C. A., and Relles, D. A. (1995), *Estimating Eye Care Provider Supply and Workforce Requirements*, MR-516-AAO, Santa Monica, CA: RAND.

Lehman, A. F., and Cordray, D. S. (1994), "Prevalence of Alcohol, Drug, and Mental Disorders Among the Homeless. One More Time," *Contemporary Drug Problems,* 20, 355–383.

Lewis, E., and Rolph, J. E. (1993), *The Bad Apples? Malpractice Claims Experience of Physicians with a Surplus Lines Insurer*, P-7812, Santa Monica, CA: RAND.

Los Angeles Times, Orange County Edition, Editorial, Metro Section, August 7, 1988, p. 12.

Los Angeles Times, Orange County Edition, Editorial, Metro Section, December 5, 1993, p. 6.

Los Angeles Times, Orange County Edition, Editorial, Metro Section, December 28, 1993, p. 1.

MathSoft, Inc. (1997), *S-PLUS for Windows, Version 4.0*, Seattle, WA: Data Analysis Products Division.

McAuliffe, W. E., Rohman, M., Breer, P., Wyshak, G., Santangelo, S., and Magnuson, E. (1991), "Alcohol Use and Abuse in Random Samples of Physicians and Medical Students,*" American Journal of Public Health*, 81, 177–182.

McAuliffe, W. E., Rohman, M., Santangelo, S., Feldman, B., Magnuson, E., Sobol, A., and Weissman, J. (1986), "Psychoactive Drug Use Among Practicing Physicians and Medical Students," *The New England Journal of Medicine*, 315, 805–810.

Melnick, G., Mann, J., and Serrato, C. (1988), *Hospital Costs and Patient Access Under the New Jersey Hospital Rate-Setting System*, R-3601-HCFA, Santa Monica, CA: RAND.

Mensch, B. S., and Kandel, D. B. (1988), "Underreporting of Substance Use in a National Longitudinal Youth Cohort: Individual and Interviewer Effects," *Public Opinion Quarterly*, 52, 100–124.

Meyer, M. M., and Fienberg, S. E. (eds.) (1992), *Assessing Evaluation Studies: The Case of Bilingual Education Strategies*, Washington, DC: National Academy Press.

Morris, C. N. (1979), "A Finite Selection Model for Experimental Design of the Health Insurance Study," *Journal of Econometrics*, 11, 43–61.

———— (1983a), "Parametric Empirical Bayes Inference: Theory and Applications," *Journal of the American Statistical Association*, 78, 47–65.

———— (1983b), "Sequentially Controlled Markovian Random Sampling (SCOMARS)," *The IMS Bulletin*, 83t-62, 234.

Morris, C. N., and Rolph, J. E. (1981), *Introduction to Data Analysis and Statistical Inference*, Engelwood Cliffs, NJ: Prentice–Hall.

Moses, L. (1992), "Statistical Concepts Fundamental to Investigations," in *Statistics in Medicine* (2nd ed.), eds. J. C. Bailar III and F. Mosteller, Waltham, MA: New England Journal of Medicine Press.

Moskowitz, J. (1989), "The Primary Prevention of Alcohol Problems: A Critical Review of the Research Literature," *Journal of Studies on Alcohol*, 50, 54–88.

Murray, D. M., O'Connell, C. M., Schmid, L. A., and Perry, C. L. (1987), "The Validity of Smoking Self-Reports by Adolescents: A Reexamination of the Bogus Pipeline Procedure," *Addictive Behaviors*, 12, 7–15.

Nathan, G., and Holt, D. (1980), "The Effect of Survey Design on Regression Analysis," *Journal of the Royal Statistical Society, Series B*, B42, 377–386.

National Institute of Justice (1995), *Drug Use Forecasting, 1994 Annual Report on Adult and Juvenile Arrestees*, Washington, DC: U. S. Department of Justice, Office of Justice Programs, National Institute of Justice.

National Institute on Drug Abuse (NIDA) (1992), *National Household Survey on Drug Abuse: Population Estimates 1991*, DHHS No. (SMA) 93-1980, Rockville, MD: ADAMHA, U. S. Department of Health and Human Services.

Neter, J., Wasserman, W., and Kutner, M. (1990), *Applied Linear Statistical Models, Regression, Analysis of Variance, and Experimental Designs* (3rd ed.), Burr Ridge, IL: Irwin.

Newell, N. E., Newell, R. E., Hsiung, J., and Wu, Z. (1989), "Global Marine Temperature Variation and the Solar Magnetic Cycle," *Geophysical Research Letters*, 16, 311–314 .

Newhouse, J. P., and the Insurance Experiment Group (1979), "Design Improvements in the Second Generation of Social Experiments: The Health Insurance Study," *Journal of Econometrics*, 11, 117–129.

_____ (1993), *Free for All? Lessons from the RAND Health Insurance Experiment*, Cambridge, MA: Harvard University Press.

Newhouse, J. P., and Morris, C. N. (1976), *Site Selection for the Health Insurance Study*, RAND Working Note prepared for the Department of Health, Education, and Welfare, Santa Monica, CA: RAND.

Nicholls, N., Gruza, G. V., Jouzel, J., Karl, T. R., Ogallo, L. A., and Parker, D. E. (1996), "Observed Climate Variability and Change," in *Climate Change 1995: The Science of Climate Change*, eds. J. T. Houghton, L. G. Meira Filho, B. A. Callander, N. Harris, A. Kattenberg, and K. Maskell, Cambridge, UK: Cambridge University Press, pp. 133–192.

Normand, S., Glickman, M. E., and Gatsonis, C. A. (1997), "Statistical Methods for Profiling Providers of Medical Care: Issues and Applications," *Journal of the American Statistical Association*, 92, 803–814.

Office of Applied Studies (1993), *National Household Survey on Drug Abuse: Main Findings 1991*, DHHS No. (SMA) 93-1980, Rockville, MD: SAMHSA, U.S. Department of Health and Human Services.

Office of Management and Budget, Subcommittee on Small Area Estimation, Federal Committee on Statistical Methodology (1993), *Indirect Estimators in Federal Programs*, Statistical Policy Working Paper 21, Washington, DC: Statistical Policy Office, OMB.

Osler, W. (1892), *The Principles and Practice of Medicine*, New York: D. Appleton & Company.

Park, E., Brook, R., Kosecoff, J., Keesey, J., Rubenstein, L., Keeler, E., Kahn, K., Rogers, W., and Chassin, M. (1990), "Explaining Variations in Hospital Death Rates: Randomness, Severity of Illness, Quality of Care," *Journal of the American Medical Association*, 264, 484–490.

Penner, J. E., Dickinson, R. E., and O'Neill, C. A. (1992), "Effects of Aerosol from Biomass Burning on the Global Radiation Budget," *Science*, 256, 1432–1434.

Rolph, J. E., Kravitz, R. L., and McGuigan, K. A. (1991), "Malpractice Claims Data as a Quality Improvement Tool: II. Is Targeting Effective?" *Journal of the American Medical Association*, 266, 2093–2097.

Rosenbaum, P. R. (1995), *Observational Studies*, New York: Springer-Verlag New York, Inc.

Rosenbaum, P. R., and Rubin, D. B. (1983), "The Central Role of the Propensity Score in Observational Studies for Causal Effects," *Biometrika*, 70, 41–55.

———— (1984), "Reducing Bias in Observational Studies Using Subclassification on the Propensity Score," *Journal of the American Statistical Association*, 79, 516–524.

———— (1985), "Constructing a Control Group Using Multivariate Matched Sampling Methods That Incorporate the Propensity Score," *American Statistician*, 39, 33–38.

Rossi, P. H. (1989), *Down and Out in America: The Origins of Homelessness*, Chicago, IL: University of Chicago Press.

Rossi, P. H., Fisher G. A., and Willis G. (1986), *The Condition of the Homeless of Chicago: A Report Based on Surveys Conducted in 1985 and 1986*, Amherst, MA: Social Demographic Research Institute, University of Massachusetts at Amherst; and Chicago, IL: NORC, A Social Science Research Center.

Santer, B. D., Wigley, T. M. L., Barnett, T. P., and Anyamba, E. (1996), "Detection of Climate Change and Attribution of Causes," in *Climate Change 1995: The Science of Climate Change*, eds. J. T. Houghton, L. G. Meira Filho, B. A. Callander, N. Harris, A. Kattenberg, and K. Maskell, Cambridge, UK: Cambridge University Press, pp. 407–443.

Sarason, S. B. (1982), *The Culture of the School and the Problem of Change* (2nd ed.), Boston, MA: Allyn and Bacon.

Schaps, E., DiBartolo, R., Moskowitz, J., Palley, C., and Churgin, S. (1981), "A Review of 127 Drug Abuse Prevention Program Evaluations," *Journal of Drug Issues*, 11, 16–43.

Scheiber, S. C. (1983), "Emotional Problems of Physicians: Nature and Extent of Problems," *The Impaired Physician*, eds. S. C. Scheiber and B. B. Doyle, New York: Plenum Medical Book Company.

Schlesinger, M. E., and Ramankutty, N. (1994a), "An Oscillation in the Global Climate System of Period 65–70 Years," *Nature*, 367, 723–726.

—— (1994b), "Low-Frequency Oscillation," *Nature*, 372, 508–509.

Scuderi, L. A. (1993), "A 2000-Year Tree Ring Record of Annual Temperatures in the Sierra Nevada Mountains," *Science*, 259, 1433–1436.

Sherbrooke, C. C. (1992), *Optimal Inventory Modeling of Systems*, New York: John Wiley and Sons.

Shore, J. H. (1987), "The Oregon Experience with Impaired Physicians on Probation: An Eight-Year Follow-up," *Journal of the American Medical Association*, 257, 2931–2934.

Single, E., Kandel, D., and Johnson, B. D. (1975), "The Reliability and Validity of Drug Use Responses in a Large Scale Longitudinal Survey," *Journal of Drug Issues*, 5, 426–443.

Sloan, F. A., Githens, P. B., Clayton, E. W., Hichson, G. B., Gentile, D. A., and Partlett, D. F. (1993), *Suing for Medical Malpractice*, Chicago: The University of Chicago Press.

Steffy, K. R. (1984), "The Group Sampling Model: A Computer Program for Statistical Experimental Design," Masters Thesis, University of Texas at Austin.

Stein, C. (1955), "Inadmissibility of the Usual Estimator for the Mean of a Multivariate Normal Distribution," in *Proceedings of the Third Berkeley Symposium (Vol.1)*, Berkeley, CA: University of California Press, pp. 197–206.

Talbott, G. D., Gallegos, K. V., Wilson, P. O., and Porter, T. L. (1987), "The Medical Association of Georgia's Impaired Physician Program: Review of the First 1000 Physicians, Analysis of Specialty," *Journal of the American Medical Association*, 257, 2927–2930.

Thomas, N., Longford, N., and Rolph, J. (1992), *A Statistical Framework for Severity Adjustment of Hospital Mortality*, N-3501-HCFA, Santa Monica, CA: RAND.

Thompson, S. K. (1992), *Sampling*, New York: John Wiley and Sons.

Tsonis, A. A., and Elsner, J. B. (1992), "Oscillating Global Temperature," *Nature*, 356, 751.

Tufte, E. R. (1983), *The Visual Display of Quantitative Information*, Cheshire, CT: Graphics Press.

—— (1990), *Envisioning Information*, Cheshire, CT: Graphics Press.

U. S. Bureau of the Census (1995), *County and City Data Book,* Washington, DC: U. S. Bureau of the Census.

Velleman, P. F., and Hoaglin, D. C. (1981), *Application, Basics, and Computing of Exploratory Data Analysis*, Belmont, CA: Wadsworth.

Vernez, G., Burnam, M. A., McGlynn, E. A., Trude, S., and Mittman, B. S. (1988), *Review of California's Program for the Homeless Mentally Disturbed*, R-3631-CDMH, Santa Monica, CA: RAND.

Wagner, H. M. (1969), *Principles of Operations Research, with Applications to Managerial Decisions*, Englewood Cliffs, NJ: Prentice–Hall.

Walker, W., Chaiken, J., and Ignall, E. (eds.) (1979), *Fire Department Deployment Analysis*, New York: Elsevier North Holland.

Watson, R. T., Zinyowere, M. C., and Moss, R. H. (eds.) (1996), *Climate Change 1995: Impacts, Adaptations and Mitigation of Climate Change*, Cambridge, UK: Cambridge University Press.

Weisberg, S. (1985), *Applied Linear Regression*, New York: John Wiley and Sons.

Williams, C. L., Eng, A., Botvin, G. J., Hill, P., and Wynder, E. L. (1979), "Validation of Students' Self-Reported Cigarette Smoking Status with Plasma Cotinine Levels," *American Journal of Public Health*, 69, 1272.

Contributors

ALLAN F. ABRAHAMSE, *RAND*

JOHN L. ADAMS, *RAND*

ROBERT M. BELL, *AT&T Labs–Research*

PHYLLIS L. ELLICKSON, *RAND*

LIONEL A. GALWAY, *RAND*

JAMES K. HAMMITT, *Harvard School of Public Health*

JENNIFER L. HILL, *Department of Statistics, Harvard University*

JAMES S. HODGES, *University of Minnesota School of Public Health*

CATHERINE A. JACKSON, *RAND*

PAUL P. LEE, *Duke University Eye Center*

DANIEL F. MCCAFFREY, *RAND*

KIMBERLY A. MCGUIGAN, *Merck-Medco Managed Care, LLC*

CARL N. MORRIS, *Department of Statistics, Harvard University*

SALLY C. MORTON, *RAND*

DANIEL A. RELLES, *RAND*

JOHN E. ROLPH, *Marshall School of Business, University of Southern California*

NEAL THOMAS, *Pharmaceutical Research Institute, Bristol-Myers Squibb Company*

Index